Adversity Quotient @ Work
Paul G. Stoltz, Ph.D.

"*Adversity Quotient @ Work* introduces a powerful set of tools to address the greatest challenge of our times—hiring and retaining the best people to drive success."
—CHRIS POWELL, director, workforce planning and performance, Marriott International, Inc.

"In a world that rewards those who best manage change, *Adversity Quotient* has given my staff a better sense of their personal capacity to embrace [adversity] and the confidence to more effectively work through a change agenda. *AQ* is considered mandatory reading in my shop and the LEAD Sequence has been integrated into all aspects of our day-to-day operations. Read the book, institutionalize the precepts, and good things will happen."
—IAN M. BURGE, vice president, Customer Development, Mott's

"In the era of swift change and unremitting uncertainty, the challenge for executives and entrepreneurs is not only how to avoid crisis but mainly how to weather and defy adversity. Dr. Stoltz shows that success in converting adversities into profitable opportunities is related to our ability to move forward despite what appears to be insurmountable obstacles."
—GIDEON MARKMAN, PH.D., assistant professor of entrepreneurship, Lally School of Management and Technology, Rensselaer Polytechnic Institute

"Paul Stoltz has done it again. This time he applies AQ theory to the workplace in even greater depth. I think AQ theory should be a required part of any business school curriculum. Thanks, Dr. Stoltz, for giving us something of practical value for college students and working professionals."
— STEWART L. TUBBS, Darrell H. Cooper Professor of Leadership, Eastern Michigan University, and author of *A Systems Approach to Small Group Interaction*

"It is not coincidental that Adversity Quotient is first on the list of new millennium quotients; this is the base from which other wisdom springs, whether it is building or rebuilding your life, your business, or your country—something we in South Africa know so well!"
— LISA ASHTON, BIOSS Southern Africa

"This book inspires, informs, and equips you for success. AQ strengthens and unleashes human endeavor, spirit, and success."
— COLONEL WINSTON LIM, director, Outward Bound Singapore

"This book transcends cultures, countries, and industries. AQ is fundamental to business and leadership in any country, culture, or industry in the global New Economy."
— DR. SHIRLEY LIM, president, Research Communication International

"*Adversity Quotient @ Work* always raises an entire team's performance. AQ is the most surefire way to sustain exceptional results. Thank you, Dr. Stoltz, for helping us to raise the bar of achievement during these challenging and exciting times."
— JOE SASSO, president, Team2Learn

"*Adversity Quotient @ Work* is a must for any individual or organization that wants to unlock their human potential immediately!"
— DEAN D. HOHL, president and cofounder, Leading Concepts, Inc.

"Yet again, powerfully, Paul Stoltz has shown us the true meaning of bravery, responsibility, and leadership. He achieves this with wit and with his rare understanding of what really makes anyone into a high achiever both personally and professionally."
— J. W. KAEMPFER, CEO, BAA McArthurGlen, UK Ltd.

"In today's workplace, new problems, information overload, and immediate decision points are coming at us at a faster and faster pace, with no leveling in sight. AQ doesn't stop the flow, but does expand your capacity to deal effectively with these issues in a practical and habitual manner."
  —TODD ROSSEL, principal and director of human resources, Management Solutions and Services, Deloitte & Touche

"Most of us encounter almost twenty-four adversities every twenty-four hours! Having a manual to survive such conflict and stress is not only essential, it's critical. *Adversity Quotient @ Work* will not only help you grasp the personal frictions in your life, it will smooth them out for you. After this book, you won't have less adversity in your life, but you will have more peace—and success!"
  —TOM BROWN, MG, The "New Ideas" Webzine (*www.mgeneral.com*)

"We've been using AQ for years to grow and keep the best people. It's been invaluable to our success. Now *Adversity Quotient @ Work* puts these world-class strategies into practical terms for everyone to use."
  —STEPHEN J. BURILL, partner, Deloite & Touche, LLP, and Healthcare Industry Leader–Pacific Southwest

"During my career I have instinctively tried to recruit employees who could overcome adversity but never had the tools. With the tools and principles provided in *Adversity Quotient @ Work,* I now make more informed judgments about this most critical trait. AQ helps my people *and* the bottom line."
  —BRUCE MERRICK, CEO, Dant Clayton Corporation

"In *Adversity Quotient @ Work,* Paul Stoltz once again demonstrates his unconditional commitment and passion to encourage us all to succeed and Climb higher."
  —BILL CORDASCO, president, Babbitt Ranches

"Clear, thoughtful, and action-oriented, *Adversity Quotient @ Work* will change the way you conduct business and manage your personal life—a must-read."
  —GEOFFREY S. BARNARD, president, Grand Canyon Trust

"We each yearn to find our life's work, our calling. Paul Stoltz has a deep appreciation of what gets in the way of the deep challenge of living our purpose and how we can persevere into that unfamiliar territory each and every day."

—RICHARD J. LEIDER, founding partner, The Inventure Group, and author of *The Power of Purpose* and *Repacking Your Bags*

"This book has global appeal and lays the foundation for the future and an optimized life. It is the blueprint of the human journey to a life well lived and the world well occupied by climbers."

—PROFESSOR CARLITO E. BALITA, president/training director, Executive Center for Professionals, Republic of the Philippines

"Paul Stoltz has hit a home run with his new book *Adversity Quotient @ Work*. In a business where failing seven out of ten times can still make you an all-star, increasing a player's and a team's AQ is essential for Major League success."

—GARY MACK, president and CEO, SportsAssist, and team counselor, Seattle Mariners

"Learning to Climb and leading others through their Climb becomes an essential skill for leaders in the new millennium. The wisdoms of Stoltz's work are that we all have the potential to do both."

—BOB WEIGAND, director of management training and development, St. Luke's Hospital and Healthcare Network

"Finally! A book that shows exactly how to bring the best out of employees in today's organizations. *Adversity Quotient @ Work* provides readers with the essential tools they need to invent their own futures and to control their own destinies on the job—taking their organizations to new heights. Get this book—before your competition does!"

—PETER ECONOMY, coauthor of *At the Helm: Business Lessons for Navigating Rough Waters* and *The Complete MBA for Dummies*

"The key to career success in any organization is not just skill mastery or even political savvy. It's all about AQ, Paul's principles, and managing workaday adversity, nonstop, with focus and grace."

—BEVERLY KAYE, organization consultant, and author of *Up Is Not the Only Way*

"We all should be aspiring to climb our own Mount Everests in the workplace. *Adversity Quotient @ Work* masterfully and powerfully helps us with our ascents. . . . Climb on!"
—Dr. CHRISTOPHER C. ROLAND, managing principal, Roland/Diamond Associates, Inc.

"The contents of this book build upon a wealth of scientific and practical knowledge. From this background Paul Stoltz has synthesized a very practical and efficient approach that offers a true precision to the development of culturally successful organizations."
—CHRISTOPHER COOKE, Hidden Resources

"At last, someone has clearly delineated a viable method to assess and address the adversity that we each face day to day in our personal and organizational lives. The most compelling and appealing aspects of Dr. Stoltz's book are not only the combination of a self- and organizational-assessment tool to measure your adversity response, utilizing the Adversity Response Profile QuickTake, but the use of CORE/LEAD Sequences that can be considered prescriptions to pull yourself and your organization out of the ruts to achieve new heights. With today's rapid pace of organizational and technical change, this book is a solid resource for assessing and managing adversity that we face at every corner. This book is a must-read for the organizational leader, entrepreneur, and the student of success. Why Camp when we can Climb!"
—RONALD D. MCFARLAND, PH.D., professor, UCLA, and founder of Sheltersoft.org

"In today's world great leaders are perhaps not best measured by their success, but by how they deal with failure. In *Adversity Quotient @ Work* Paul Stoltz has created both a thought-provoking [discussion] of the issues facing managers as well as a pragmatic guide for dealing with chaos and challenging situations. This book will certainly change the way you think and it may very well change your life."
—JON V. PETERS, president, The Institute for Management Studies

"*Adversity Quotient @ Work* is the text for success in the twenty first century, from the science of AQ to the application of the AQ techniques and methodology. A must for effective management and corporate operations. . . . I recommend this text as a guidebook to success for every corporation."
  —JOHN CIRELLO, PH.D., P.E., president and chief executive officer, Florida Water Services Co.

"*Adversity Quotient @ Work* provides a life-changing method and measurement that will give [our] and other employees a new energized perspective on their jobs and on their lives."
  —BRIAN TURCHIN, president, Turchin Consulting, Inc.

"For the sales manager, *Adversity Quotient @ Work* is an invaluable tool for hiring hungry, never-say-die salespeople. It is essential to initiating corporate change. For the individual, it can reshape your life, pushing your limits and helping you soar."
  —RENE BROOKBANK, assistant vice president, sales, GAB Robbins North America, Inc.

"I thoroughly enjoyed this book. It advanced my workshop experience and reminded me why the Adversity Quotient is such a simple and effective answer to many of today's personal and organizational challenges."
  —TOM BARRY, managing director, The Blueprint Organization, Ltd., London, UK

"The Norwegian army is facing the biggest adversity in a long time and we have looked into AQ as one of the elements to prepare our people to meet these challenges. *Adversity Quotient @ Work* will be a great contribution to help us overcome the adversity."
  —OBLT. RUNE BREKKE, leader of the Army Competency Center, Norway

"Work is becoming increasingly complex, and the need for individuals to overcome organizational uncertainty is critical for success in today's world of work. *Adversity Quotient @ Work* provides practical applications for reengaging employees and increasing employee potential. *Adversity Quotient @ Work* gives specific tools to strengthen an entire organizational system. [It's] a powerful book about how individuals can become more productive and how organizations can improve their overall performance."
  —TAMAR ELKELES, PH.D., vice president, learning and development, QUALCOMM

"*Adversity Quotient @ Work* provides substantial, proven, and practical insights for leading others in complex, fast-changing times. AQ is a core competency in the global New Economy. The AQ principles transcend cultures, countries, and industries."
  —FRANKLIN C. JESSE JR., international attorney and principal, GrayPlant Mooty Law Firm

"Our organization has embraced the AQ for personal and business development and coaching because the process provides tools essential to handling the day-to-day challenges that confront us."
  —MARIE SCHILLY, manager, sales and executive development, Cypress University

"Investing in knowledge-intensive startups requires tools to find the entrepreneurs that have what's needed to overcome the adversity they meet on their climb. *Adversity Quotient @ Work* helps investors look for the right skills and the entrepreneurs to meet the challenges."
  —JAN TAUG, venture capitalist, Scandinavia

ADVERSITY QUOTIENT
@ WORK

Also by Paul G. Stoltz

Adversity Quotient: Turning Obstacles into Opportunities

ADVERSITY QUOTIENT @ WORK

Make Everyday Challenges the Key to Your Success—
Putting the Principles of AQ into Action

Paul G. Stoltz, Ph.D.

WILLIAM MORROW
An Imprint of HarperCollins*Publishers*

FIRST EDITION

Designed by Michael Mendelsohn at MM Design 2000, Inc.

Printed on acid-free paper

Library of Congress Cataloging-in-Publication Data

Stoltz, Paul Gordon.
     Adversity quotient @ work : make everyday challenges the key to your
success—putting the principles of AQ into action / Paul G. Stoltz.—1st Morrow ed.
        p.   cm.
     ISBN 0-688-17759-X (alk. paper)
     1. Success—Psychological aspects.   2. Self-management (Psychology)   3.
Work—Psychological aspects.   I. Title: Adversity quotient at work.   II. Title.

BF637.S8 S695 2000
158.1—dc21
                                                                    00-032463

        03   04   /   10   9   8   7   6   5   4   3   2

To my bride, Ronda,
who embodies and inspires the highest
principles of AQ and its author

Big success is not built on success.
It's built on adversity, failure, and frustration,
sometimes catastrophe,
and the way we deal with it and turn it around.

—Sumner Redstone,
chairman of the board, Viacom, Inc.

CONTENTS

CHAPTER 3 | Measuring Your AQ

CHAPTER 4 | The CORE of the Climber

CHAPTER 5 | Developing Response-Able Climbers

CHAPTER 8 | Hiring Climbers

CHAPTER 9 | Building Climbing Teams

CHAPTER 10 | Building a Climbing Culture

CHAPTER 11 | Forward and Up!

EXHIBITS

ACKNOWLEDGMENTS

This book represents a confluence of the thoughts, tears, vision, failures, contributions, and greatness of many people. This abbreviated and predictably incomplete list is meant to highlight those individuals whose roles have been most significant. There is no way to express adequate gratitude for all that they added to bring this vision to print, except to say that it would not exist without them.

Heartfelt appreciation to:

You, the reader, for having the courage to lift your gaze beyond the warm comfort of the Campground to the higher aspirations and gifts you have left to explore, and for taking on the mountain until your final breath.

Dr. Ronda Beaman, for the tenacity and purity with which she delivers her spirit to the planet, despite all adversity, elevating all she can reach. For her incisive mind and bulldoggish protection of the higher purpose AQ can serve. For who she is and how it shaped the author and this book.

My sons Chase and Sean, for their love, big hearts, outrageous humor, and for having the courage to ascend with purpose in their lives when so many hang on the rope.

Mildred Gordon Haniford, for modeling how a high AQ can help one age with grace, dignity, and a boundless spirit. She inspires us all.

Dr. Sabina Thornton, for refusing to let adversity get in the way of contributing deeply to the planet.

Dr. Jeff Thompson, my partner in Climb, for his courage to become a Lead Climber, and for his long nights, countless hours, and bottomless dedication to this project. His soul, sweat, and integrity are on every page.

Michael Gaines, for his resolve, passion, and success in offering AQ to an expanded business audience worldwide.

Harry Gaines, for his insights and faith.

Miriana Clark, PEAK Base Camp Coordinator, who keeps our Climbing Team moving forward and up along our mountain.

Henry Ferris, my editor at Morrow, who approached this book as more of a cause than a project. If it makes sense, thank Henry.

Lisa Queen, for putting AQ at the forefront and for all that she has done to release the worldwide AQ brand.

Margret McBride, the most gifted literary agent and a true Climber—and the McBride team—for letting AQ become a part of her, not just another plaque on the wall.

Patti Danos, Climber and publicist, for dedicating her rare blend of integrity, precision, authenticity, and professionalism to bring AQ to the planet.

Stephen Stern, for his lifelong friendship, dedication, and sacrifice in helping this manuscript mature into a book, and for the mountain cabin in which some of the richer portions of this book were crafted.

Phil Styrlund, my brother, who makes elevating humanity his full-time cause, for his generosity of spirit in making AQ a part of his mission. Together we Climb.

Steve Burrill, for being an early believer in AQ, me, and the mountain.

Marie Schilly, for her strength of character and vision in helping thousands harnness adversity for their own growth.

Joe Meade, for elevating AQ to an art form and way of life.

Oprah Winfrey, for resonating with and sharing this message with the planet, and for modeling what a Climber can become, do, and contribute to humanity.

Peter Economy, a substantial author in his own right, for his editing expertise on the initial proposal that helped launch this book.

Dr. Jeri Grandy, for elevating quantitative research to an art form and for helping to shape the continuous improvement of the AQ measures.

Scott Jern, our high-AQ building contractor, for his relentlessness, vision, and can-do spirit, and for building PEAK's home.

Dr. Gideon Markman, assistant professor at Rensselaer Polytechnic Institute, for his breakthrough research on AQ and entrepreneurship, AQ and wealth, as well as AQ and innovation.

Bob Wiegand with St. Luke's Hospital and Dr. Laura Murray, for their groundbreaking research on AQ and kidney disease.

Dr. Alex Genora of Australia, for his breakthroughs in exploring AQ and chronic pain.

Jan Taug and the Core team, for bringing AQ to Scandinavia with integrity and passion.

Dr. Shirley Lim and the Research Communication team, for launching AQ in Asia with commitment and heart.

The PEAK certificatees who have expanded the AQ universe through their interest in using the Adversity Response Profile to hire and grow people with boundless capacity.

The PEAK clients, many of them pioneers, whose stories fill these pages and who have inspired us to evolve, strengthen, and grow AQ into the future.

Climbers everywhere, for the quiet sacrifices you've made and will continue to make along your ascents, and for inspiring countless others to get "on rope."

The countless great thinkers, researchers, and pioneers whose work and ideas have formed and advanced this foundational science.

My parents, Gary and Sandra, generous beyond measure, who helped me hardwire the AQ required to take on the unknown and Climb through adversity, and for sharing in the ascent.

ADVERSITY QUOTIENT
@ WORK

CHAPTER 1

EXPANDING YOUR CAPACITY

The Human Operating System

IN AN AGE when we face an average of twenty-three adversities a day, most of us are ill-equipped to manage, let alone thrive, amid such unprecedented demands.

Before 7 A.M. you may be sipping your morning coffee and scanning the morning paper only to discover some megaconglomerate is interested in buying or merging with your company. Another story reports that children now spend forty-seven hours per week in front of some form of uncensored media, and you think about the implications for your own son and daughter.

Despite your best efforts to outwit traffic, getting anywhere is a hassle. What will it be today? Perhaps the parking lot is full, or your flight is delayed, and you miss a connection. When you arrive at work, you are met with fifty-one E-mail and twenty-three voice-mail messages. Another eighty-two messages will bombard you by the end of the day. There is no way to answer them all. You sift through the junk and, although several messages are important, you are able to respond curtly to only a few before you dash to the morning meeting. The meeting runs long, and tensions are high; people jump in and out of the discussion to respond to the constant cacophony of beepers and cell phones. On the way back to your desk you are handed the latest financials for your department and make a mental note to peruse them before tomorrow's budget meeting, asking yourself, "Yes, but *when*?"

At your desk, you whip open your organizer and see that fifteen items have increased to nineteen, seven of which you'll complete today, barring any unforeseen events, but there are *always* unforeseen events! As you prioritize, your son's school nurse calls; he has a fever. You can't miss the client meeting scheduled for lunch, but even so, you have to.

Rumors of the reported merger or buyout color the day, and the leaders are conspicuously absent. You wonder how hard you should work on today's strategic imperative when it may now be irrelevant. At home that evening, you sit down to sift through some papers after a quick bite to eat, and you hear your son coughing. He seems to be getting worse. It's going to be another late night.

Welcome to the realities of the entrepreneurial, high-velocity New Economy. Each day demands greater speed, capacity, and capabilities. Few can keep up without taking a tremendous toll upon themselves and those around them. It takes more than strong coffee and high-speed Internet lines to meet today's demands, but what about tomorrow's? *USA Today* reports that in a typical day office workers send and receive 163 messages via phone, fax, E-mail, postal mail, interoffice mail, and cell phones. That number doubles every year.

In 1967 Gordon Moore, one of the founders of Intel, predicted that computers would double in speed and capacity every eighteen months. For more than thirty years, Moore's Law has held true. We may attribute the breakthroughs to human ingenuity, but we have created our own prison. We, the consumers, *demand* greater speed and capacity from our technology. The latest pocket-size Palm Pilot organizer has greater horsepower than the computer I used to write my doctoral dissertation. We consistently upgrade our computers to meet our new demands.

Of the more than 100,000 people I have polled, who represent a wide range of careers, industries, and countries, 98 percent predict a more difficult, chaotic, and uncertain future. As this impending reality unfolds, hope, innovation, aspirations, and momentum are all increasingly at risk.

If we don't upgrade our *human operating systems* in a similar manner, the cost will continue to be enormous. Performance, agility, resilience, problem solving, decision making, innovation, optimism, and health all will be degraded. Nowhere in our training or upbringing were we given a viable way to upgrade our operating systems so that we could tap ever-greater speed and capacity to meet ever-greater demands. Yet, *upgrade we must.*

Imagine running your desktop machine on a 1967 operating system. Its capacity would be severely compromised and would fall far short of what you require it to do. The same is true of the human operating system as it attempts to process an endless flow of information and to perform increasingly complex and demanding tasks. Like your computer, your human operating system drives everything else. All learning, skills, capabilities, knowledge—*the human software*—are driven by your hardwired operating system.

It is also impossible to meet today's ever-increasing demands simply by adding more software in the form of information, knowledge, and skills. The only way to meet these demands is to upgrade your operating system by optimizing your existing software and expanding your capacity for storing more software. And you must go beyond the traditional approaches and standard methods. You must upgrade your operating system by understanding and strengthening your Adversity Quotient (AQ).

THE AQ DISCOVERY

Your AQ describes your hardwired pattern of response to all forms and magnitudes of adversity, from major tragedies to minor annoyances. It is about how you respond to adversity in the deepest and most automatic recesses of your brain and every cell in your body. AQ is also a theory of human performance deeply rooted in several sciences and grounded in roughly 1,500 research studies from around the world.

I began my research twenty years ago, when I first explored the patterns of success among top-performing entrepreneurs and students. I discovered that none of the standard predictors of success, such as test scores or people's backgrounds, held true, and that there appeared to be a hidden element that was determining their enduring success. Ten years ago I posited the theory of AQ: those who respond most effectively to adversity will prevail in work and in life. My team also began conducting quantitative studies with athletes, students, leaders, and salespeople. We discovered that AQ was an exceptionally robust predictor of success. After additional studies, we also discovered how to measure and permanently strengthen individuals' AQs. It was time to share these methods with the world.

On the basis of this evidence, we presented the AQ theory and initial AQ-strengthening methods in the book *Adversity Quotient: Turning Obstacles into Opportunities.* We were pleased to see it so well received around the planet. It became apparent that adversity crosses all cultures, genders, and industries. Yet AQ remained largely unknown. At the time of our first book we had measured the AQs of 5,000 people. Since its publication we have measured the AQs of 100,000 individuals, provided training and consulting at dozens of organizations, and put tens of thousands of people through the AQ-strengthening protocol presented in this book. We have also learned a great deal along the way.

Over time we discovered that most training is tantamount to upgrading or adding new software. But "running" this new software on an over-taxed operating system doesn't work. Many people's hard drives are full of impressive software that lies dormant or underutilized because their personal operating systems are stressed, incompatible, or corrupted by a deeper virus.

Our research directed us to confront a key issue: Why do some people turn mediocre training into enduring lessons for improvement? Even when not provided with training, why do they still seek ways to grow and improve? These people are among the few who possess an operating system that allows capacity and capabilities to grow. We found that AQ predicts who will grow their capacity and who will stagnate.

The most encouraging facet of our research and your potential with AQ is that you need not be born with a high AQ in order to prevail. AQ can be permanently and substantially improved, regardless of your starting point. In fact, my team discovered that AQ-strengthening methods not only endure but also deepen over time. Ninety days after AQ training, when people remeasure their AQs, a 20 to 25 percent increase in AQ is common. As you will discover, these improvements in AQ are manifested in decreased turnover and sick days and improvements in sales, performance, disposition, and responsiveness to change.

AQ technology provides tools for expanding, improving, and navigating an adversity-rich future. It

- influences all facets of human endeavor
- can be validly and reliably measured
- tells you how well you withstand adversity and measures your ability to surmount any crisis
- can be permanently rewired and improved
- determines the value people receive from training
- is a valid predictor of sales, performance, agility, problem solving, and long-term success
- can be used to reduce turnover and improve hiring
- predicts who will quit and who will climb
- plays a powerful role in all relationships

In this book I am pleased to introduce the latest evolution of the AQ theory and technology for an expanded menu of workplace-related applications. *Adversity Quotient @ Work* is about (1) expanding upon and "putting to work" the ideas I presented in my first book, *Adversity Quotient*, and (2) applying AQ at work, since this is where we dedicate so many of our best hours. It is not mandatory for you to have read the first book, nor does it matter if your "workplace" is at home, complete with bunny slippers, or at the top of a gleaming office tower. Wherever you work and whatever you do, you will be able to apply *AQ @ Work*—and beyond. I hope that you will use AQ not only to assess and strengthen your enterprise but also to discover and expand your capacity with renewed energy to persevere in the pursuit of your highest aspirations.

There's more to life than increasing its speed.
—Mohandas Gandhi

REDEFINING HUMAN CAPACITY

Human capacity is composed of talents, aptitudes, skills, experience, knowledge, and will. Theoretically, human capacity is boundless. Yet if capacity does not expand quickly enough, enterprise and aspiration can grind to a halt. In fact, as adversity, complexity, and uncertainty continue to rise, we face the very real threat that, individually and collectively, we will lack the capacity to meet the world's demands.

Among the great challenges facing any leader is growing and tapping other people's full capacity. Consider the three forms of capacity. *Required Capacity*, which is what is required of you to meet the day's demands, is constantly increasing and expanding. *Existing Capacity* defines all that a person is *capable* of delivering. This can also be thought of as his or her software (knowledge, skills, aptitudes, talents, experience, etc.). Existing Capacity defines what you could offer if you were to tap your full potential. Not surprisingly, as the demands the world places upon us continue to grow (Required Capacity), it gets harder and harder to find people with enough Existing Capacity to meet those demands, let alone grow their own capacities. In addition, the challenge is magnified because most people do not tap their full capacity. The portion they tap in a given day is what I refer to as their *Accessed Capacity*. Successful leaders and individuals must unleash all forms of capacity to maintain an edge in today's market and to further their ascent.

In a recent *USA Today* poll, CEOs in Europe, Japan, and the United States reported that among their top worries are "the ability to increase flexibility and speed," while "reducing costs" and "competing for top talent." And as a result of these requirements, what is demanded of their workers continues to expand.

For example, a customer service representative at Sun Trust Bank must not only provide assistance but also sell products and services. His or her Required Capacity has increased. To meet that demand, both the Existing Capacity and the Accessed Capacity must increase, ideally beyond the mere requirements. Otherwise, the employee may be perceived as obsolete to the company's new vision.

It is disturbing that as adversity mounts most individuals' Existing and Accessed Capacities *shrink*. As a gap grows between what is demanded and what is available or tapped, people shut down—their hard drives crash—and they fail.

This book will explore human capacity in greater depth and provide practical tools for using AQ to expand it in all of its forms. As you and your coworkers expand your human operating systems, you will see how to exceed the demands of tomorrow so that your enterprises can flourish, and you, the people who drive them, can become something more than your jobs.

A person asked Confucius, "What surprises you most about mankind?" Confucius answered, "They lose their health to make money and then lose their money to restore their health. By thinking anxiously about the future, they forget the present, such that they live neither for the present nor for the future and they live as if they will never die, and they die as if they never lived."

THE TOLL ON THE SOUL

Today everyone faces mounting adversities, and these increasing demands on human capacity require us all to develop new capacity in the form of higher-level skills and accessible wisdom. If we aren't able to do this, there will be a growing toll on the soul, an unnecessary artifact of the times. We see this toll manifested today in briefer human interactions, increases in stress-related disease, shorter vacations, and new language like "multitasking" becoming a standard part of conversation.

Just as rigorous exercise requires greater nutrition, adversity-rich times demand a strong AQ. Your AQ fortifies your operating system, allowing it to perform optimally under today's demands. This AQ-based upgrade of the human operating system is long overdue.

How much of your software or capacity are you and your coworkers able to tap each day? How much lies dormant? In moments of truth, do you and your coworkers rise to the challenge, dig deep, and show greatness? Are you unfazed by daily annoyances, challenges, and uncertainties? Or, as adversities mount, do you get mired in the mess, become demoralized, and compromise core values and the purpose once so revered?

Blaming, whining, deflecting accountability, risk aversion, and resistance to change are but a handful of symptoms of the adversity-beaten individual and organization. More serious indicators include individual and collective helplessness, organizational turnover, and general stagnation.

But the damage extends far beyond the climate-controlled cubicles of the corporate world. The deeper toll can be discovered in relationships, hopes, and aspirations. While many organizations slowly dampen, even crush, the spirit of their workers, others will occasionally stand head and shoulders above the rest. These high-AQ organizations encourage employees to "climb the mountain," which is defined as their purpose in life and work. They help people strive to go a step further—to do and become a bit better than before.

As you upgrade AQ, you will build new strength and capacity to deal with and overcome adversity. The end result improves your ability to climb the mountain and lead others to do the same.

Begin by assessing the current toll adversity takes on you, your team, and your organization by completing the following snapshot of your organizational operating system (Exhibit 1.1, Parts One and Two).

Please reflect and answer Yes or No to each of the *five statements within each section* by circling your response.

How much of a toll does adversity take upon you?

- At the end of the day, I am typically energized.   Yes   No
- I thrive on challenges and am relatively unfazed   Yes   No
  by most difficulties.
- Most people consider me optimistic, resilient,   Yes   No
  tenacious.

• When adversity strikes, I keep a cool head and focus on resolving the situation.	Yes	No
• I constantly strive to learn, grow, and improve.	Yes	No

Your team?

• We have a high-performing team.	Yes	No
• We avoid blaming, complaining, and criticizing.	Yes	No
• We focus on solving problems, no matter how substantial they may be.	Yes	No
• People seek us out to take on the toughest challenges.	Yes	No
• We remain energized and focused when faced with a setback.	Yes	No

Your organization?

• When something goes seriously wrong among my immediate group, people rarely point fingers.	Yes	No
• People here accept and learn from failure, so they are comfortable taking risks and trying new things.	Yes	No
• When we're really under a lot of pressure, the leaders in my organization let people retain the same level of control in decisions and daily action.	Yes	No
• When we face change, people quickly join in the creative process of how to make it as effective and positive as possible.	Yes	No
• People rarely waste time whining when they could be improving the situation.	Yes	No

Exhibit 1.1 How Is Your Organizational Operating System?
Part One

Score your responses by counting how many you marked "Yes" for each section.

You

4–5   You probably deal with adversity better than most of the people you work with. You are likely the one they rely on to assist with challenges and setbacks that might demoralize others. You may be dragged down or frustrated by low-AQ people.

2–3   You deal well with moderate levels of adversity but may be suffering an unnecessary toll when adversities pile up and demands increase. Increasing your AQ will help you remain strong in challenging times.

0–1   Adversity takes a real toll on your soul. You can substantially improve your outlook, performance, and strength by measuring and strengthening your AQ.

Your Team

4–5   Your team probably enjoys high performance and synergy. It solves problems, makes decisions, and takes action. Adversities rarely slow you down and may be welcome sources of opportunity and learning.

2–3   Your team fares best when conditions are predictable and moderately demanding. When adversities pile up, people may behave poorly and the team may start to fray at the edges. Improving Team AQ can strengthen your team's ability to grow and tap its full capacity.

0–1   Your team is easily beaten down by challenges and does not rise to meet new demands. There is likely to be a lot of conflict, and some people are mentally checked out of the process. Measuring and strengthening your Team AQ can produce dramatic improvements in team morale and performance.

Your Organization

4–5   You probably have an agile, high-accountability culture, which does not get mired in the same muck many of your competitors seem unable to avoid. You can learn to strengthen this vital factor with the principles in this book.

2–3 You probably have a moderate-AQ organization, which takes longer and works harder than necessary to implement change. Some of your top people may come and go. You can strengthen your people, teams, and culture with the assessments and tools provided in this book.

0–1 You probably work for a moderately low-AQ organization that dampens spirit, morale, and innovation. Over time, many "real doers" leave, and problems drag on longer than necessary. Training doesn't seem to solve the problem. People may be becoming somewhat jaded. Even you may be uninspired or have a hard time envisioning being there for long. This requires a fundamental shift in the culture. The good news is, as you employ the deeper strategies offered in this book, people will start to rekindle their hope and effort. You may inspire some Campers to Climb.

Exhibit 1.2 How Is Your Organizational Operating System? Part Two

Behold the turtle. He makes progress only when he sticks his neck out.

—James Bryant Conant

Now that you have had the chance to consider the toll adversity may take on you, your team, and your enterprise, consider the three categories of how people respond to the daunting challenge of the ascent.

Quitters, Campers, and Climbers

Quitters are the people who retired years ago but just never bothered to tell anybody. At some point Quitters were overwhelmed by the challenge of the ascent and gave up on their higher pursuits. They ignore, mask, or desert their basic core human drive to ascend and, with it, much of what life offers. Unfortunately for them, and for those around them, Quitters often are bitter and depressed about their lot in life. They are resentful of the Climbers, and even the Campers, around them. When adversity strikes, Quitters' operating systems freeze or crash.

Campers, for the most part, are retired Climbers. They get the job done sufficiently; they simply don't strive as hard or sacrifice as much as they once did. They've lost the edge. Their operating systems get bogged down, or they have reached some limits beyond which they seem unable to go. They perform the basic functions but do not demonstrate the same speed, capacity, and capabilities they once had. Campers represent half-tapped potential. At some point in their careers and lives, they understandably got tired of the ascent up the mountain and they found a nice, comfortable place to sit out their remaining years. They have sacrificed their highest aspirations and contributions for the security and stability they now may enjoy. I say "may" because, ironically, the mountain is far from stable. The campground is continually rocked by an avalanche of change that causes Campers great consternation and fear. More tragically, while Campers may have been successful in reaching the campground, once they abandon the ascent they gradually atrophy and lose their ability to Climb, assessing an incalculable cost on themselves and their organizations.

Climbers are dedicated to a lifelong ascent. Their operating systems drive an inner relentlessness that immunizes them from adversities. Climbers make things happen. They are tenacious and refuse to accept defeat for long. They step into the very fear that paralyzes so many others. Although they may face more adversity than others, they continue to think in terms of possibilities and rarely allow any internal factor or external obstacle to get in the way of their ascent. They are fueled by challenges and refuse to be insignificant in their work or their relationships. Because of their operating systems, they simply learn from each challenge, adapt, grow, and move on to the next mountain.

The Trail and Tribulations of Adversity

How would you classify yourself? Your coworkers? Your employees? Who do you hire, work with, and lead? Are they Quitters, Campers, or Climbers? What do you see in their operating systems when new demands are placed upon them, or when they face adversity? What roles do each of them play in the morale and momentum within your organization?

CEOs and managers worldwide report that 80 percent (or more) of their employees are Campers. As adversity mounts more people Quit or

Camp. Yet these leaders are aware that they *must* hire, grow, and become *Climbers* in order to gain ground in this new millennium. This requires the creation of a new kind of workforce and work culture that will rise to meet the challenges of the New Economy.

A recent restructuring within the organization of one of our clients crystallized the differences among Quitters, Campers, and Climbers. The restructuring was fairly broad and deep. It was a nationwide effort that affected all facets of this financial institution. It was further complicated by a rumor of the company's demise; this rumor threatened to preempt efforts to communicate the restructuring.

No one disagreed that the company was faltering; however, the leaders hadn't expected performance to plummet when the rumor arose. Even with little or no information, employees of the firm assumed that they would all suffer as a result. Sick days increased, and a general malaise pervaded the workforce. People seemed burdened with the certainty that the change would wreak havoc, uprooting their campground.

The chief operating officer characterized the rumor's response as follows: "Fifteen percent of the people are inconsolably panicked. It's eating them alive, and we have not even announced the plan! Seventy-five to eighty percent of the people seem resigned, as if certain of some awful fate. They drag around in a haze, shuffling under the weight of their burden. In contrast, a minority are genuinely excited that we are finally taking courageous action to remain competitive."

Some crash, others bog down, while a minority continues to flourish. This is the direct result of each person's AQ.

THE TOOLS OF AQ @ WORK

Over the past several years, my team and I have developed a variety of proven models and tools to assess and upgrade individual, team, and organizational AQ, which we would like to teach you in this book. We tested these models and tools throughout the world, and our clients now use them for a broad range of applications, including hiring, training, mentoring, and coaching, as well as accelerating change, improving performance, developing leaders, and strengthening organizational culture. You will learn about and apply the models and tools introduced below, among others, to address your adversities and further your ascent.

Measuring AQ is how you will get a precise read of how well you, your team, and your organization currently respond to adversity. Using abbreviated versions of the full AQ assessments, you will measure AQ at each of these levels so that you have a precise and meaningful starting point from which you can learn and apply specific AQ-strengthening tools.

You will also learn how to include and measure AQ in your hiring practices so that you can hire high AQ Climbers to join your Climbing Team.

Your CORE describes the four dimensions that make up your AQ and your operating system. You will learn about and graph your CORE so that you can learn to strengthen your CORE response to adversity, as well as your overall AQ and Response Ability. This is one of the most important and useful lessons about AQ.

The Hierarchy of Control articulates the quest toward greater Response Ability and explains why most people communicate and behave poorly when adversity strikes. This model will challenge you with the lifelong ascent toward greater response control and personal effectiveness. It sheds light on unproductive outbursts and frames a new, more effective approach.

Response Ability—the outgrowth of your AQ—is your capacity to respond effectively to whatever comes your way. Or, more precisely, it is your capacity to maintain clarity, focus, and direction in adversity-rich times. It is a new conceptual framework for strengthening ourselves and others for long-term, not just short-term, effort.

Most people have been trained to listen, assume accountability, solve problems, make decisions, and craft a plan. Yet how well do the people you work with access this important software in moments of truth, when adversity strikes? This book teaches the discipline of Response Ability by providing precise insights into what your response to challenges is composed of and how to permanently rewire this pattern so that your operating system performs optimally under the onslaught of the day.

You will assess and strengthen Response Ability in your team and your culture. You will also learn to assess the Response Ability and AQ of potential job applicants through a variety of new methods that will strengthen your overall search-and-hiring process.

The LEAD Sequence is the precise model and tool you will use to help your-self, others, and your teams to rewire, raise, and strengthen your AQ. You will first apply this scientifically grounded approach at the individual level, but you will also go to Climbing School and learn to apply these techniques as a coach, mentor, and leader. You will then advance your skills to the team level.

The Significance Scale is a model and tool for assessing what helps a per-son matter in the quest for the grander cause. It introduces significance as the deepest human motivator and one of the vital facets of a Climbing Culture. You will use the Significance Scale to reach the heart of the Climber and to coach, lead, and grow other people toward greater contri-butions, fulfillment, and influence.

The Wisdom Pyramid will explain how noise, data, and information cre-ate Infofog, which may cloud your ability to make clear decisions and solve problems. The Wisdom Pyramid will challenge you to refocus your ener-gies beyond knowledge to timeless truths, or wisdom.

Together, these models and tools can fundamentally strengthen your hiring process, your training, your coworkers, your teams, your culture, and the way you view and approach all adversities.

ADVERSITY QUOTIENT @ WORK AND BEYOND

Florida Water Services almost sank. This privately held company with-stood record winter rainfall, which led to a severe falloff in customer demand and a precipitous drop in revenues. It threatened the survival of the business during a time of tremendous change. The employees felt like they were getting hit from all sides.

An initial assessment of the organization's AQ revealed it to be moder-ate, or slightly below average, when compared with that of others in the industry. The goal was to strengthen its AQ and upgrade its individual and collective operating systems, thereby improving morale, performance, and profitability. My team and I were pleased to discover that, following inten-sive training in the principles of AQ @ Work, Florida Water Services avoided imminent disaster and quickly achieved even greater profitability. The training took the form of the extended version of Climbing School introduced in this book.

First, we measured the individual and collective AQs of the entire leadership team and examined their initial level of Response Ability. Graphing the CORE dimensions of their AQs revealed some individual and general weaknesses and strengths upon which we could build. We saw some immediate improvements in their Response Ability, which sparked momentum and greater interest in exposing the entire workforce to Climbing School.

Next, we walked the employees through their own AQ and CORE Profiles and developed specific plans to strengthen the CORE dimensions of their AQs. They defined their mountain and implemented specific steps to improve their AQs so that they could ascend through any challenge. Early in the training, Mercedes Guzman, vice president of human resources for MP Water Services, noted, "The change is significant. It is impressive to see employees follow through on commitments to implement what they have learned, not only at work but in their personal lives, too. I have noticed the improvement in attitude and their sense of ownership. We have had several successful years in a row and, in my opinion, the employees' improved AQ and approach to challenges has been instrumental to the success of the corporation." They were now accelerating their change agenda and good-naturedly bragging about each adversity they would conquer.

We then applied AQ at the team level to strengthen team resilience, problem solving, and decision making. We wanted to create some Climbing Teams. Leaders began to use AQ to coach, mentor, and lead Climbers. They also applied the Hierarchy of Control model to strengthen their ability to control their own responses and outbursts. They used the Significance Scale to assess and deepen each person's sense of significance on the job and within the workplace. Each person was trained in the LEAD Sequence and Action Funnel as an efficient problem-solving model for dealing with adversity of any magnitude. This method was used to help rewire individual patterns of response to all kinds of adversity. We helped organizational leaders develop an AQ-based performance appraisal system and provided the tools to implement AQ in the hiring process—all provided in this book.

The results were immediate and enduring, according to company president John Cirello. "It was precisely the wake-up call and tools we needed to rewire how we dealt with more and more adversity," he said. "Our outlook before this training was pretty dismal. Today it has never been brighter. Through upgrading our operating system with AQ, our business, people, and entire culture have been transformed."

While the workforce attended AQ Climbing School, the strategic leadership team learned, selected from, and implemented a series of methods for creating a high-AQ culture—also provided in this book. This strengthened the culture, shrank the campground, and nurtured the Climbers.

Overall, Florida Water Services used the methods presented in this book to create a holistic approach to AQ, resulting in short- and long-term impact on profitability and performance. A reassessment of the company AQ over months, and now years, reveals a significant and consistent strengthening of the culture and the workforce, poising the company to thrive despite the quickening pace of acquisitions, entangling regulations, and the reinvention of the entire industry. Sure, they still have problems. In fact, they face more than they did five years ago. Through implementing the AQ principles and methods provided in these pages, they deal with problems more effectively and efficiently. Previously, any challenge could slow them to a grinding halt; today, nothing gets in their way.

But the results go deeper than the bottom line. Catherine Walker, an engineer for the company, was diagnosed with breast cancer months after the training. At the time of the training, she had an AQ that was slightly above average. I knew she really "got it" when she came up to me after the program to explain some of the ways she could use it right away. I remember that she was especially excited about using the LEAD Sequence to strengthen her own AQ and to help coach others. She also admitted that she felt that she had been camping in some facets of her life, and it was now time to climb. She believed the AQ training could help her sustain the motivation and effort to take on her greater aspirations, one of which was to run a marathon. For Catherine, as for so many people, it seemed that the simple awareness of her AQ coupled with the LEAD Sequence was enough to spark significant change in her Response Ability and overall resilience. Then the breast cancer was diagnosed.

I was curious to see how Catherine would respond to the adversity, since she had already seen a 21 percent improvement in her AQ. She now scored in the moderately high range, but would it make a difference?

Catherine directly applied the CORE dimensions of AQ. She focused on what she could control, took ownership of her recovery, and developed specific strategies to limit the reach and endurance of the cancer.

She also focused on her own mountain, or purposes, knowing it had to be keenly in mind in order to ascend through her current adversity. In short, she harnessed the adversity, using the cancer to elevate her purpose and fuel her determination. She knew chemotherapy would be brutal but refused to let it hold her down. She set her sights on running a marathon and raising money for other victims. She made it her driving purpose to teach her seven-year-old daughter Nicole and her coworkers a lifetime lesson.

"I contemplated death only briefly. Then I got a grip and said, People don't die from breast cancer anymore! I'm going to get through this. I've got as good a chance as anyone to get through this," Catherine explained.

It was inspiring to see AQ put to use at such a personal level and in such a poignant way. It was also wonderful to see how AQ can be contagious, sparking others to consider adversity in a new light. Even in the throes of chemotherapy and her multiple surgeries, Catherine somehow ran and inspired her coworkers in the form of notes and E-mail. Some days she was able to run only a single block, but she refused to give in to the cancer.

Recovering more completely than expected and in half the predicted time, Catherine went on to run her marathon and is now in complete remission. Currently, she is training for the Disney Marathon. Reflecting on her experience today, she said, "It seems odd, but I'm grateful for the cancer. I could never be the person I am today without having gone through what I did. I'm lucky to be alive, and I am stronger for what I went through. I think people respect me more as a leader at work because of how I learned to deal with and continue to handle adversity. Now others want to learn how."

Tools for understanding and growing AQ provided in this book have sparked many such stories and comebacks, each with dramatic impact on the person and the workplace.

The good news is that AQ is not something innate and instilled only in the "chosen." It's quite the opposite. Once you understand AQ, you can upgrade your own, your team's, and your organization's—enlarging your capacity for all challenges, as Catherine did.

Specifically, you will go through the steps of assessing, graphing, and understanding your own AQ. You will then learn about the practical science of AQ to better understand and teach these concepts to others. I will guide you through Climbing School, first for yourself, then to coach and lead others. You will learn how to find and hire Climbers using AQ in all facets of the hiring process. As your expertise grows, you will apply advanced Climbing School skills to create high-AQ Climbing Teams and a high-AQ culture. In short, you will learn a comprehensive approach to strengthening your own AQ and that of your enterprise.

You will explore how adversity inspires, strengthens, and defines people and their organizations so that they can fulfill their greatest potential and highest aspirations. Indeed, this is at once the hope and the promise of the Adversity Quotient. Open yourself to these lessons and you too will harness the blessing and power of adversity.

"On rope!"

Topographical Map of Chapter 1
Expanding Your Capacity: The Human Operating System

Adversity is on the rise.
- Individuals face an average of twenty-three adversities each day. Ninety-eight percent of the individuals predict a more difficult, chaotic, and uncertain future.
- You must upgrade your human operating system to remain viable and strong.

Adversity Quotient (AQ) defines the human operating system.

Response Ability is one's capacity to maintain clarity, focus, and direction in adversity-rich times. It defines the extent of your ability to respond effectively to whatever comes your way.

There are three types of human capacity.
- **Required Capacity**—all that is required of a person to meet the world's demands.
- **Existing Capacity**—the full extent of a person's skills, aptitudes, talents, knowledge, and experience.
- **Accessed Capacity**—the portion of Existing Capacity that is actually tapped or delivered.

A successful leader will unleash all forms of capacity to maintain an edge in today's marketplace and to further the ascent.

- **The Mountain**—represents your purpose. Individuals and organizations have distinct mountains.
- **Climbers**—Those who remain relentless in their ascent. They continually strive, improve, grow, learn, and enlarge their capacities.
- **Campers**—Those who settle into their comfort zones. They become motivated by predictability, security, and limited change. They and their capacities atrophy.
- **Quitters**—Those who have abandoned their ascent. They are often bitter and avoid change. Their Accessed Capacity is very limited.

AQ can be used to accelerate change; improve performance; grow resilience; improve hiring; reduce turnover; coach, mentor, and lead others; strengthen teams; fortify your culture; and turn Campers into Climbers.

CHAPTER 2

THE SCIENCE OF AQ

If you watch how nature deals with adversity,
continually renewing itself, you cannot help but learn.
—Bernie Siegel, M.D.

HARNESSING ADVERSITY:
THE HIDDEN ELEMENT OF SUCCESS

My personal journey to AQ began twenty years ago and was influenced primarily by two life-changing events. I had begun researching issues of business success in my undergraduate days at the University of California and read much of the conventional wisdom in this field. My first job upon graduating was working with a prominent venture capitalist and author in Santa Fe, New Mexico. As his assistant I was responsible for collecting data on entrepreneurs and profiling them and their common traits of success for his upcoming book. I had gathered dozens of stories from his clients and contacts. Sitting alone in the main room of his historic adobe office, reviewing my notes, I was dumbstruck. These self-made entrepreneurs, who had essentially brought their dreams to life, did not fit the conventional description of success. These entrepreneurs had not cornered the market for intelligence, past performance, GPA, education, technical competence, or special upbringing.

In fact, most of these successful entrepreneurs *violated* the conventional wisdom on success at every turn. Many had had trouble in school; some had dropped out. They had unconventional résumés, which would have made it tough for them to find a job. Most had not had great home lives, schooling, and privilege. The most amazing finding to me was that every single successful entrepreneur had faced some terrible setback in his or her life. Those setbacks came in every variety, from emotional (abuse, alcoholism, divorce, etc.) to physical (disabling injuries, addiction, heart attacks, etc.) to professional (being fired, several failed businesses, etc.). My boss explained, "They each have some sort of chip on their shoulder, something to prove. It gives them the fire in the belly."

The successful entrepreneurs had come the closest to crafting and living their dreams than any category of professionals I had encountered. Unlike many of their peers, these people were taking meaningful risks, living adventurously, going up against terrible odds. Why?

That was the day I set my old research on human effectiveness on the shelf like a high school yearbook—a fond memory, but of fading relevance—and began to explore the role of adversity in success with the same relentlessness these people had inspired in me through their stories.

Five years later, with a Ph.D. almost in hand, I conducted staff training for Outward Bound in the Boundary Waters of northern Minnesota—a place where the state bird, the mosquito, reigns supreme. Outward Bound is an organization based in Garrison, New York, that uses adventure-oriented activities in wilderness settings to teach teamwork through group decision making, assignment of duties, and coordinated action.

At that time in my life, I, like most people, found as many things to complain about as I did to appreciate on any given day, sometimes more. Although relatively upbeat, I would on occasion find myself whining about some pretty meaningless concerns. I often let things get to me, bother me, even drag me down.

During the course of this fateful day with Outward Bound, I witnessed an odd phenomenon—an event that would forever change the way I look at life, my research, and how I approach my everyday trials and tribulations.

I had been climbing all morning with my team of Outward Bound leaders-in-the-making. As noon approached, we decided to take a break, and we gathered together in the shady forest, near a stagnant pond. As I reviewed the lessons on leadership, we were being reviewed by a swarm of mosquitoes that invaded us like some demonic cloud straight from the gates of hell. At first we held strong—there were the occasional swats—but within minutes, they became unbearable. Soon these outdoor-hardy leaders were inventing new curse words as they danced like whirling dervishes to fend off the clouds of bloodthirsty attackers. With each angry swat, the prospect of continuing that day's ascent became more and more remote. I looked around the group, and no one seemed able to stand his or her ground, let alone focus on the lesson at hand—that is, except for one man.

Over to the side of the group stood Jake, who was dressed only in a T-shirt, shorts, and sandals. Despite the same cloud of mosquitoes buzzing relentlessly around his exposed arms, legs, head, and neck, he was attentively taking notes. He was clearly amused at the antics of the rest of the group but literally unfazed by the event. Somehow, some way, Jake was able to rise above the adversity, take in the beauty of the deep, virgin forest, and appreciate the sweet, pine-scented air. The mosquitoes crossed his face, went in his ears, landed on his nose, but he refused to let them divert him from the learning at hand. In a strange way, he almost seemed to thrive on the aggravating assault. Jake demonstrated a Zen-like clarity and steely calm. While the rest of us were ready to tear our skin off, forgetting all about the next leg of our ascent, Jake alone was prepared to continue the climb.

How was this possible?

Exasperated, others asked, "Don't they *bite* you? Can't you feel it?" It was obvious that we all envied this hidden power that Jake seemed to wield over the very forces of Mother Nature.

Jake shrugged and said, "I can't make the mosquitoes go away, so I make them irrelevant."

Irrelevant? But how could that be? Clearly, some mosquitoes were dive-bombing Jake's exposed limbs and face, taking bites of flesh, draining blood, again and again.

But something else was taking place within Jake. Not only did he make the adversity irrelevant, he used it to somehow *strengthen* himself. I could see the resolve in his eyes—and we were all moved by his intensity. What if we could all learn to let life's mosquitoes become irrelevant? How much easier might each day be? How much greater might our focus, energy, and momentum become? We all wanted to learn his secret. At that moment, I knew that something larger was happening. It was the ability to harness adversity, and my curiosity to determine how to harness adversity would forge my research, career, and life.

My curiosity was piqued by my experiences with entrepreneurs and Jake, as well as by the tremendous implications for individuals and organizations. So I dedicated my life to understanding and refining this amazing ability to *harness* the hidden forces of adversity. After twenty years of research and ten years of measurement and business application with more than 100,000 people in every type of organization, I found that—especially in adversity-rich times—success at work and in life is determined primarily by a person's Adversity Quotient.

THE AQ ADVANTAGE

At its most basic, *AQ is the precise, measurable, unconscious pattern of how you respond to adversity*. But AQ is much more than a measure. It contributes a vital piece to what is becoming a grand unification theory of human behavior, drawing from nearly four decades of wisdom and scientific research from some of the world's top thinkers. Once you get a picture of how AQ works, you will be able to apply the following science to unravel some of the fundamental mysteries of individual and collective endeavor.

AQ AS A WORKPLACE MEASURE

As virtually every industry becomes more competitive, leaders are under mounting pressure to measure and substantiate their investments and efforts. Whereas it was once good enough to provide business-relevant training, you must now demonstrate the impact the training has upon the enterprise. The same mandates apply to investments in new hiring methods or organization-wide initiatives.

One of the most compelling aspects of AQ and our work is that it and the improvements are *measurable*. This is a true distinction of AQ, especially given the statistical strength of the measure (see Appendix A). You will find many uses for the ability to measure AQ. I have listed a few examples to spark your thinking.

AQ and Income

AQ is a predictor of wealth. A study by Dr. Gideon Markman, professor of entrepreneurial studies at Rensselaer Polytechnic Institute, revealed a strong relationship between the AQs and incomes of entrepreneurial inventors. So far, other studies on AQ and entrepreneurialism indicate that higher-AQ people appear to earn more.

AQ and Sales

Of all types of performance, sales is one of the most measurable. We are, therefore, frequently asked to use AQ as a predictor of sales performance. SBC Telecommunication provided my research team with three perform- ance measures, including percentage of: (1) top-line sales (new sales), (2) quota, and (3) net sales. We discovered that those in the top half of AQ scores outsold those in the bottom half by 166, 150, and 106 percent, respectively. These results are typical, although the differences between high- and low-AQ salespeople may vary from 90 to 320 percent, or more, depending on the industry.

AQ and Performance

Deloitte & Touche was voted by *Fortune* magazine as one of the top ten employers. To strengthen its position as "employer of choice," leaders in Deloitte & Touche's Great Lakes Region began to explore how AQ might help them predict performance and promotability for their new experi- enced hires. Over the course of two years we have found that the AQs of their top performers exceed those of the lower performers by 17 points (a significant difference). Also, those promoted had the highest AQs. Pilot studies on the AQ training with different levels of managers revealed an 18 percent increase in AQ as a result of the training.

AQ and Hiring

Like so many industries, the world of financial services has been com- pletely redefined—putting intense pressure on the remaining players to hire people who can thrive in an environment filled with uncertainty and demands. In a sample of 278 employees in the retail bank division, Sun- Trust Bank discovered that, on average, the high-AQ people tended to out- perform the low-AQ employees. SunTrust is now moving toward measuring the AQ of every applicant.

Measurable and Behavioral Change

Applying the principles provided in this book, people improve their AQs by an average of 23 points, or roughly 16 percent, representing a broad range of initial scores. Some improve substantially more, some less. But what I find most inspiring, beyond the score, is the change in *behavior* that results from the higher AQ. As people respond more effectively to adversity, it begins to influence all facets of their lives and has the general effect of lightening their burden. To understand and create behavioral change, we must start with a discussion of patterns.

THE GAMES PATTERNS PLAY

We are all deeply driven to make sense of the world. There may be instances when you are perplexed by how others are making sense of things and how different their view is compared with yours. We each have a distinct *explanatory style,* or pattern of responding to life's events. The nature of the pattern determines how we react and all that follows. For example, those who believe that a given setback is far-reaching and long-lasting are more likely to believe that what they do will not matter. This pattern is also known as "learned helplessness."

It has taken close to thirty-eight years of research into how patterns of thought and emotion—such as explanatory style—affect human behavior for it to be fully acknowledged. But after more than 1,500 studies into these patterns we have gradually and fundamentally changed how we view our species. As a longtime student-turned-practitioner of human performance, I have seen the concrete, measurable benefits these understandings and breakthroughs can provide.

Martin Seligman, Ph.D., of the University of Pennsylvania, is most prominent among the dozens of accomplished scientists who have contributed to this field of research. His groundbreaking work on the landmark theory of "learned helplessness" opened a flood of research into depression, optimism, health, and performance.

Applications of these patterns of response, or explanatory style, go beyond the typical workplace. According to Seligman, "Basketball teams, optimistic baseball players, and baseball teams all do better than they're expected to, particularly when the chips are down." Dr. Christopher Peterson of the University of Michigan adds, "The pessimistic individual puts himself or herself in situations where bad things might happen, and they eventually do."

The dozens of researchers in this area have given us new insights into the tragic disease of "give-up-itis." They also provide us with some potential ways to immunize people against learned helplessness.

Seligman says that those with these destructive response patterns "are a group of people who reliably, when bad things happen, say, 'It's going to last forever, going to undermine everything I do, and it's my fault.' " However, those who perceive the same setback as limited and fleeting are more likely to respond to the challenge positively and optimistically. The research of Seligman and others clearly indicates that *these patterns are learned*. More important, it has been determined that these patterns can be permanently rewired and strengthened. These discoveries contribute to our understanding of the Adversity Quotient.

AQ is the next generation of understanding how we explain or respond to life's events. It expands the original research on learned helplessness and related concepts, pulling together for the first time those elements that most precisely predict and influence human effectiveness. To optimize these patterns we must understand how they are formed.

> Our character is basically a composite of our habits. Because they are consistent, often unconscious patterns, they constantly, daily, express our character.
>
> —Stephen Covey

HARDWIRING YOUR BRAIN—THE ORIGINS OF AQ

Patterns such as your AQ are learned and hardwired into your brain during your impressionable youth when you watch others deal with life's difficulties. As you unconsciously absorb and adapt these responses, you form your own, unique response pattern, or AQ. We hardwire all sorts of patterns, including speech, music, and laughter.

As we develop a history of responses, we literally alter the molecular structure of our brains. This is the physiology of learning. The brain is ideally equipped to hardwire patterns of thought, emotion, and behavior. *Hardwiring patterns is one of the great capacities of the brain.*

A recent study of cabdrivers in London—long renowned for their ability to navigate anywhere without a map—revealed a difference in their brains. The portion of their hippocampus related to spatial abilities was actually larger. They had altered the wiring and structure of their brain. And the longer they drove, the larger this section of the brain became. I believe the same is true of our AQ—how we respond to adversity. As it strengthens, we change the wiring and structure of our brains. There is an increasing pool of evidence for how we hardwire patterns.

As brain-imaging and -mapping technology becomes increasingly sophisticated, neuroscientists are greatly improving their understanding of how the brain functions and communicates. Researchers at Cold Spring Laboratory have recently employed a new type of microscopy to see how some facets of hardwiring occur and how brains change in structure based on their stimuli, which are triggered by response patterns. Mirjana Maletic-Svatic, Roberto Malinow, and Karel Svoboda, a Cold Spring Lab research team, discovered that new dendrites (the hairlike ends on a nerve cell) that communicate and connect with other neurons can be generated and thickened based on their stimuli. This is one of the ways that hard-wiring occurs.

At Mankato State University brain researchers discovered a group of nuns who were able to remain sharp and professionally viable well into their eighties and beyond. The nuns donated their brains to scientific research upon their death so studies could be conducted on their mental staying power. Scientists discovered that by engaging in brain-active hob-bies like music, bridge, and Scrabble, the nuns formed new pathways or hardwiring until their final days. This ability to grow new dendrites is what provides genuine agility, flexibility, and adaptability in a changing world.

Can hardwiring be habit-forming? Each day we go through a complex series of hardwired patterns of grooming, washing, communicating, and eating—all without thinking about how we perform them. But if the brain had not hardwired such patterns, we would constantly have to renavigate the same terrain. Hardwiring is your brain's way of improving, growing, and adapting to life's demands.

Some hardwired patterns are highly personal, with no real implica-tions for your performance. Laughter patterns vary widely; they probably do not influence your ability to confront life's challenges. However, other patterns, such as your AQ, do influence a broad range of factors, including recovery time from surgery, pain threshold, ability to solve problems, com-petitiveness, optimism, decision making, sales performance, leadership selection, team performance, agility in responding to change, resilience, and staying power.

Medical research is just beginning to acknowledge that these patterns can have as much or *greater* power over a patient's health as the treatment one receives. Dr. Lisa Aspinwell of the University of Maryland discovered that people with more constructive response patterns prior to heart surgery "were likely to get up and walk around their rooms sooner and return to work and the normal activities more quickly." Medical issues columnist Stephen Cohen summarized the power of hardwiring in an article on brain-related breakthroughs: "It appears that physical pathways in the brain may dictate much, if not all of human behavior."

As a specific, hardwired pattern, AQ influences human behavior more dramatically than any other pattern we have discovered to date. It defines what occurs between any given event and your resulting behavior. This is why AQ affects all facets of human endeavor, including vitality and health. To grasp the holistic effect of your AQ, it is helpful to explore how it works at a microscopic level.

THE CHEMISTRY OF PERFORMANCE

Imagine a six-year-old girl holding a baseball mitt; nearby there are two balls—a red one and a blue one. You pick up the red ball and gently toss it to her. She giggles as she catches the ball, which fills her little mitt. She calls out, "Now, toss the blue one!" So you gently lob the blue one. She sticks out her glove and watches as the blue ball bounces off the red one still in her mitt. She looks surprised. You explain that she *has* to drop the red one to catch the blue one.

Scientifically, this game of catch is played countless times every second through every cell of the body. Each cell has its own variety of baseball mitts, called *receptor sites,* which are designed to catch whatever floats by. The informational substances that link to these receptor sites are called *peptides.* Peptides are strings of tiny proteins—amino acids—that can enhance or deplete your cells' functions. The type of peptides a specific receptor site "catches" or links determines what happens to that cell and that part of the body. Once a peptide links to a receptor site, it prevents another from doing so.

"That is why you cannot hold opposing emotions at the same time," according to Candace Pert, Ph.D., professor of biopeptide research at

Georgetown University and author of the breakthrough book *Molecules of Emotion*. In a recent conversation, Dr. Pert explained to me that the combinations of different peptides and receptor sites have different effects. For example, one kind of peptide may strengthen your immune system, while another will sap your energy or give you the common cold.

The powerful twist to this theory is that the hundreds of peptides coursing throughout your body and linking to these receptor sites are profoundly influenced by your *patterns of thought and emotion*. These patterns are largely influenced by how you experience and explain your life's events; therefore, the adversities you face, are not what determine the consequences you suffer. Your experience of—and response to—those events is what matters and what will influence all systems in your body.

Peptides are among the most diverse and potent chemical transmitters in the brain. People who experience depression are not just mentally sad; they are *systemically* depressed. Their entire chemistry is depressed, which influences everything that happens in the body. That is why depressed people often do not feel hungry, cannot sleep, or, conversely, oversleep, and why seemingly minor tasks seem to require herculean effort.

Peptides also drift and perhaps leap through all systems of the body. Brain-imaging technology shows that the cerebral spinal fluid carries these informational substances from the brain down the spinal column out to the skin. Each cell affects that area of the body for which it is specially designed; this is why different organs respond differently to their receptor sites.

For example, when the peptide for thirst (angiotocin) is sprinkled in the brain of a rat, it flushes to all systems in the body, affecting the muscles, nerve cells, brain, and more. As a result, the rat engages all of its systems and drinks furiously. Since the peptide flushes through *all* systems, the lung cells conserve water, kidney cells concentrate urine, and so on. Every facet of the rat is affected as the peptide spreads throughout its entire system.

The same peptide flush takes place inside of you as you respond to life's events. By the time you experience an emotion, your peptides are already at work, affecting every system in your body. Your AQ therefore triggers the chemical interplay throughout your body. Beyond understanding its implications on your mental and physical strength, you can influence and fortify these reactions as you improve your AQ. We can see the positive influences patterns can have when we examine people who achieve optimal states.

The function and health of every cell of your body-mind is
influenced by how you respond to life's events.

The Flow Experience

When a person is so fully immersed and engaged in a task that he or she loses all sense of time, this optimal state is known as *flow*. The term was coined by Mihaly Csikszentmihalyi, author of *Flow: The Psychology of Optimal Experience*. He explains that a person in flow is likely to experience extraordinary clarity of thought, boundless energy, and a deep inner calm. The heart pumps strongly, the muscles are fluid and relaxed, breathing is deep, and the mind is alert. This "relaxation response," studied at length by Dr. Herbert Benson of Harvard University, was found to be the opposite of the "fight-flight response" that triggers such powerful stress responses in the body as rapid heartbeat, sweaty palms, a rise in blood pressure, and a narrowing of the eyes. In flow the body-mind network is creating an optimal experience, elevating the body, and generating top performance.

Clearly, your pattern of response to any event influences your entire thought process and physiology. The most important concept derived from this research boils down to this: *The function and health of every cell of your body-mind is influenced by how you respond to life's events*. Why, then, is this book not about the Good Luck Quotient or the Joy Quotient? As it turns out, among all kinds of events, adversity plays the most potent role, making your AQ the most vital pattern.

The Brain's Adversity Bias

Research on the chemistry of performance indicates that adverse events appear to have a significant and influential impact on the human brain. For example, psychologist John T. Cacioppo, Ph.D., discovered that the brain has a negative bias—that is, we respond much more strongly to negative events than to positive events, even in the earliest stages of brain development. As a result, *adversity plays a predominant role in the brain*, and in the resulting flood of peptides. It is as if we hear adversity with greater volume and intensity than we do more pleasant events. Arguably, this could be why the evening news reports a lot more bad news than good news. The brain is drawn toward adversity. We naturally assign adversity great importance, putting all systems on guard, as if poised for an attack. This explains why your response to adversity is of paramount importance.

A constructive pattern of response, or higher AQ, can keep all systems vital, strong, and functioning optimally. A destructive pattern of response, or lower AQ, can create both short- and long-term consequences. In the short term, a lower-AQ individual suffers all the symptoms of stress, worry, and perhaps fear. Beyond the elevated blood pressure, sweaty palms, and tensed muscles may be rushed decisions, risk-averse behavior, and catastrophizing. This can drag down the individual and those with whom he or she is in immediate contact. In the long term, a person with a low AQ may suffer from a depleted immune system, fatigue, resignation, loss of hope, depression, or worse.

The brain's bias explains why, ultimately, your pattern of response to *adversity*, or AQ, profoundly influences the functioning of the entire human organism, which in turn affects your entire system and all that you think, feel, and do. Recent breakthroughs explain this phenomenon as well as how and why you are constructed more like the Internet than a machine.

Ultimately, your AQ profoundly influences the functioning of the entire human organism, which in turn affects all that you think, feel, and do.

THE MYTH OF THE HUMAN MACHINE

Many of us think of our bodies as the machine that transports our brain from place to place! However, new findings reveal the body-mind to be much more of a symphony or like the Internet.

According to one expert, the brain does not exist just in our head. Ever have a gut feeling or butterflies in your stomach? Dr. Michael Gershon, author of *The Second Brain* and a neurobiologist at New York's Columbia-Presbyterian Medical Center, states that we have 100 billion neurons in the gut (the same number as in the brain) that signal stress and influence health. Dr. Paul Pearsall, author of the best-selling book *The Heart's Code,* has documented evidence to suggest that many of our decisions and reactions *do* come directly from the heart! Additionally,

Candace Pert's research on peptides shows that both the heart and gut have high concentrations of receptor sites.

Dissecting the human body into discrete and independent systems is as limiting as thinking of the Internet as mere computers, wires, servers, and electric current. While all of these components exist, they fall well short of describing the essence of the Internet, which is so much more than the sum of its components, just as the separate systems of the body fall well short of explaining its holistic nature.

In fact, Dr. Pert argues, "The body is organized as a *network*. . . . Peptides communicate to and connect all facets of the network, making the body a single functioning whole." As the groundbreaking researcher in the area of peptides, Dr. Pert helps us rethink the role of the brain: "The brain does not rule. . . . There is no center . . . and the network can be accessed *anywhere*."

The cerebral spinal fluid around the spinal cord is in direct communication with every nerve in the body out to the skin. Our reactions to life's events evoke certain peptides, which get dumped into the cerebral spinal fluid and flow to all of our tissues. *We literally bathe in our thoughts and emotions.* Molecules of emotion are found everywhere and they influence everything.

This linkage of peptides and receptor sites also influences your memories and beliefs. They trigger a specific menu of memories and beliefs— shaping the way you see the world at that moment. Perhaps that is why low- and high-AQ people experience and view the world in distinctly different ways. We see this every day at work. When a major change is announced, AQ comes into play. One person is utterly convinced it will hobble the organization, while another sees it as a genuine opportunity.

It is as if everything you say, feel, think, and do affects every facet of your own Intranet. The brain does not dominate. Your AQ is the spark that ignites all that follows. Despite these new findings, some people feel that any effort to improve themselves is hopelessly overshadowed by the daunting force of genetics.

THE MYTH OF SELF-DETERMINATION

One of the great backlashes of the turn of the millennium is coming from genetic researchers and evolutionary psychologists who have determined that who we are and what we do is influenced by our genetic code. The hardwiring from this code, some argue, may date back 200,000 years or more, to the origins of human presence on the planet.

These experts come from fields like evolutionary psychology and they believe that we carry in our brains ancient imprints as hunter-gatherers, that have not evolved as quickly as the environment in which we live. It was a mere 10,000 years ago that the invention of agriculture changed the way we lived, not nearly long enough for the brain to evolve new circuitry. They argue that the brain learned to trust instinct over reason, allowing us to respond immediately to an impending danger or wild predator. Since the brain is wired to give emotion primacy, we have a natural aversion to loss, which is why we may resist change, or why people act desperately or panicky when directly threatened. We are also programmed to classify things rather than think holistically. Moreover, we are programmed to fight or flee in the face of danger. Evolutionary psychologists argue that when we try to civilize ourselves out of these patterns we are fighting tens, if not hundreds, of thousands of years of circuitry.

Geneticists have an important role in this argument. With studies now encompassing many hundreds of sets of identical twins separated at birth, as well as adopted children, geneticists believe they can pinpoint, with almost eerie precision, the degree to which our genetics influence certain factors.

For example, geneticists believe that assertiveness is 60 percent inherent, and happiness is 80 percent genetic, having little to do with wealth, achievement, or marital status. Some geneticists also argue that genes influence how much coffee we consume, yet they have no effect on our tea consumption. Body size is largely genetic, while, overall, personality traits are roughly 50 percent heritable.

These messages have crept into the mainstream consciousness, sometimes with negative consequences. For instance, many obese people have given up on their health, having been told they will eventually lose their battle with genetics. We have also discovered that depression, violence, happiness, and serenity are more than emotional states—they are part of our genetic imprints. The ultimate question is this: are we simply playing out a genetic screenplay, or does AQ play a role?

The Reptilian Brain in a Suit

We all carry around a reptilian brain—the most primitive, instinctual part of this organ, which reacts strongly and is the source of several mechanisms largely unwelcome in the twenty-first century. Among these are violence, sexual domination, selfishness, and rage. While all of these served vital functions for primitive humans, today they threaten the fabric of our society. Evolutionary psychologists argue that it takes more than a suit or an education to overcome the reptilian brain.

So, for those of us who grew up in the era of self-determination, believing that "if you believe it, you can be it," the geneticists and evolutionary psychologists retort, "Not so!" They argue that you can take the man out of the cave, but you cannot take the caveman out of man. The danger in this comes when we camp out with genetics—making it an excuse for giving up the fight to be better, stronger, and more of a Climber. Why fight genetics, *right*?

But not all scientists agree, including psychologist Dr. Stanley Greenspan. "When a trait appears to be influenced by genes, people assume it's not changeable," Greenspan said. "Well, we can't change genes, but we can change the way genes express themselves. We *can* change behavior."

We have to get past the expression "I was made this way, so this is how it will forever be"—at least when it comes to our behavior. AQ is the tool for transcending these embedded ancestral codes to make powerful, clear, and spontaneous choices to handle any situation to the highest benefit. It interrupts and steps outside these old codes, enabling new, more appropriate patterns of thought to take over. *AQ changes behavior.*

The important lesson from the geneticists and evolutionary psychologists is that we can influence some things more easily than others. This gives us the information needed to focus our efforts on those parts of ourselves that we can most easily and dramatically strengthen for the benefit of our internal network and, ultimately, our world. The highest-leverage change comes with improving your AQ. With the help of AQ, you can influence *the structure of your own brain.*

IMPROVING AQ AND THE MYTH OF THE DYING BRAIN

If the doors of perception were cleansed the world would appear to man as it is . . . infinite.

—William Blake

Many of us grew up believing that over our life span we lose (or kill) a finite number of brain cells. In college I was told that an ounce of alcohol would kill 5,000 brain cells that would never be replenished. School officials were convinced that this explained most campus behavior! Aging people are told that their not-so-instant recall and short-term memory loss are the result of aging brain cells.

If the brain were a static dying organ, changing your AQ would be next to impossible. Fortunately, nothing could be further from the truth. The latest findings in brain research indicate that the dwindling brain is a complete myth. Even an elderly brain has the capacity to generate new brain cells throughout its remaining days. In fact, the frontal cortex, the most highly evolved part of the human brain, is not fully developed until the age of twenty-three. So, if your teenager seems like she has lost her mind, it may be that she does not yet completely have one!

According to Dr. Fred Gage, a neuroscientist at the world-renowned Salk Institute, you can actually alter the *structure* of your brain! "The actual structure of our brain is modified by our experiences," he said. "It turns out we have more control over our biology than we thought." The physical structure of our brain is modified by how we *experience* experiences. In other words, how you respond to life's events literally shapes your brain. Certain patterns of thought play a powerful role—particularly *the way you respond to adversity*. This is why AQ can also shape your reality.

THE NOCEBO EFFECT—THE LOW-AQ VIRUS

Most people are familiar with the placebo effect. It occurs when the expectation or belief that something will have a positive effect actually *creates* the positive effect. The placebo effect has been well documented in medical studies for decades. People are given sugar pills in pharmacological studies to see if the expectation of a drug's specific effect is strong enough to produce the actual effect. If it is, the placebo effect occurs.

Recently, doctors and practitioners have started to pay attention to the placebo effect's dark sibling, the *Nocebo Effect*. This may be a new term, but you are probably familiar with how it works. When the makers of Olestra, the fat substitute, announced that it may cause gastrointestinal problems, a wave of people suddenly began to experience the symptoms. Every time officials announce another breakout of *E. coli*, the dangerous bacteria found in tainted meat, far more people get sick than actually contracted the bacteria. This is the Nocebo Effect, which occurs when negative expectations create negative results.

In a study at Harvard University, researchers randomly selected people and put them into one of two groups. Group A was to receive a pill that would dilate or expand their bronchial tubes. Group B was to receive a pill that would constrict their bronchial tubes. But researchers lied to half of each group, telling them they were receiving the opposite treatment. The negative expectation was roughly as powerful as the pill. In the group who were given the bronchial dilator but told it was a constrictor, roughly half experienced constriction. The same result occurred among the other group of deceived participants.

Pointing the Bone

Acclaimed medical doctor and health care pioneer Deepak Chopra tells the story of the Nocebo Effect among aborigines of Australia. He discovered that when a person from one tribe slighted someone of another tribe, one would go to his witch doctor and ask for a curse against his antagonist. The witch doctor would go to the enemy and *point the bone,* declaring, "You will die within two weeks!" Within days the enemy would fall ill, and within two weeks he would die. Dr. Chopra wanted to go to the authorities to stop this murderous practice, but he realized that Western doctors also point the bone. The Nocebo Effect takes hold when a doctor says, "Take this pill; it may make you nauseous, but it should help your headache," and five minutes later you feel nauseous regardless of whether the pill caused it. More seriously the bone is pointed when a surgeon says, "You have cancer. You have two months to live." This is fundamentally different from saying, "Eighty-three percent of the patients with this condition die within two months. Some survive. I can share their strategies with you, if you would like to try." Every time a doctor or leader predicts demise, he or she is pointing the bone.

The Nocebo Effect can have the same dire consequences on an organization. You may know leaders or coworkers who point the bone by saying something like, "This merger could devastate our company," "That department will never be profitable," or "We can't possibly compete with Microsoft!"

This phenomenon is so powerful that the day will come when doctors *and leaders* may be held liable for how they explain a prognosis to their patients or enterprises. Knowing that good or bad patterns of response can literally create the reality they set in motion is a powerful revelation that can no longer be ignored.

There is a direct relationship between the Nocebo Effect and what I call a "low AQ." Low-AQ people propagate the Nocebo Effect. Because they are more likely to believe their low-AQ response and predictions, they suffer from the Nocebo version of reality. As you will discover in Chapter 4, the CORE dimensions of a low AQ result in someone being a carrier of the Nocebo Effect within his or her relationships, teams, and organizations. The Nocebo Effect demoralizes good people in good organizations every day. It's what takes place on the faces of those around you when your team member says, "We'll never get this project in on time," or when your coworker blurts out, "This acquisition is going to be the death of us." The Nocebo Effect is the virus that a low AQ can spawn and spread. To avoid such consequences and to strengthen your AQ, Response Ability is imperative.

THE RESPONSE IS EVERYTHING *(I CHING)*

Given the decades-long study of response patterns, the human brain, and how peptides influence cellular functions, we know now that how we respond to adverse situations *is* everything. Given the brain's bias against adversity, your AQ has the most profound role of all patterns in what you think, how you feel, what you do, and who you become.

As you examine Exhibit 2.1, you can see that your AQ drives and determines all that follows throughout the network of the body-mind and beyond. To better understand how this happens, you will need to explore your CORE.

Bad times have scientific value. These are occasions a good learner would not miss.

—Ralph Waldo Emerson

ORIGINS OF CORE

In Chapter 4 you will explore your CORE response to adversity in great depth—Control, Ownership, Reach, and Endurance, the four dimensions that make up your AQ. To fully appreciate their value, you must understand their origins.

These dimensions are derived from the research mentioned in this chapter as well as our field studies. Beyond the list of researchers mentioned in this chapter, the AQ technology is drawn from the roughly

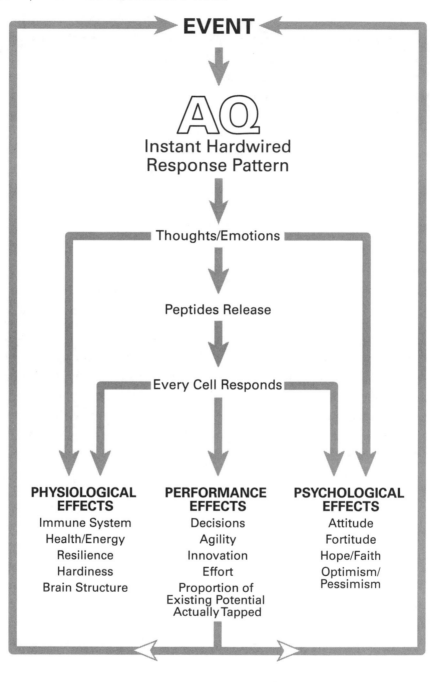

Exhibit 2.1 **The Effect of Your Response**

10,000 leaders and 100,000 professionals the PEAK team (see Appendix D) has interviewed and/or surveyed to form the ever-evolving twenty-year base of AQ-related research. Additionally, our knowledge expands through the dozens of AQ-related research projects under way worldwide. We have tested our methods for ten years, over which time we have seen the evolution and statistical validation of new AQ factors.

Specifically, we know that Control, Ownership, Reach, and Endurance play the central role in remaining resilient and optimistic in the face of adversity. Beyond the research mentioned in this chapter, studies in learned helplessness, hardiness, self-efficacy, resilience, biological psychology, optimism, and attributional theory confirm conclusively that three of these dimensions—Control, Reach, and Endurance—are strong predictors of human effectiveness. Our early work on AQ brought these dimensions together for the first time, and we discovered that they did predict performance and success reasonably well.

Yet, in our studies, we suspected that there was a missing element. This element had to do with blame and accountability. Earlier research had suggested that people should blame others for bad events in order to remain resilient. I was immediately concerned about these findings and had reservations about teaching these concepts to business leaders. It made no sense to train people to deflect accountability. This is why some of the most powerful entrepreneurs would bomb the earliest measures of AQ that incorporated the research on blame. We discovered that the most effective people took ultimate accountability for dealing with a problem, regardless of what caused the adversity.

After additional research and measures, my team and I discovered that our gut suspicion was true. More important than who one blames is to what extent people take it upon themselves to better the situation. This made great intuitive sense and held true in the new measure of AQ, bringing it to a high level of statistical reliability and validity.

In short, we now know that when adversity strikes, the higher one's AQ, the more likely one is to perceive some way to influence the situation (Control), take it upon oneself to make it better (Ownership), and perceive it as limited and fleeting (Reach and Endurance). The lower one's AQ, the less control one perceives, and the less ownership one will take for dealing with what appears to be a far-reaching, long-lasting setback.

Each of these CORE dimensions has its unique attributes, as verified by statistical analysis and common sense. The superiority of one over another will be determined by their relative importance to your value system and culture. Each contributes equally to the overarching measure and notion of AQ.

PUTTING IT ALL TOGETHER

You now understand that how you navigate life is fundamentally influenced by your AQ. Among the countless patterns that influence your behavior, you know that some, like learned helplessness, lead you to give up, while others—a high AQ—lead you to persevere. At the microscopic level, your AQ influences the chemistry and function of every cell in your body. These chemical messages and reactions are communicated throughout your body as if on an internal Internet, or Intranet.

As a child you hardwired these patterns, which we now know are the strongest driver of human behavior. Some scientists argue that we are destined to operate from primeval impulses. Instead, you can use your AQ not only to transcend some of these primitive impulses, like emotional outbursts, but also to strengthen the structure of your brain.

We can see the potential positive influence of certain patterns by studying optimal states, such as "flow," where we see the opposite of the destructive effects stress has on most people. But, for most of us, life is filled with adversity, not with optimal experiences. In fact, your brain is wired with a natural bias toward adversity, hearing it with greater intensity and volume than you do good news. This ancient survival mechanism plays an important role in keeping you sharp, and it explains why of all patterns, your AQ is the most global predictor of your success.

You also understand how AQ can influence the tenor and climate of an organization. It determines your ability to expand your capacity to meet tomorrow's demands. Low-AQ leaders may inadvertently "point the bone" by introducing dire predictions that come true as a result. They shrink collective capacity. Low-AQ coworkers can compromise the progress and performance of their teams. The Nocebo Effect is a low-AQ virus that can infect collective endeavor. Fortunately, you can immunize yourself and your organization against the Nocebo Effect by strengthening AQ.

Topographical Map of Chapter 2
The Science of AQ

Patterns of thought, emotion, and explanation in response to life's events affect the function of every cell in your body and the structure of your brain. These patterns have a profound impact on performance, memories, outlook, beliefs, health, and behavior.

Your brain has a natural bias for adversity. Adverse events make a stronger imprint than do good events.

AQ is the measurable, precise, unconscious pattern of how you respond to adversity.
- AQ is triggered *before* thoughts and words are formed.
- AQ is hardwired in your youth.
- Hardwiring can be permanently changed.
- The brain possesses the capacity to generate new brain cells and patterns throughout life.
- AQ can help us to transcend the more primitive, volatile, and uncivilized responses we have imprinted in our reptilian brains.

The Nocebo Effect takes place when a negative consequence occurs as a result of someone predicting the adverse consequence.
- In organizations, the Nocebo Effect takes place when lower-AQ people respond to change, uncertainty, and all forms of adversity.
- The Nocebo Effect can demoralize, deflate, and devastate.
- A high AQ can immunize a person against the Nocebo Effect.

AQ can be reliably measured using the Adversity Response Profile and can be permanently improved using the tools in this book.

Chapter 3

MEASURING YOUR AQ

O NE OF THE most powerful steps you can take to upgrade your operating system is to measure your own AQ. This chapter provides an abbreviated version of the Adversity Response Profile (ARP) instrument, the full version of which we use to measure AQ for hiring, coaching, training, and development. You will find the measure brief, easy, and highly useful, and the remaining tools in this book will help you to understand it and to strengthen it.

ASSESSING YOUR AQ

As you work through this condensed adaptation of the ARP, you must be as honest as possible. If you find you are getting stuck on any question or response, you are working too hard. To gain the best results on your AQ, you should complete this assessment when you have ten to fifteen minutes to spend in an environment that is conducive to uninterrupted thought.

Remember that this is *for* you and *about* you. It's about your operating system, and it is the key to upgrading your effectiveness, performance, and overall happiness. This is *just* a snapshot, not a tattoo. Dedicate some time to reap the most benefit you can from this human-performance technology.

The Adversity Response Profile* (ARP) QuickTake

Instructions:
- Imagine the following events as if they were happening right now.
- Vividly imagine what will happen as a result of each event (the consequences).
- Circle the numbers that represent your answer to the question below each situation.

Example:
1) Situation: You lose your favorite pen.
   (Imagine this happening to you. Picture it in your mind).
2) Imagine what will happen as a result. *"I'll never have a pen like that one again. My dad will be so upset when he finds out I lost it."*
3) Circle the number that represents your answer to the questions below each situation.

   To what extent can you influence this situation?
   Not at all   1   2   3   4   5   Completely

ARP QuickTake

1) **You suffer a financial setback.**

   To what extent can you influence this situation?
   Not at all   1   2   3   4   5   Completely

2) **You are overlooked for a promotion.**

   To what extent do you feel responsible for improving this situation?
   Not responsible 1   2   3   4   5   Completely responsible
   at all

3) **You are criticized for a big project that you just completed.**

   The consequences of this situation will:
   Affect all   1   2   3   4   5   Be limited to
   aspects of my life   this situation

4) **You accidentally delete a very important E-mail.**

   The consequences of this situation will:
   Last forever   1   2   3   4   5   Quickly pass

5) The high-priority project you are working on gets canceled.

The consequences of this situation will:

| Affect all | 1 | 2 | 3 | 4 | 5 | Be limited to |
| aspects of my life | | | | | | this situation |

6) Someone you respect ignores your attempt to discuss an important issue.

To what extent do you feel responsible for improving this situation?

| Not responsible | 1 | 2 | 3 | 4 | 5 | Completely responsible |
| at all | | | | | | |

7) People respond unfavorably to your latest ideas.

To what extent can you influence this situation?

| Not at all | 1 | 2 | 3 | 4 | 5 | Completely |

8) You are unable to take a much-needed vacation.

The consequences of this situation will:

| Last forever | 1 | 2 | 3 | 4 | 5 | Quickly pass |

9) You hit every red light on your way to an important appointment.

The consequences of this situation will:

| Affect all | 1 | 2 | 3 | 4 | 5 | Be limited to |
| aspects of my life | | | | | | this situation |

10) After extensive searching, you cannot find an important document.

The consequences of this situation will:

| Last forever | 1 | 2 | 3 | 4 | 5 | Quickly pass |

11) Your workplace is understaffed.

To what extent do you feel responsible for improving this situation?

| Not responsible | 1 | 2 | 3 | 4 | 5 | Completely responsible |
| at all | | | | | | |

12) You miss an important appointment.

The consequences of this situation will:

| Affect all | 1 | 2 | 3 | 4 | 5 | Be limited to |
| aspects of my life | | | | | | this situation |

13) Your personal and work obligations are out of balance.

To what extent can you influence this situation?

| Not at all | 1 | 2 | 3 | 4 | 5 | Completely |

14) **You never seem to have enough money.**

The consequences of this situation will:

Last forever   1   2   3   4   5   Quickly pass

15) **You are not exercising regularly when you know you should be.**

To what extent can you influence this situation?

Not at all   1   2   3   4   5   Completely

16) **Your organization is not meeting its projected goals.**

To what extent do you feel responsible for improving this situation?

Not responsible 1   2   3   4   5   Completely responsible
at all

17) **Your computer crashed for the third time this week.**

To what extent can you influence this situation?

Not at all   1   2   3   4   5   Completely

18) **The meeting you are in is a total waste of time.**

To what extent do you feel responsible for improving this situation?

Not responsible 1   2   3   4   5   Completely responsible
at all

19) **You lost something that is important to you.**

The consequences of this situation will:

Last forever   1   2   3   4   5   Quickly pass

20) **Your boss adamantly disagrees with your decision.**

The consequences of this situation will:

Affect all   1   2   3   4   5   Be limited to
aspects of my life   this situation

---

*Note: This is an abbreviated version of the Adversity Response Profile. For more information on the complete ARP, see Appendix A.

Congratulations! You have just completed the ARP QuickTake.

Botanists say that trees need the powerful March winds to flex their trunks and main branches, so that the sap is drawn up to nourish the budding leaves. Perhaps we need the gales of life in the same way, though we dislike enduring them. A blustery period in our fortunes is often the prelude to a new spring of life and health, success and happiness, when we keep steadfast in faith and look to the good in spite of appearance.

—Jane Truax

Scoring the ARP QuickTake

STEP ONE: Insert the number you circled for each of the above questions into the corresponding boxes below. For example, if you circled 4 for question number 2, you would insert the number "4" next to question number 2 below.

C	O	R	E
1.	2.	3.	4.
7.	6.	5.	8.
13.	11.	9.	10.
15.	16.	12.	14.
17.	18.	20.	19.

STEP TWO: Insert the total for each column in the grid below.

Total C +	Total O +	Total R +	Total E =	Total from CORE

STEP THREE: Add the four totals from Step Two, then multiply that number by 2. Insert your answer in the triangle.

———————————— x 2 =

Total from CORE

△ AQ

YOUR AQ QUICKTAKE™ SCORE

INTERPRETING YOUR RESULTS

We'll now interpret your results in two parts. First, in the remainder of this chapter, you will learn the implications of your AQ. Then in Chapter 4 you will continue the second part of interpreting your results as we learn about and graph the CORE dimensions of your AQ. Together, you will get a comprehensive picture of your own results, which will lead you to strengthening your AQ, CORE, and Response Ability throughout the remaining chapters.

High Versus Low AQs

Dozens of case studies and tens of thousands of individual AQ performance tests show that the higher one's AQ, the more likely one is to demonstrate the characteristics of a Climber. Moreover, the higher one's AQ, the more likely one is to turn adversity into opportunity.

> The higher one's AQ, the more likely one will:
> - Be resilient in the face of adversity
> - Be a top performer and sustain high performance
> - Be *authentically* optimistic
> - Take necessary risks
> - Thrive on change
> - Remain healthy, energetic, and vital
> - Take on difficult and complex challenges
> - Persevere
> - Innovate to find solutions
> - Be an agile problem solver and thinker
> - Learn, grow, and improve

In contrast, we find that the lower one's AQ, the more of a toll adversity is likely to take upon one over time.

The lower one's AQ, the more likely one will:
- Give up
- Become overwhelmed
- Become depressed
- Not tap one's full potential
- Feel helpless
- Suffer illness
- Propagate the Nocebo Effect
- Get mired in problems
- Avoid challenging jobs and situations
- Leave good ideas and tools unused
- Camp

High AQ (178–200): If you score in this range, you are among the elite who routinely face and overcome adversities of all magnitudes. Setbacks are likely to be short-lived and contained. You probably demonstrate strong accountability for dealing with difficult situations and are an agile problem solver. People are drawn to your natural resilience and optimism. But there is still room at the top. You can further fine-tune your AQ and use your abilities to coach and guide others.

Moderately High AQ (161–177): If your AQ falls in this range, you are already more effective than most people at dealing with difficulties and setbacks. You probably remain resilient and persevere when faced with most challenges. There may be moments when adversity piles up and becomes more of a burden than is necessary. By strengthening your AQ, you will become even more agile and able to take on greater challenges.

Moderate AQ (135–160): The majority of people fall in this range. If you have a moderate AQ, this suggests that you probably fare well with many difficulties. However, when adversities mount and you become fatigued, they may wear you down unnecessarily. You may at times become demoralized or overwhelmed. As you strengthen your AQ, you will discover newfound strength and fortitude in dealing with all sorts of challenges.

Moderately Low AQ (118–134): If you score in this range, you may handle some setbacks relatively well. However, as your world becomes increasingly complex, chaotic, and challenging, you may be suffering unnecessarily. You can reduce the toll adversity takes and strengthen your resilience by raising your AQ.

Low AQ (117 and below): If you have a low AQ, *do not despair!* It simply explains why life can seem so overwhelming and difficult at times. It also provides you with a firm starting point. As your AQ increases you will experience the most dramatic results in how you view, respond to, and experience challenges in your work and life. Improving your AQ may become a transformational experience as you discover a large pool of untapped potential and enjoyment.

Difficulties strengthen the mind, as labor does the body.

—Seneca

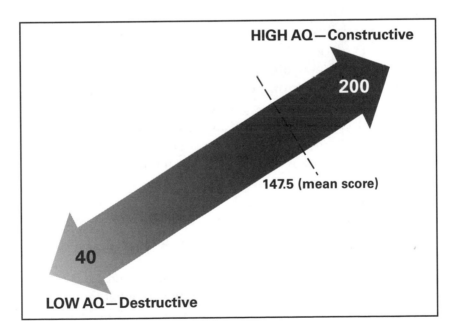

Exhibit 3.1 The AQ Continuum

The AQ Continuum

AQ scores fall between 40 and 200 points. They make up a strong bell curve, or normal distribution. This means the vast majority of AQs fall in the moderate ranges. Therefore, the further the score is from the middle, the more extreme the resulting impact of AQ is likely to be. The following examples will shed light on these extremes and what role AQ plays when a person faces adversity.

The High-AQ Bankruptcy

Marie Schilly is training manager for the sales and marketing division at a major semiconductor company. She has a moderately high AQ of 167. She demonstrates many of the characteristics of a high-AQ person. Although she is exceptionally busy, she is reinventing her entire job, expanding her training efforts to the entire company, and, on her own initiative, creating a corporate university.

Her company has been enormously successful, and, as a result, Marie set aside some money to invest in the stock market. Acting on what seemed to be a solid tip, Marie invested heavily, most of it on margin.

While she was away on vacation her dream became a nightmare. Her stock completely bottomed out and she lost her entire investment. She assumed wrongly that her stockbroker would call with any concerns. Marie had plenty of reason to be devastated. The stress could have made her ill or depressed, and she could have missed several days of work. Instead, Marie refused to let this ruin her. Coincidentally, on the day she received the news of her financial disaster, she was attending an AQ training session. No one had a clue that her world had been turned upside down that day. Inwardly she struggled to keep her footing. But her AQ helped her through the day and the ensuing months of difficulty.

Marie's moderately high AQ suggests that she would handle her loss reasonably well, but that it would still take more of a toll than if her AQ were even stronger. That day she confided that she briefly imagined her world crumbling around her. She considered what would happen if she never got out of the current mess and how her whole life could be ruined. These were natural reactions, given the circumstances.

Yet as Marie learned about her AQ and her CORE, she could see how her response could make her hardship even harder. That day, she learned how to employ the LEAD Sequence, which she immediately put to use in her current adversity. It required that she strip-search her response and reconsider the evidence that supported her worst fears. Using what she learned, Marie decided to take Ownership for making the situation better. Even though the broker may have had some accountability, she decided to focus her energy on her recovery, so she could limit the Reach and Endurance of the adversity.

Later that day, she turned to me and said, "I know there must be a reason for this. I don't yet know what it is, but I do know this cannot last forever and that this will represent a whole new life for me. In an odd way, I'm looking forward to it."

Marie found a way to refinance her house, filed for bankruptcy, and is on the road to full financial recovery. She attributed her resilience to strengthening her AQ. "Learning about AQ and LEAD enabled me to respond to the adversity in the most constructive way. I honestly am glad this happened, because I know I will be strengthened by this experience." She added, "I already am!" Her plans for a corporate university are right on track, and, with training, her AQ has since risen to 186!

Trudging Through the Low-AQ Divorce

In a recent AQ program there was a woman who had a dramatically low AQ of 69. I noticed her after the program, while she was waiting in line to talk with me. She was visibly trembling, had deep-set circles under her eyes, and looked as though she had not slept in days. When she came up to speak to me, she blurted out, "I'm still here." I asked her what she meant.

"My husband left me and took all the money and I lost my job and I'm raising the kids by myself, and I'm going to graduate school trying to get good grades and . . . I'm still here," she explained, trembling from what was probably a bad concoction of caffeine and damaging peptides.

I could not help thinking, Yes, but for how long? I asked her how long ago her husband had left. "A little over a year," she replied, holding back the tears. "I wake up every day knowing my life has been destroyed and my children will never be happy, but somehow, I get out of bed. Sometimes it is so hard, I can't even move. But I'm doing all I can!" she pleaded.

True, this poor woman was digging deep inside herself to pull out all she could to forge forward with her life amid great adversity. She was trying to Climb. Yet her low-AQ score showed that she was magnifying the effects of the adversity throughout her body. Her peptides were likely causing systemic chaos. One year after her husband left, she was tormented by the low-AQ-triggered belief that her life and her children's lives were ruined. She was clearly depressed, sleep-deprived, and physically exhausted. While her adversity was real, the toll for her ascent was unnecessarily great, rendering her current strategy unsustainable. By raising her AQ, she would be able to focus on limiting the Reach and Endurance of the adversity, reducing the tremendous toll adversity was taking on her health, strength, and spirit.

Success at What Price?

True, AQ is a predictor of success. However, it is entirely possible for an entrepreneur with an AQ of 118 (moderately low) to be building a company. The question is, *At what price?* The lower a person's AQ, the greater the toll adversity is likely to take upon him or her, especially over time. The woman whose AQ was a dismally low 69 was struggling with all her might. However, the adversity she was facing was literally killing her.

This is why increasing your AQ can have such a powerful effect on your ascent and overall well-being along the way. It provides a sustainable model, an upgrade of your system for working and living in increasingly demanding times.

NEXT STEPS IN THE AQ ASCENT

Now that you have measured and scored your AQ, you are ready to interpret your results. In the next chapter you will discover and graph your own CORE Profile—the building blocks of your AQ. Equipped with this understanding, you will coach, mentor, and lead those around you to greater heights.

Topographical Map of Chapter 3
Measuring Your AQ

The ARP QuickTake is a condensed snapshot of your AQ.
- The full version of the Adversity Response Profile must be used for hiring, coaching, and training.
- You measured your AQ and CORE.
- These scores serve as a starting point for strengthening your AQ and upgrading your operating system.
- These scores provide insight into your Response Ability.

Insert your scores below:

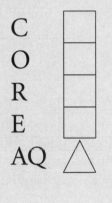

CHAPTER 4

THE CORE
OF THE CLIMBER

Always bear in mind that your own resolution to succeed
is more important than any other one thing.
—Abraham Lincoln

SIX FEET FROM the edge of a 1,000-foot drop-off, I can hear the wind
howl. Through patches of dense fog, I see waves crashing hard on the
shore. From the day I laid eyes on this mountaintop acreage, I realized it
was home. And, despite the adversities of turning this vision into reality, I
knew it was meant to be.

I wanted an inspirational and relaxed setting for clients and the PEAK
team. I envisioned a high-ceilinged, open-air barn to house our international headquarters. However, the road up to this building site is so steep
that only one of a dozen contractors even considered it. Within moments
of seeing the entryway to the job site, nearly all the contractors simply
laughed out loud. Others offered diplomatic excuses. Most were apologetic
and were suddenly booked for months ahead. Gravel haulers, lumber-
yards, movers, electricians, delivery businesses, as well as a slew of vendors
and construction firms, all turned down well-paid offers for their services.

But finally, one contractor reacted differently. He had an instant spark
in his eye and seemed undaunted, if not intrigued, by the road. "Let's take
a look at the top," he declared as he started up the hill. Upon arriving at the
top, he exclaimed, "I guess I can see why you would want to build *here!*" He
then laid out the practical steps involved in the project, as if it were any

other structure, not a mountaintop retreat. I just had to ask him about the road.

"It will have its challenges, but nothing we can't handle" was his reply. I pushed further, asking about every kind of challenge I could imagine we might face, including mudslides, erosion, trucking, materials, wind, and floods. "Oh, sure, that just comes with the job," he answered matter-of-factly to each. He also did not see any reason we would face any additional expense or delays. Unlike all the other contractors, he was *inspired* by the adversity and recognized that it would be up to his resourcefulness to keep the project on time and within budget. He could not wait to get started. "I do a lot of projects," he explained, "but *this* one is exciting. I hope we can get started soon."

The ascent to this land is so extreme that visitors must be shuttled to the top in an appropriately equipped four-wheel-drive vehicle. The well water, while safe and delicious, is rich with clay, which clogs our filters and can distastefully discolor our toilets and sinks. When there is a power outage, we are last to regain service; it can take days, even weeks, to get back on line. Today, an appliance delivery person said that if he had known which road he had to drive, he *never* would have agreed to make the trip.

Living and working here can be a daily test of one's AQ. As a result, it serves as a perfect mini-lab to assess how people respond to the apparent challenge.

One client said, "Oh, Paul, this is just unbelievable! I mean *really*, have you lost your mind? Do you realize that when there is a fire, you're *trapped*? This whole dream could go up in flames in an instant and you with it, and there's nothing you will be able to do to prevent it. And don't tell me that the local fire station won't be quick to find reasons not to come up *here*. Not to mention, you'll *never* sell this place if you face a financial emergency. . . ."

This person saw the adversity as encompassing, enduring, and uncontrollable to the point where our dream was a nightmare to her. I recognized in her heartfelt response the precise factors that can convert one person's challenge into another's unbearable adversity. I paused, acknowledging that her response was exposing her *CORE*. More precisely, she was displaying the four dimensions of anyone's response, which make up a person's AQ and ultimately intertwine to form the four central strands of the DNA of human fortitude. Like your DNA, these CORE dimensions form the human operating system and its ability to function optimally under pressure. We see people's COREs come to life daily in our work-places.

You scored your CORE dimensions of AQ in the last chapter. In this chapter you will learn about each dimension and graph your CORE Profile to get a deeper and more precise view into your pattern of response to adversity, or AQ.

YOUR INNER CORE

Based on the research presented in Chapter 2, you know that there are four CORE dimensions that make up your AQ. CORE includes *Control, Ownership, Reach,* and *Endurance,* which combine to form a person's AQ and his or her response to any given adversity. Your CORE ultimately determines how you handle every deadline, conflict, injustice, setback, challenge, and opportunity—life's everyday realities.

C = Control

Control has two facets. First, *to what extent are you able to positively influence a situation?* Second, *to what extent can you control your own response to a situation?*

Control is so transformative that many clients have suggested we formulate a self-standing instrument that assesses nothing but Control. Looking at life through a Control lens can permanently alter and ultimately strengthen your approach to any situation. Research studies show the growing importance of Control as a vital ingredient in our outlook, performance, health, and long-term success. This ingredient most directly determines our propensity to strive or take meaningful action in the course of a given day or in response to a certain challenge.

As powerful as Control is in our effort to be effective, its evil twin—*helplessness*—is the cancer of human endeavor. As Martin Seligman has pointed out, helplessness is the belief that what you do does not matter. It is a crisis of insignificance. Those who lack Control have weaker health, a greater tendency toward depression, and are more likely to become violent. Helplessness is the antithesis of empowerment. This syndrome describes why so many who receive the empowerment mantra at work are immune to its lure, so mired are they in the quicksand of helplessness, which mounts with the demands, complexity, and uncertainty of the modern workplace. Now, more than ever, we must do all we can to immunize our coworkers against such insidious and ravaging ills. Such immunization begins with *Control*. Without it, empowerment becomes as cruel as yelling "Come here, boy" to a lame dog.

Vital to understanding Control is your ability to set aside past understandings of Control. And in the context of AQ, you must first be clear on what it is *not*. You may think of Control as a subtle and often abused power, overt domination, perhaps an iron grip, or even a genuine cause for concern. Some think of Control as the damage it causes when someone has "control issues" in a relationship. Or that it's related to your position or station in life.

For our purposes, Control is none of these things. When I use Control in conjunction with your AQ, it is a very precise and powerful source of freedom, not oppression or constraint.

Control is about (1) your perceived ability to alter a situation and (2) your *Response Ability*, which is the ability to control your own response to anything that may arise.

The extent to which a person is able to improve an adverse situation is called positive influence. It nurtures the seeds of contribution, significance, and action. Those with higher AQs are like skilled gold miners, relentlessly sifting through the muck to find the single nugget or facet of the situation they can improve. Control affects us even in the most fundamental aspects of life.

Jon Kabat-Zinn, Ph.D., a pioneer in introducing meditation techniques in medical treatments, was called into a novel study on psoriasis, a common and often devastating skin condition. Because the symptoms are external (scaly, red patches of skin), researchers can easily monitor the effects of their treatment, which typically involves hours inside a modified tanning booth. The treatment is time-consuming and can be detrimental to the patients, bombarding them with ultraviolet radiation.

Dr. Zinn developed a meditation audiotape that patients use to control their claustrophobia and increase their comfort. It also taught them how to concentrate on and influence their own healing. As a result of the improved Control these patients felt over their health, their treatment time was cut in half.

"The patients' perceived control over their condition played a central role in their often dramatic improvements," Dr. Kabat-Zinn explained. Other studies show similar results.

Early seeds of Response Ability were unearthed years ago by researcher Suzanne Kobasa. She studied the elements that make up a stress-hardy personality. Her group of telecommunications executives was facing a major industry-wide shake-up. Many of the predictable stress-related symptoms emerged, including heart attacks, anxiety, and sleep loss. However, some people seemed to be immune to the adversity. Among those executives found to be most hardy were those who felt a sense of Control in their lives; even if they could not control the external events in their lives, they could at least control their own response to whatever occurred.

A study conducted by Edward McAuley, a professor of kinesiology at the University of Illinois, showed that people who feel the most Control over their physical exercise program are least likely to experience fatigue. But those who perceive minimal Control lose their motivation and, as a result, succumb to the discomforts. They feel more tired and are more likely to quit.

David Nordstrom, Ph.D., a professor of epidemiology at Boston University, found in his study of carpal tunnel syndrome that subjects who felt the least influence over their work had almost three times the risk of developing numbness or burning in their hands as those who felt the most influence.

As the Serenity Prayer reminds us, there is wisdom in recognizing the difference between those things we cannot control and those we can. However, there is great danger in erring on the wrong side of that equation. AQ plays a pivotal role in determining on which side you might find yourself: you have a choice between being actively involved in bettering what is and simply accepting what is, even if it could be better. As a graduate student at Assumption College in the Philippines stated in a recent E-mail message, "I recognize there is much in life we cannot prevent from happening, but I now realize the enormity of control I have over how I respond. This revelation has unleashed in me entirely new freedom and responsibility. I never dreamed the two were so closely linked."

Consider the list of things we *cannot* control. Death, taxes, natural disasters, war, weather, crime, and disease are certainly common entries on the list of uncontrollables. To any one of these you might throw your arms up and say, "Well, there's nothing I can do about it, what's done is done." Yet, within each, there are facets we can positively influence, even in dire situations.

If a loved one is diagnosed with a fatal illness, you may not be able to prevent, or even control, her demise. However, imagine all the positive things that could be done to influence her remaining days, her peace of mind, and the legacy she leaves behind. In a sense, there may be no greater opportunity to be significant than in being the one who takes charge of these precious details. In those final weeks, months, or even days, you can help that person live out her days with dignity and more meaning than she may have felt in all her preceding years. The perceived ability to positively influence at least one part of the situation is what keeps some people strong, as well as sane, in the most horrible circumstances.

You may not like taxes, but you can influence how hard they hit you, how well you plan, and how creatively you strategize within the ethical confines of the law. This influence is an essential form of Control. Also, you may not be able to avoid having your entire division eliminated at work, but you can control how quickly you develop other options and whether or not you use this adversity to explore a pent-up dream to do something else. You may not be able to save your wood-frame house from being leveled by an imminent high-grade hurricane, but you *can* greatly influence whether or not it ruins your life, how quickly you recover, not to mention your neighbor's level of hardship by providing him or her with a helping hand. You may not be able to change that truly negative person at work, but you can influence how much he affects you and others. These forms of Response Control are manifestations of a high AQ in the most difficult situations.

In 1999 some Bosnian refugees, while unable to escape the horrors waged upon their people, dramatically influenced their health, sanity, and the well-being of others. A newscast showed a Bosnian refugee who had lost his children, witnessed his wife being raped, and had his arm amputated in a mine blast. He told the reporter, "We will make a new life. Look around," he said, scanning the refugee camp, "at all the children who need us now. They are our future, and we must all help."

Another news segment showed a man of similar age who had lost his home and possessions but had his family. He was too despondent to form full sentences. "They take everything . . . all is gone . . . no way to live . . . nothing we can do . . . *nothing.*"

In these responses we see bold evidence of how profoundly different one's perceived influence can be over dire events. Imagine their lives one month down the road. One has discovered a new purpose in helping those who suffer, while the other is branded by his far less severe loss, tattooed with the word "victim," and tragically uses his brand as cause for self-pity and stagnation. They experience such different fates—all stemming from the moment of response.

What about those things we cannot control at work? Mergers, acquisitions, vendors, distributors, customers' loyalty, the economy, competitors, and so on. Yet, any of these business challenges can be improved. Your response ultimately determines the fallout of any given event.

In short, there is almost *always* some way a situation can be made better. That's Control. To stay focused on what *can* be influenced instead of what cannot is called Response Ability. Not only does Response Ability strengthen your operating system, it provides virus protection against panic, debilitating worry, and helplessness.

Focusing on the positive influence facet of Control can be such a delicate, even offensive, topic because it directly challenges the excuses and rationales we give ourselves for inaction or mediocrity. You have heard the responses:

"I hurt my knees running, so I can't work out."

"They don't promote women here."

"As if a minority guy with a limited education could ever make vice president!"

"I have a slow metabolism, so I'll always be large."

"I was diagnosed with a learning disability, so I can't do those kinds of projects."

"I've never been good with computers."

"I get eyestrain headaches, so I don't read."

"She has such a terrible temper, so I never say how I feel."

You get the picture! You may think I'm insensitive because I see these legitimate challenges as wimpy excuses for inaction. Yet the best thing I can do for you is to stop you from arguing for your frailties. Instead, you should recognize, grow, and influence situations in a positive way. As you do, you will shrink, if not eliminate, the limitations that might have handcuffed you to mediocrity.

As John Hogan, president of ADP Brokerage Services Division, puts it, "There's no time for victimhood. Even in the toughest situations, as soon as I have a plan, I know it's going to be okay. So I don't waste time worrying about what cannot be done."

It always surprises me that, despite a large expanse of land, my dogs take comfort in their cages. Don't you know people who, despite boundless opportunity, take comfort in their own little cubicle, both literally and figuratively? True, constraints often provide comfort. Yet opportunity expands the soul. But, with opportunity comes adversity. This ability to control our response to the adversity is what enables us to welcome and create new opportunities.

> Argue for your limitations and they are surely yours.
> —Richard Bach

Two Components of Response Control: There are two general types of Response Control. One type is *delayed control*—the most common form. You've probably had moments when you became irate, threw a tantrum, said things you later regretted, or lost Control the moment some unexpected event occurred. After the outburst, you may regain your senses and are able to respond more sensibly. That's delayed control.

Control
I *Perceived Influence* to improve the situation
II *Response Control*
 • Delayed Response Control
 • Spontaneous Response Control

Even more subtle body language such as rolling eyes, sighing—signs of contempt, anger, and exasperation—followed by more constructive responses, are indications of delayed Response Control.

Recovering from an emotional outburst, even a minor flare-up, is certainly better than no damage control at all. Unfortunately, some of the most significant damage can occur in the gap between the response and the recovery, even if it lasts only a few seconds. You probably can remember the most hurtful words certain people have spoken to you. They may have been very brief. Yet for many, they last long past the lengthier apologies and excuses. Someone offers an idea, and a coworker snaps, "When are you going to get a clue?" or "You worked that long for *this*? That's worthless!"

Fatigue, worry, anger, misunderstanding, and false assumptions are all highly human and viable excuses for outbursts, but they do little to eliminate the scars such eruptions may produce. We are capable of evolving to a higher level.

Psychologist Fern Lippert explains how some outbursts relate to perceived Control. "Habitual cursing is a sign of an unhealthy state of mind," she begins. "When people feel they cannot control their situation, they are more likely to swear. The louder they become, the more in control they feel." Such outbursts usually carry a heavy price tag for that person and those around him or her.

In his landmark bestseller, *Emotional Intelligence,* Daniel Goleman describes these outbursts as typical of someone with less than ideal emotional restraint. Of course, we shouldn't restrain our emotions so that they fester and wreak havoc on our body-mind. Rather, emotional intelligence involves, in part, the momentary restraint and proper use of our emotions. This is where emotional intelligence and AQ most directly intersect.

My finding is that people with higher AQs have much greater emotional restraint. They are more likely to demonstrate the second, superior type of Response Control—*spontaneous control.* As its name indicates, those with spontaneous control are able to grab, consider, manage, and even optimize their response at the very moment adversity strikes.

Ideally, you are able to control the thoughts the instant they form. These thoughts will determine your words and action. One step shy of the ideal is the ability to restrain the negative reaction before it is unleashed through words and/or behavior. In other words, in the transition between your private and public self, something powerful happens. You may have a horrible private thought or internal reaction, which you restrain, assess, and alter before it exits and becomes public in any form.

It is better to be thought a fool than to speak out and prove it.

—Confucius

Spontaneous Response Control is the ultimate form of control. Think of spontaneous Response Control as the one feature in your operating system that you can upgrade automatically as new demands, software, and adversities arise. It is the gateway to serenity—both individual and interpersonal—and one of the most authentic sources of trust, respect, and leadership. Spontaneous Response Control can prove useful in the most unexpected circumstances.

Mark and his wife, Charlene, were on their way to an important meeting, driving down the interstate at 75 miles per hour, when they spun out on a large patch of black ice. Their car spun just beyond one complete turn and slammed into the guardrail with the rear end sticking out into oncoming traffic. Mark immediately guided the car out of harm's way, then turned to Charlene and asked, "Are you okay?"

"I'm fine," she replied. He then walked to the front, saw what was merely cosmetic damage, got back in the car, and resumed the conversation as if nothing had happened. Charlene was stunned by how cool-headed he was. "You're not even upset!" she declared.

Mark explained, "Hey, once I knew you were fine, what was there to worry about? Worrying is not going to repair the car, and if we had panicked, we could have been killed, right?" Mark was right: if he had thrown up his hands, panicked over the spin, or catastrophized over how the car was now ruined, they could have been killed in those precious seconds. His spontaneous Response Control saved their lives.

Response Control is a power *anyone* can wield, and it is different from stoicism, which we associate with passive indifference. Response Control is not the assassin of passion. In fact, Response Control is the loyal guardian of the precious passion that can erode as one encounters countless adversities. Passion is often considered a gift of the young, which, like exuberance and all youthful characteristics, dies a slow death. This does not have to be the case.

If the goal is to die young—as late as possible—we must work to preserve our youthful gifts, like passion, for the duration of life. Joy, exuberance, enthusiasm, wonder, curiosity, amazement, and passion are all too easily killed by life's adversities. Once snuffed out, these gifts are difficult to rekindle—making spontaneous Response Control all the more important. This ability mitigates the toll each adversity takes upon your soul, preserving these essential traits. As you improve your Response Control, you will *fortify* passion, joy, innovation, optimism, and hope.

The true test of spontaneous Response Control is adversity. It is one thing to think and respond constructively when all is ideal. It is quite another when you come home from a long day at the office and your two-year-old son comes in the room and joyously flings a cup of sticky apple juice all over you and the new carpet—or when the laser printer jams, a vital meeting is canceled, and so on.

Through spontaneous Response Control, you can immediately connect with positive influence. Moreover, you can draw from, even select, your CORE response, from which all else emanates or ripples. Ultimately,

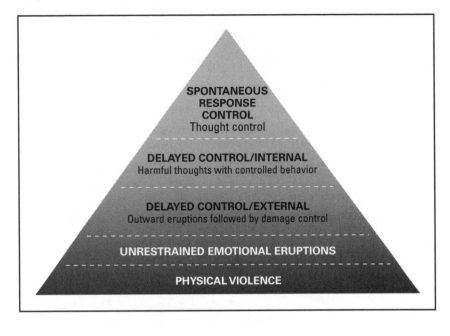

SPONTANEOUS
RESPONSE
CONTROL
Thought control

DELAYED CONTROL/INTERNAL
Harmful thoughts with controlled behavior

DELAYED CONTROL/EXTERNAL
Outward eruptions followed by damage control

UNRESTRAINED EMOTIONAL ERUPTIONS

PHYSICAL VIOLENCE

Exhibit 4.1 **The AQ Hierarchy of Control**

these thoughts translate into words, which focus on positively influencing the person next to you, your team, or your company, creating a strong, vibrant environment.

Control influences all that follows from adversity, as well as the price you pay from the moment it strikes. The greater the adversity, the greater the potential toll, and the more profound the benefits of positive influence and Response Control.

O = Ownership

Ownership helps us redefine accountability in highly constructive and practical terms. This dimension of your AQ assesses *the extent to which you take it upon yourself to improve the situation at hand, regardless of its cause.*

After reviewing hundreds of diverse work environments, I have come across one common theme and concern: *accountability.* It is more vital today than it was yesterday, and even more vital for success in the future.

Why? Because of the growing mandate for interdependence, agility, and trust as we shift from Campers to Climbers.

In order to operate as a true Climbing Team, where the fate of all Climbers on the rope is dependent on the focus and effort of one another, you must take Ownership of not only your role but also the overall success of the team. Otherwise, such necessary interdependence is impossible, resulting in dire consequences. Ownership implies that whatever goes wrong, you play a role in the recovery, regardless of fault or cause. If a Climber makes a mistake, stupid or otherwise, which results in injury, you still have to carry him off the mountain. If bad weather sets in and endangers the team, you can't just save your own neck; everyone must play a role in the survival of the team. If you must reroute because of someone else's error in judgment, you play a role in getting back on track. Blame is irrelevant. Learning and ascending together are crucial to your success.

Agility, the capacity to think and act quickly, can also be killed by blame. Blame occurs when people get caught up in assigning fault rather than learning from the behavior and moving on. Teams and organizations that point fingers get mired in adversity. Furthermore, vital resources are wasted probing into who did what wrong rather than making necessary adjustments to avoid the same mistakes.

Motorola has long prided itself on Total Customer Satisfaction, creating the sacred acronym "TCS." Each year they hold local, regional, and global competitions showcasing teams that have gone the furthest to create measurable improvements in TCS. I was asked to work with a specific team that had accomplished some astonishing feats. This team had devised a new system for disseminating benefits information and accessing services, which would save human resources tens of millions of dollars. It was simple, elegant, user-friendly, and brilliant.

Yet after one visit I knew this team's chances of winning the competition were doomed. A couple of key people had developed the idea, and now their momentum was being sapped by a couple of low-AQ team members. These people had fallen into the blame game, which flared up every time any facet of the project went awry. When they were thrown a rule change midstream, the finger-pointing began immediately: "You are in charge of the competition guidelines, you should have told us this was coming. Now we're doomed," bemoaned one team member. Another team member shot back, "Yeah, well, if you had the visuals ready, we could make these changes on the spot. Now we have to rebuild our entire presentation." And so it went.

Blame kills agility no matter what the quest. I remember one actual climbing class where this lesson was painfully demonstrated. There were three guides, and we hiked several miles over three hours to the base of a formidable "pitch" or climbing route. They assembled the gear, noticed some vital pieces were missing, and a heated exchange ensued: "You were in charge of the gear! What the heck were you thinking? Now this whole trip is ruined."

About twenty minutes later, one of the guides stomped off with a "Forget you! I'm outta here!" For safety reasons the climb was called off on the spot. Blame often kills the ascent.

Blame can also uproot and topple trust—that vital sense of interpersonal safety that frees communication, sharing, and openness. If, like Motorola's TCS team, you learn that when the going gets tough, your coworker is going to start pointing fingers, you are likely to engage in all sorts of defensive and offensive schemes to make sure you emerge untainted. This is unfortunately all too common in many organizations. This low-Ownership culture breeds cynicism, mistrust, political maneuvering, and alienation—direct opposites of the synergy, trust, purpose, and excitement we all seek in our work. It results in a sad compromise of talent and potential. I am sure your own examples come to mind!

Ownership, on the other hand, fosters healthy interdependence, greater agility, and authentic trust. At its root is the reflex or response to step up and take the initiative to better the situation, regardless of its cause. When resources, energy, and effort are spent in such a positive direction, tremendous innovation, teamwork, and progress are typically unleashed.

In a recent AQ program, I was speaking to a group of 250 safety engineers. Things got highly interactive and fairly loud. To manage the crowd, I stood on a chair to guide them through the next activity. Immediately, a man came toward me from the far end of the room and declared, "Excuse me, but this is considered an unsafe act. This chair is not designed to support you in this fashion. You could fall and be injured. In order to continue this session, I am going to have to ask you to please step down right now."

"Are you the safety engineer for this facility?" I asked.

"No," he responded, "but I *am* an employee of this company, and safety is *everyone's* responsibility here." He was from a plant located across the country. I congratulated him on embodying the message. Everyone cheered. I still had to get down from the chair.

Fear, cynicism, and mediocrity are crowded out by the sustainable "can do" spirit of the ascent. Ownership in the form of taking it upon one's self to deal with the situation grows a special sort of cultural knowing. In the previous example, this came out when our engineer's words and actions filled in the blank in the following: "When someone violates the safety code anywhere in this company, people need to (say or do)_____." To the extent there is a shared answer to this question, there is cultural knowing.

A more generic statement for looking at the AQ-related behavior in your culture is: "When something goes wrong, or an unexpected setback occurs, people tend to ___ *(insert your assessment of what people say or do)* ."

In high-AQ cultures with strong Ownership norms, responses to this statement might include: "Assess and solve the problem." "Figure out how to make it as good as it can be." "Take action to stop the dangerous behavior." "Mine the adversity for opportunity." "Ascertain what went wrong so we can learn and avoid the same mistake in the future." "Come up with their best ideas!"

In lower-AQ cultures the response might be: "Point fingers." "Blame it on upper management." "Figure out reasons why it cannot be done." "Shove it on someone else's plate." Such lack of ownership clearly damages the people and the endeavor.

Deeper than words are the trust, learning, and improvement that come from Ownership. If Control is the gateway to serenity, Ownership is the catalyst for engagement. Through Ownership one becomes involved in solutions, improvement, innovation, and the long-term success of whatever one does.

Through AQ and with the help of tools like the Adversity Response Profile, people can assess and strengthen their Ownership. In later chapters, we will explore how you can strengthen Ownership within yourself, your team, and your organization.

> There have been some terrible moments in my life,
> a few of which actually happened.
>
> —Mark Twain

R = Reach

Reach explores *how far you let adversity go into other areas of your work and life.* Reach determines how large you perceive the problem to be, or its apparent extent. Logically, the larger the problem appears, the greater its potential to induce fear, helplessness, apathy, and inaction. The smaller and more manageable the challenge, the greater one's propensity for remaining unfazed by its presence, and the stronger one's influence in resolving or surmounting any obstacle.

The research on attributional or explanatory style describes how your patterns of internal explanation of certain events can determine whether or not you react to adversity as if it were a catastrophe. When you catastrophize, you allow adversity to rage like an emotional wildfire, allowing it to cover vast psychic acreage before it is ever controlled. It can happen in an instant.

In London I sat on the train next to a relatively upbeat systems analyst with Amoco, who was apparently on holiday with his wife. I had brought a copy of the *Wall Street Journal,* the front page of which announced the merger of British Petroleum and Amoco. Apparently he had not read the news, because the moment he read the headline, he instantly threw up his hands and exclaimed, "There goes our whole department. Now they'll lay off thousands! What a disaster." He turned to his wife and said, "Amoco just ruined the entire holiday."

If people are indeed facing increasing numbers of adversities, then catastrophizing over one adversity can render you incapable of taking action on any. The toll of letting adversity reach any further than necessary can go deep. But imagine if our train passenger possessed greater Response Ability. The subconscious wiring of his AQ might translate into the following response: "This is certainly big news. Well, thank goodness we're on holiday. That will give the big guns time to work it out before I return. I imagine there may be more to deal with when I return, so let's enjoy every moment." This response would offer a number of benefits. His health would remain robust, his attitude upbeat. His vacation would go unscathed, and his relationship with his wife would likely be strengthened through the respect she felt for him and the gratitude he felt for her. Their time together would be made more precious by the uncertainty of what lay ahead, and he would feel a positive anticipation about the opportunities the merger may present.

Reach is also a frequent source of strain in relationships. One person may consider a new project as an exhilarating challenge that will test and strengthen the mettle of the department, while another coworker may insist that the project is impossible to accomplish and may ruin the whole department. The resulting conflict may be damaging to their ability to work together.

Two coworkers might hear the same televised business report on a new economic downturn. One person may genuinely respond to the downturn as a temporary blip, while the person next to her might view it as the beginning of the end—an insidious virus that will slowly devour the financial flesh of their vibrant business.

Reach, like all of the CORE dimensions of your AQ, is a highly private matter. First, the initial trigger of AQ takes place internally, within your brain and cells. Second, according to social norms, we are much more likely to catastrophize in our thoughts than in our spoken words. Often, people monitor or filter their thoughts before they become words; some better than others, of course. The intensity of this filter might be influenced by your workplace or societal culture. Some people may have a response pattern that indicates the adversity will be far-reaching, but they may not let it show. Nonetheless, the fallout can be substantial. People may even have high Control and a delayed internal response, but because of their poor score on Reach they may be devastated *inside*.

I recently sat next to a Singaporean at a business presentation. The presenter used the word "kvetch"—a Yiddish word for complaining. She turned to me and asked, "Please, tell me, what is 'kvetch'?" I explained. She paused and responded, "I think there is good reason why this word does not exist in Singapore. People don't often complain. That would be considered weak." However, in the Singaporean culture, one might keep the Reach of the adversity private to avoid embarrassment, but the consequences of responding to adversity as far-reaching remain the same.

Remember, AQ is not about putting on a smile and saying happy things to yourself or others. It is about altering the response pattern, which is hardwired in your brain, so that your words and actions are a natural and positive outgrowth of your high-AQ response pattern. Improving your AQ eliminates, or at least reduces, the tendency to kvetch in the first place.

Reach determines how much emotional real estate a given adversity can potentially devour or damage. It is also the dimension where we see the power of self-fulfilling prophecy brought to life most dramatically. People who predict that a computer crash means utter disaster are much more likely to experience disaster than those who see it as a limited annoyance. One spurs helplessness; the other brings on action and potential resolution.

As consultants and trainers, my team and I frequently travel and must deal with the accompanying delays and hassles. The mantra we have adopted for every delay or flight cancellation is, "There is *always* a way." Again, this is not some artificially recited positive affirmation—it's the natural outgrowth of a high-AQ team and high-AQ individuals. They take pride in remaining undaunted when adversity strikes. It becomes a game. Their high AQs limit the Reach of the adversity and spur action that improves the likelihood of a positive outcome.

Reach is also the dimension that can evoke the most fear and worry. Fear and worry are close siblings—both are based on negative assumptions about the event at hand. Those who perceive adversity as far-reaching are often flooded with fear and consternation over all the bad things that may (or "certainly will") ensue. The sad irony is that more sleep is lost over the response to an event than most events ever warrant. Chronic fear and worry can so weaken a person that he or she becomes incapable of optimal action.

When the phone system crashed at a client's office, the receptionist said, as she threw down her pen, "I guess I can forget my lunch break. Everyone is going to blame this on me. I'm telling you, if this isn't fixed soon, we'll be out of business!" With each passing moment I could see her mind whirring like a computer stuck on a corrupt file, calculating new and disastrous fallouts stemming from this one misfortune.

In contrast, I called the contractor who was building the PEAK office to see how it was going. "Oh, okay, I guess." He laughed. "The lumberyard called and they refuse to bring up the load on account of the hill. I've called each propane place three times, and none of them will bring up propane. The sheet rockers are three days late and won't return my calls, and the roofers brought up the wrong material. Oh, and the electrician nearly slid into the canyon. I don't think he'll be coming back anytime soon. So, every day there's a new challenge," he said brightly. "Nothing we can't deal with, though." It is easy to see how his CORE helped him finish the job on time and within budget.

The stark contrast in these two examples is clear. On one hand, we have a receptionist who is forecasting impending doom because of a single mishap. On the other is the contractor—facing far greater challenges—who remains amused and increasingly determined as the adversities continue to mount. It is the response from which all else ripples. How far you perceive the adversity will reach greatly influences how far the ripple will go.

> The mind is its own place, and in itself
> Can make a heaven of hell, a hell of heaven.
>
> —John Milton

E = Endurance

In the early 1900s British explorer Ernest Shackleton assembled a team to be the first ever to sail to Antarctica and cross the entire continent by dogsled and skis. Their boat, the *Endurance,* became permanently lodged in the ice floes and sank. Shackleton and his crew were forced to brave the Arctic winter camped on the ice floes, facing their imminent demise. Thomas Ordes-Lees, a scientist on the expedition, calculated accurately by all the data available that they were doomed. His facts were well grounded, but he didn't account for the only ingredient that can transcend the odds—the human spirit.

The AQ research indicates that this crew's perception of how long the adversity would endure would affect how long *they* would endure. Shackleton's relentless optimism and ability to see past the adversity, despite all "evidence" to the contrary, caused them to survive these impossible odds.

Refusing to submit, Shackleton devised a plan. They sailed a small lifeboat seven hundred miles in the Arctic winter across the biggest seas on the planet. At times the boat became so encrusted with ice that it began to sink. They were hit by rogue waves—walls of water that buried the boat. Their skin was ripped open by the salt water, covered with boils, and their throats were so swollen from lack of water that they could not eat. Their clothes were constantly soaked and threadbare, and their seventeen months of survival had brought them to the edge of insanity. But all along the way Shackleton fervently believed and communicated that they would get past their predicament.

His ability to see past seemingly enduring adversity allowed the adversity to be as abbreviated as possible so that they could live to tell the tale, which to this day is considered the most heroic and astounding escape from death ever recounted by any expedition. When all around him saw nothing but despair, he saw past the current nightmare and envisioned the day they would be home.

Shackleton demonstrated extraordinary strength on the final CORE dimension, which assesses and describes *how long one perceives the adversity will endure.* Those with lower AQs are more likely to perceive adversity as enduring, and those with higher AQs possess an almost uncanny ability to see past even the most dire circumstances. Clearly, this high-AQ tendency is most dramatically advantageous when the adversity is severe.

As with the other CORE dimensions, Endurance has its own consequences, good and bad. In a recent study at Dalhousie University in Nova Scotia women were shown to be more likely than men to dwell on pain, and thus their pain threshold was lower. But when both male and female participants focused on new thoughts like "I can get through this," pain tolerance was significantly increased. Seeing an end to the pain made them stronger.

Similar stories are found in the histories of concentration camp survivors. The perception that no matter how dismal the present, it will improve, or that "this too shall pass," was vital to their resilience both during and after their nightmare.

Those who see adversity as enduring often base their case on evidence of how things dragged on in a past, perhaps similar, situation. In fact, one of the primary reasons moderate- or low-AQ people predict that change will take forever is because it has in the past. Higher-AQ people learn from history and recognize that the present need not be haunted by the past. Only on the assumption that adversity is short-lived can it ever be so. It is about *today*, the present, and what comes after. Dwelling on the past or fearing the future does not prompt action.

One need not be facing certain death on the polar ice cap to see the importance of the Endurance dimension of AQ. In some ways its strength is most profoundly experienced as the more mundane adversities of daily life arise.

A client of mine recently lost three of his key people while in the middle of unprecedented growth. His immediate response was, "It looks like three months of good, hard work ahead. By then, I should have a new team in place, ready to pitch in." His determination was visible, his optimism contagious. His ability to limit how long the adversity would endure enabled him to remain buoyant and determined. That is what Endurance is all about. Had his response been "Well, this is the beginning of the end," or "We'll *never* recover from this loss," then his words would likely have been a self-fulfilling prophecy.

THE CORE OF AQ @ WORK

The CORE of your AQ is at the heart of all you do and become. It is the center of the pond from which all else ripples. To genuinely grow and sustain certain virtues like courage, tenacity, mastery, and discipline, you must know your CORE. If you wish to alleviate the plagues of worry, stress, despair, fatigue, and apathy, you must begin with CORE. If you strive to sustain your ascent, performance, agility, and innovation, start with your CORE. Or, should you desire to coach others to greater self-reliance, accountability, and determination, you'll need to pull from CORE. If you seek to lead others through increasingly uncertain, difficult, and chaotic times, begin with CORE. If you wish to understand some of the underlying norms of your team and culture, CORE can help. You will also likely apply these revelations to yourself, as well as to your relationships both within and beyond the parameters of your work. Strengthening your CORE will allow you to begin to see the impact of AQ at work.

> **If this is a blessing, it is certainly very well disguised.**
> —Winston Churchill

Choosing Your CORE

From the beginning of history, we have been intrigued with characteristics that set us apart from the animal kingdom. Logic, love, monogamy, self-awareness, embarrassment, and pride are commonly believed to be among those uniquely human characteristics, although our sole possession of any of these could be questioned. Beyond these, one quality transcends all others—the indomitable human spirit.

While most creatures strive out of necessity, humans do so out of *choice*. And, since in striving one must face challenges, that choice starts with your CORE. Unlike other primates, we are equipped with a prefrontal cortex—the region of the brain that filters all conscious behavior and where we make decisions. As a result, there is a huge range in the choices we make, and in how far we will go to accomplish a goal, be it grandiose or mundane. When we are indomitable, it is because we choose to be so; yet it is not as simple as wanting or choosing to be relentless. The CORE of the human operating system defines how we respond to every challenge and what resources and abilities we bring to bear. Our CORE response to these challenges determines how far we will go, how deep we will dig, and how long we will ascend.

Ultimately, to improve performance, we must address our inner workings, while immunizing ourselves against the dark underbelly of adversity. Joe Meade is a living example of how you can choose your CORE response to anything that happens. As a young boy in southern California, Joe led an idyllic life with a passion for the great outdoors and for all the world had to offer.

On March 21, 1976, Joe and his high school sweetheart took a trip into the mountains for a sunny-day picnic. As they were driving home after relaxing by the river, the front wheels of his Jeep got stuck in deep ruts of mud, causing the vehicle to slowly roll end over end. Joe and his girlfriend were thrown from the Jeep, which rolled right on top of Joe, crushing many bones, rupturing his spleen, and destroying his entire face below his eyebrows. It also severed his optic nerve.

He went through several protracted surgeries just to stay alive. A doctor then reconstructed Joe's skull, using a high school photograph as his guide. What the doctors could not rebuild was Joe's eyesight, which was forever lost. He entered the hospital weighing a strong 165 pounds and left as a weakened 95-pound boy with no clue how to navigate the darkness of his new world. Though Joe had always held a positive outlook on life, he initially thought all his dreams had been destroyed with his eyesight. But his mother urged him to consider adversity in a new way. The day he arrived home from the hospital, she put him to work in the garden. When Joe experienced difficulty because he couldn't see and therefore could not complete the task, his mother set a garden hose at his feet to guide his steps, gave him a shovel, and said, "You can do this." Her lesson was more about life than the garden. Joe's mother worked with him to refute the conclusion that a loss of sight meant a loss of life. Joe picked up on her inspiring high-AQ example and began to rewire his own response to adversity. Rather than becoming mired in his limitations, Joe learned to focus on what he could control, refusing to let his setback destroy his dreams, and took responsibility for becoming a contributing member of society.

As the director of recreation, heritage, and wilderness resources in the Southwest Region of the United States Forest Service, Joe helps manage the lands he grew up loving. In this role he is responsible for 21 million acres of National Forest land in the Southwest. His conservation and land-use programs have served as models nationwide, and Joe received four top honors at the president's cabinet level, most recently the USDA's highest departmental honor, the Silver Plow, for efforts in government reinvention.

Joe went through Climbing School—the AQ program—where he focused on his CORE profile and used the LEAD Sequence to further strengthen his AQ. Today, his high AQ (173) is reflected in his words: "Over time I've found for me it is as much mind over matter as it is turning challenges into opportunity. Through AQ I have learned that much in our daily lives is basically made up from our mind-set and how we choose to feel about any given event. The daily task of dealing with chronic pain and selecting to not permit it to take charge of me has left me with a powerful awareness of just how much we can empower our mind over daily events. You can get past anything. I use AQ to remind myself that we often make basic choices to let things affect us, how we feel, and much of this can be back in our control."

In Joe's response you can hear optimal Control ("much of this can be back in our control"), Ownership ("We often make basic choices to let things affect us . . ."), and Reach and Endurance ("turning challenges into opportunities . . . The daily task of dealing with chronic pain . . . has left me with a powerful awareness . . . You can get past anything").

The ideal of measuring and rewiring how one deals with adversity is quite simply the foundation of all human endeavors. It decodes the human operating system so everything that is demanded of you can be performed at optimal effectiveness. It pinpoints and enlightens us about the ultimate choice—your CORE.

The meaning that you give an event is the event.
—Deepak Chopra

Swim with the Salmon

You need not coach a salmon to swim upstream. The DNA of its operating system comes from deep within. Its relentlessness goes beyond human understanding. To strive toward one's destiny against such insurmountable odds and, ultimately, its imminent demise, is more than we can expect of others or ourselves. Yet, we admire the salmon for its sheer persistence and its noble quest to ensure its legacy—admirable traits regardless of the goal. How often do you or the people you work with display such fortitude? If your answer is "less than I would prefer," then let us consider why.

Every salmon is programmed in its DNA to swim upstream, while we humans are given the blessing and curse of *choice*. When you were a child, you were given no choice but to go to school, so most likely you attended. Yet once school is perceived as optional, attendance generally drops, often precipitously. The same can be said for most human striving. Unlike salmon, a rare few individuals will *choose* to persevere when the current becomes formidable, or continue to ascend when the conditions and incline are less than ideal. The farther you go from the main campground and visitors' center in most national parks, the more rigorous and uncrowded the trails tend to become. Despite traffic and noise, most people stay in the crowded tourist area, missing much of the grandeur and sublimity.

It is a mystery why most people, when required to perform, do not demonstrate salmon-like tenacity, especially when the fulfillment of the goal will be rewarding. We often rationalize this behavior by saying it is a matter of *importance*. To many, it does not *matter* enough to hike the extra miles away from the visitors' center. Is it fair to compare ourselves to the salmon? Few things we pursue have such elevated importance as the biological imperative to survive. So why strive, unless it is really important? There is clearly a hidden danger in letting our choices be driven by what we see as the importance of the goal.

We use importance as an escape clause to avoid giving our best. It becomes a commonly accepted rationale for mediocrity. Many people are deluded into thinking, "If it really mattered, I could and would put forth my best effort, but . . ." However, in the *mundane* challenges, setbacks, and adversities, one's true nature is revealed. When we face adversity, the limitations of our operating system become most apparent. It is far easier to become courageous when facing an impending tornado than to remain undaunted by the daily onslaught of demands, difficulties, challenges, setbacks, and annoyances. The dramatic inspires what the mundane requires.

Those who are in the "not important enough" camp get caught in a spiral of making fewer and fewer things matter, thus draining much of the joy and passion from life and work. This also creates conflict when the project they are working on is of much greater importance to someone else. If importance is the basis for motivation, it will be difficult, if not impossible, for you or your people to *draw deep* and bring your finest efforts to bear. The boss's demands are rarely enough to draw out your best.

Once you get caught in the choice trap, carefully selecting fewer and fewer endeavors worthy of your best efforts, you miss out on most opportunities and have already decided to Camp. Climbers, on the other hand, have the uncanny tendency to make the mundane matter. They elevate normal tasks to noble quests, inspiring others in the process.

We must understand that one effort does not matter more than another. We assign significance to an effort based on its relevance to our mountain, or personal quest. How important is it to what's most important? In other words, *mattering is a choice.* Those who Camp within their apathy destroy much of the day-to-day, moment-to-moment significance of life.

Our CORE response to any event determines our capacity for having things positively matter. The higher one's AQ, the more likely one is to assign positive significance to a given event. The lower one's AQ, the more likely one is to assign negative significance to the same event. This is why your CORE reveals and determines your tendency to forge forward when besieged with annoyances. As you improve your AQ and strengthen your CORE, you make better choices. Our CORE response determines how steep a mountain we are willing to climb, if we are willing to climb at all. It is what enables us to enjoy the advantages of being salmon-like without facing such an unfortunate end!

AQs AND LEADERS

A recent doctoral dissertation compared the AQs of educational leaders (administrators) and business leaders (executives and managers). One discovery indicated that the educational leaders on average had significantly lower AQs. It is important to note that AQs are not situational or likely to be changed over the course of one's life without proper awareness and training to strengthen one's CORE and Response Ability.

One explanation for these results may stem from these individuals' original career choices. Those with lower AQs tend to choose careers where they perceive that they will face less adversity and a greater opportunity to Camp. They intuitively know that they are less equipped for adversity-rich careers. However, those with higher AQs do not necessarily choose more challenging lives. Many high-AQ people choose to go into education because they want to have a purposeful and rewarding career. It is in alignment with their mountain. Based on our analysis of turnover among teachers, we discovered that many reasonably high-AQ people discovered how difficult it is to implement change in a bureaucratic environment. So some of the Climbers rerouted to other careers, possibly reducing the overall AQ mean among those who remain. In one case, lower-AQ individuals may have sensed that their operating systems could not handle the same capacity as those with higher AQs, so they sought jobs that they believed would be less demanding only to find out that education is rich in adversity. Or, in another case the educational establishment was seen as an overhang, nudging the higher-AQ Climbers to seek other ways to live their mountain. AQ can fundamentally influence one's career choice (regardless of industry), passion for one's work, the difficulty one is willing to take on, and one's patience with inertia.

Our town has a weekly farmers' market, which takes over the downtown for an entire evening. It features the most beautiful display of flowers, fresh produce, gourmet foods, and music one could hope to find in a five-block area. One week, after filling our baskets, my wife, Ronda, and I saw a woman selling bouquets of flowers. Judging by her weathered skin and white ponytail, she was probably in her sixties. She greeted us with a warm hello. I casually asked her if she sold flowers as a hobby or for a living. She told us that she made her living by "bringing joy to people's lives at the farmers' market every week for twenty-one years!" I later learned that she had lost her husband and their horse ranch in a terrible fire. Her spirit seemed indomitable.

Within 20 yards were six other booths bursting with flowers of the same or better value. It was highly competitive. Yet she was nearly sold out. In an instant I knew why. In her eyes, I saw the love she felt for her flowers. She described each as a living miracle and sold them by helping her customers experience the flowers as she did. She said, "These are a very special strain of begonias. Have you ever seen such oranges and pinks together? . . . *Feel* these sunflowers, aren't they soft? And *smell* the lavender; isn't it just *intoxicating*?" It is incredibly difficult to make ends meet in our community by just selling flowers. Yet the attitude emanating from what I guessed to be a high AQ was clearly creating a self-fulfilling prophecy. She did what she could to make the impossible possible. As a result, she was successful. To her the flowers, the customers, the display, the *smiles* all mattered. Her passion was contagious.

As you strengthen your CORE, you too can enhance your capacity for joy in what you do, regardless of the hardships involved, and have an infectious and positive impact on those around you.

One of the best ways to understand your own CORE and AQ is to learn to spot it in others. You learn to look and listen for it in everyone you meet.

Consider the road-weary marketing manager seated next to me in an airport. He appeared to be in his midthirties but carried himself like someone twice his age. He dressed the part and was armed with a client dossier. Our flight was delayed, so we began to chat. I asked where he was heading. "Oh, some meeting," he sighed, waving it away like a fly with a flick of his wrist. After some prodding, he told me about his urgent client meeting in Denver and how it represented 25 percent of his company's business. It was clearly a make-or-break event for the customer, who had apparently threatened to take its business elsewhere. He was under the gun to save the account, and if he failed, his bonus would be killed, maybe even his job. He explained this assignment with such a tone of weariness and resignation, it was as if he were being asked to hand-mop the entire runway. Rather than being fired up for the challenge, he was clearly beaten before he took off.

When the airline announced the cancellation of our flight, it was as if someone had let the air out of him. He sagged in his chair even further, sighed deeply, and seemed temporarily immobilized. It was as if his hard drive froze. After a few still moments, he folded his overcoat over his arm and slowly began to turn away. I asked him where he was going, and if he wanted to find an alternative route by talking to my travel agent on the other end of my cell phone. "That's okay," he said. "They [the customer] were probably going to bail on us anyway." When I listened to his CORE, I heard *a classic low-AQ response*—low Control, no Ownership—the customer was gone!

Numerous thoughts simultaneously flashed through my head. First, what was he like ten years ago? Had he always been so fatalistic and willing to throw in the towel, or had years of adversity worn down his youthful resolve? This often happens in people with moderate AQs. Additionally, what would his boss say if this man's ready resignation in the face of a challenge were revealed, especially given the consequences of standing up a room full of valued customers in a meeting he could have made? This obviously mattered to someone! Last, I thought, even when it "matters" some people are not motivated to overcome the next adversity to reach new heights. His operating system simply could not bear the added demand, regardless of what "mattered." His CORE was too weak. If he were a salmon, he would have died before fulfilling his destiny. Because he is human, he must choose to ultimately strengthen his CORE or spend the rest of his life as a Quitter.

GRAPH YOUR CORE

Graph your CORE Profile to learn more about how your pattern affects your Response Ability and the strength of your operating system (see Exhibit 4.2). Insert your four CORE Totals from Chapter 3 in the boxes at the top of the columns. Next, graph your CORE Profile by plotting those points on the number lines below the boxes and connecting the dots. This is your CORE Profile.

As you explore your CORE Profile, you can go beyond the basic understanding of these CORE dimensions by considering the often powerful interplay among them. Like chemicals, together they sometimes form something distinct from and more powerful than what exists separately. These CORE combinations determine your level of worry, hope, optimism, and fortitude.

One of AQ's and CORE's most important insights is that they help you see *at what toll* you live your life and survive your workplace challenges. The higher your AQ, the more likely you are to be strengthened by a given setback—the more likely you are to Climb. The weaker your CORE, the greater the toll that setback will take on your well-being, performance, and disposition, and the more likely you are to Camp, or even Quit. Exhibit 4.3 provides some insight into how different levels within each CORE dimension may affect you.

	C	O	R	E
	☐	☐	☐	☐

AQ

AQ label	AQ	C	O	R	E
High	200	50			50
	190	48		50	48
	180	46		48	46
Moderately	170		50	46	44
High	165	44	48	44	42
	160	42	46	42	40
Moderate	155	40	44	40	38
	150	38	42	38	36
MEAN	145	36	40	36	34
	140	34	38	34	32
	135	32	36	32	30
Moderately	130	30	34	30	28
Low	125	28	32	28	26
	120	26	30		24
	115	24	28	26	22
	110	22	26	24	20
	105	20	24	22	18
Low	95	18	22	20	16
	85	16	20	18	14
	75	14	18	16	12
	70		16	14	10
	60	12	14	12	
	50	10	12	10	
	40		10		
Means:	147.5	36.4	40.4	37.4	33.3

Exhibit 4.2 Graphing Your CORE Profile

Climbing Tendencies

There is an immediate focus on what you *can* control.	People step up and take Ownership for making things better	Adversity stays in its place.	Adversity is fleeting.
You believe you can positively influence the situation.	Focus on solutions over blame.	You keep perspective.	You see past challenges and remain optimistic.
You are resilient and tenacious.	High trust, agility.	You compartmentalize challenges.	

Camping Tendencies

You have a reasonable sense of Control.	You have a reasonable sense of Ownership.	Some things bleed into other areas.	Some things drag on.
You may get overwhelmed when adversity piles up.	You may resort to blame when tired and/or tense.	As adversities mount, it gets harder to separate each one.	Hope and faith are good, except when adversity is high.
Adversity can wear you down.	Ownership could be stronger.	You get burdened.	Realism is valued.

Quitting Tendencies

You respond as though you have little, if any, Control.	You deflect Ownership.	You get overwhelmed.	Things drag on and on.
You may develop learned helplessness.	You resort to blame, pointing fingers.	You are besieged with catastrophes.	Adversity endures more than necessary.
You may give up.	You may become guarded.	Little difficulties blow up.	Hope gives way to cynicism and sarcasm.

Exhibit 4.3 **CORE Tendencies**

Ownership and Control, for example, have distinct dimensions, but they directly complement each other. As you take more Ownership for dealing with whatever occurs, your sense of Control is likely to rise commensurately. Likewise, the more Control you feel you have, the more you may feel you must find a solution. The more Control you have, the more difficult it is to deflect accountability. The less Control you believe you have, the easier it is to deflect accountability. So Control and Ownership fuel each other.

A similar interplay exists between Reach and Endurance. When you see adversity as far-reaching, it is more likely that the adversity will endure, and vice versa. Also, the longer adversity endures, the more that *can* go wrong. Ownership and Control combine to determine your involvement in a situation; Reach and Endurance define its magnitude.

Obviously, the greater the perceived magnitude (Reach and Endurance), the less likely it is that you might feel able to positively influence the situation. A low AQ across dimensions can be like a weakly constructed house: as soon as one wall blows down, the others follow, topped off with a caved-in roof. Fortunately, the inverse is true of the CORE of a high AQ. Each wall, or CORE dimension, contributes to the structural integrity of the entire edifice.

Ian Burge draws forth those CORE dimensions most relevant to the challenge at hand. Ian is in charge of the new organization for Mott's Canada, part of Mott's North America. He has an AQ of 183. When faced with the prospect of doubling the value of the business within a few years, his response was, "The way I look at it, there's always a way to get things done. It's my job to make sure I get the best folks for the job, and to make sure we can contain and see our way past the obstacles we can't yet foresee. There's nothing we can't handle, and we just learn more as we go along." His response indicates strong Control and Ownership, while limiting the Reach and Endurance of any adversity that may arise. Through AQ training, Ian learned to use his CORE and grow his own Response Ability to influence the team's AQ and how they handle each new challenge.

When faced with some major mishaps in shipping product for his customers, Ian pulled his team together and immediately strategized on specific actions to keep the problem from becoming a disaster, getting past it as quickly as possible, and learning how to avoid similar problems in the future. This CORE response dramatically influenced their ability to get their business back on track.

Most people have a combination of relatively higher and lower scores in their CORE Profile. These can create counteracting forces in your quest to overcome a given challenge. For example, a high C and E accompanied by a low O and R might provide you with some optimism, but your fortitude is tempered by adversity that is far-reaching and for which someone else is responsible. Similarly, a high O and R accompanied by a low C and E might indicate that you feel responsible for improving a situation that is limited in scope, but over which you feel little Control and which is certain to endure. These hardwired patterns have a powerful influence on your propensity to act.

Remaining resilient in the face of adversity is, therefore, not about making politically correct "we will survive" speeches while people inwardly die. It is not about simply proffering inspirational words to yourself or others. People with high AQs really *see* the world differently and believe with every fiber of their beings that they can positively influence any situation and take Ownership for doing so, while containing the Reach and limiting how long it endures. This is what inspires them to take real action, and it's what separates the Climbers from the Campers and Quitters. As you strengthen your AQ, you will take on the Climber's mind-set and lens on the world.

> **Help people — and if you cannot help them, at least do not harm them.**
> —The Dalai Lama

Clearly, it is every leader's imperative to do no harm. That means you must avoid spreading the Nocebo Effect within your organization (see Chapter 2). When you combine the power of CORE that you have gained from these pages with the methods provided in the following chapters, you will have the choice and ability to determine how far you are willing to have your reactions positively or negatively influence, or be influenced by, others.

Because I am the architect of the AQ theory, people often assume they can or should unload their negativity on me. I am honored by their trust. However, it is difficult when they abandon their response vigilance and indulge whatever low-AQ tendencies they may possess by heaping their worries, complaints, and doubts upon me. As they put it, "Hey, you're the AQ guy. If I can't vent to you, who *can* I unload on?"

After twenty years of AQ-related research, I like to think I am reasonably well equipped to filter out emotional smog. Negativism is like secondhand smoke, and even my own high-capacity scrubbers can become clogged, or choked. In other words, when overdone, such dumping gets old, especially when people would rather bathe in their miseries than improve their lot. Even though I care deeply for each person's well-being, it can be wearisome when people simply want to whine and make no effort to resolve their predicaments. You may face similar challenges. Strengthening your CORE will not make you perfectly immune against others' negativity, but it will give you the strength to provide the compassion and coaching tools to get past whining and help them solve their own problems.

The brain research on habit formation presented in Chapter 2 validates our common sense: change starts with awareness. Awareness literally interrupts the hardwired pattern and the resulting ripple effect. Equipped with the tools that follow, you can strengthen yourself and the choices you make when faced with adversity. Hopefully, you will emerge from this chapter with a deeper and more precise awareness of the role the CORE dimensions play in everything from your outlook on life to your fortitude and ability to surmount personal and professional challenges. I trust that we have shed light on exactly what takes place within the human operating system that enables some people to grow greater capacity and tap their fullest capabilities. Now we can focus on upgrading *your* operating system.

Topographical Map of Chapter 4
The CORE of the Climber

CORE forms your AQ and response to any given adverse stimuli.

Control
- *To what extent are you able to positively influence the situation?*
- *To what extent can you control your own response to a given situation?*

Response Ability is enhanced by:
1) Delayed Control
2) Spontaneous Control

Ownership
The extent to which you take it upon yourself to improve the situation at hand, regardless of its cause.

Reach

How far do you let the adversity reach into other areas of your work and life?

Endurance

How long do you perceive the adversity will endure?

On which CORE dimension(s) did you score highest?

On which CORE dimension(s) did you score lowest?

What does your CORE Profile indicate about how you respond to adversity?

CHAPTER 5

DEVELOPING RESPONSE-ABLE CLIMBERS

A journey of a thousand miles must begin with a single step.
—Lao-tzu

YOUR AQ IS not about taking on a veneer of false optimism or about thinking happy thoughts. To strengthen your AQ, you must rewire your pattern of response to adversity. While some improvements happen instantly, upgrading your operating system requires what we call *Climbing School*. Response Ability is a lifelong quest to respond more effectively to whatever comes your way. Climbing School is where you begin.

Strengthening your Response Ability—and as a consequence rewiring your AQ—requires a disciplined approach. In this book you will experience Climbing School as a private tutorial, but the curriculum is designed to be taught to groups of people. The complete Climbing School program can be taught to groups of as many as several hundred people. The lesson we've learned, after teaching thousands of people to strengthen their AQs, is that everyone is a potential candidate for AQ Climbing School.

This chapter will focus on part of the CORE Climbing School curriculum for strengthening AQ. Climbing School will be presented in two sections. In the first section it's essential that you learn why most training efforts fail. This will help you modify your approach to growing Response-Able Climbers. The second section provides two levels of training to *rewire* and strengthen AQ and Response Ability.

WHY TRADITIONAL TRAINING OFTEN FAILS

Personal and corporate training in the United States is roughly a $250 billion industry annually. Globally, that number grows to several hundred billion dollars. Add the substantial time and resources invested in informal training, and the amount reaches significantly higher.

With so much money on the line, it's hard to admit that the end result does not guarantee a more measurable, definable impact on individuals as well as organizations. Based on an informal study we've conducted over ten years, we've determined that the proportion of training that is actually effective in improving individuals or organizations is between 1 and 20 percent. And 5 percent is the most common response.

One of the reasons for the low percentage is that most training is geared toward the neocortex, the cognitive area of the brain. It does not acknowledge the role hardwired patterns play in allowing or preventing new lessons to take hold. Most training ignores AQ as a way to enhance all learning. Though cognitive training improves knowledge of such things as product information, it falls short of creating the imprint and wiring change that most training requires.

If I accept you as you are, I will make you worse; however, if I treat you as though you are what you are capable of becoming, I help you become that.

—Johann Wolfgang von Goethe

Software Versus Operating System

In the same way that there is a software solution for everything you want your computer to do, there is likely a training solution to address each of the skills, attributes, and contributions you demand, expect, or hope to get from your coworkers. Leadership development, team building, sales skills, managerial skills, supervisory skills, and computer skills are all forms of human software. Yet you must decide which vendor provides the best training in each, or which software you want to load onto your hard drive. Too much software or the wrong software merely bogs down or overloads the system, compromising its performance and value.

The software (training) may offer tremendous function and many practical benefits. However, if your operating system (AQ) is insufficient or overtapped—the computer (person) will not be able to access, let alone run, the new software. Each time we add new software (or even upgrade it) we demand even more of our overloaded operating system.

For 80 to 95 percent of people, new skills or upgrades are being loaded onto operating systems that are already overtaxed. This is why so many people say the vast majority of training dollars are wasted. Very few people can handle the demands, let alone optimize the opportunity, for greater capacity, speed, and proficiency. But what happens when a low- or even moderate-AQ person receives more training?

At best, the lower-AQ person learns all the knowledge and skills. In other words, he or she could pass a test on proficiency and comprehension. This might lead the trainer mistakenly to assume that the training is successful. However, there is a big difference between just understanding content and actually *implementing* new skills and ideas. Putting most new ideas and skills into practice is inherently difficult, especially when they challenge entrenched cultural norms. One's Response Ability determines how easily one can take that challenge in stride, or to what extent it becomes a true obstacle.

Implementing new skills before they become hardwired is difficult, because it requires so much more effort than it does after they become a part of your response system. When a low-AQ, less Response-Able person is faced with the difficulty of implementing new skills, along with twenty-three other daily adversities, he most likely recoils from the challenge. Even when the person recognizes that the new skills might help, he may be reluctant to make the extra effort. He knows it's the right thing to do, but thinking and doing are two different creatures. Even a moderate-AQ person is less likely to persevere in applying, let alone mastering, a new skill.

Even so, we know that anything worth doing is likely to be difficult. Whether you're faced with resistance from a customer, coworker, or boss, or the undertow of the culture, it's never easy to integrate improved or new beliefs, behaviors, and processes into your job. You *will* face adversity—your Response Ability will determine how well you hardwire the new ways into your brain and your work.

For less Response-Able people the new software becomes corrupted on their hard drives. It is infected by their lower-than-ideal AQ, as are all of their functions. Even the best software can be crippled or rendered useless by a strong enough virus in the operating system. As a result, the new software may ultimately bog down the system, making it *less* effective overall.

"Discretionary effort" is what Holly Threat, managing director of quality and process improvement at Federal Express, calls that something extra a person must put out to achieve desired results. Training is often designed to draw forth more discretionary effort from a system. But training less Response-Able people in new skills and knowledge can be a lose-lose proposition. The trainee simply cannot successfully put the new practices into full operation. It's like the old adage "Do not teach a pig to sing. It frustrates the teacher and irritates the heck out of the pig!" When you subject your workforce to ever more training, the organization often mourns its investment as performance goes unchanged. The trainees also feel like failures, and the people with the lower AQs may lose hope, dignity, and self-worth.

Running Competing Programs

Training also fails when new software is loaded onto a system that already houses a competing program. We are all programmed with expectations, beliefs, and habits that were wired through our upbringing and experiences. These programs may complement or compete with the new lessons or software.

It is difficult for a brief stint of skill training to overcome such hard-wired tendencies. If you've ever been in a relationship where you feel you are dating all your partner's ghosts from the past, you know how stubborn past programs can be. Like many programs, they operate under the surface of one's awareness and intentions.

A client recently pulled me aside with her concerns over a new wave of training on emotional intelligence. Unfortunately, this training did not do justice to the science of emotional intelligence. It was nothing more than good old-fashioned conflict management in an emotional intelligence wrapper. Her consternation arose when the trainer required the trainees to practice looking into the eyes of the person with whom they'd had a conflict. They were to directly communicate their frustrations and concerns in unvarnished language. My client had been taught to handle conflicts more diplomatically. Her earlier programming prevented her from accepting the new software. Even if the new software *was* superior to the old, the "upgrade" would be rejected due to what was already in place, which happens with much training to which we are exposed.

Training also falls short because it does not positively impact Human

Capital—the organization's most important asset in calculating its overall market value (See Exhibit 5.1).

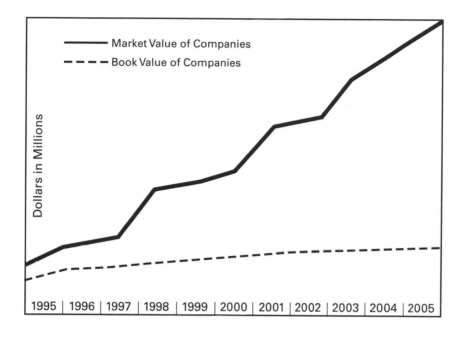

Exhibit 5.1 The Value Gap

Most Capital Is Only Human

In the New Economy, any company's dominant asset is its *Human Capital*. Today, any organization's market value can far exceed its financial capital, or book value, often by huge multiples. This has been most dramatically portrayed in the prices of technology and Internet stocks. As a result, traditional accounting or financial statements no longer communicate the true bottom line. Since the current accounting paradigm is more than five hundred years old, perhaps it is time to revise our thinking for the new millennium. We need to take a fresh look at the value we place on people and our organizations.

Leif Edvinsson, director of intellectual capital for Skandia Bank and author of *Intellectual Capital*, agrees that the missing piece in an organization's value is its Intellectual Capital. An organization's Intellectual Capital comprises Structural Capital (technology, processes) and Human Capital (people, innovation, ideas, knowledge, wisdom, experience, etc.). Human Capital is what walks out the door when the lights are turned off, or what you lose when someone leaves your organization.

Elcon Securities AS, a Norwegian insurance and banking company, wanted to sell its brokerage house. The sixty-two employees bid $100 million for the company, but the management was not satisfied and pursued other buyers. The process took a long time, and the employees (brokers) became upset. Sixty-one out of sixty-two quit, leaving only their desks and PCs. The eventual sale became the most expensive purchase of office furniture in Norway, because when the people left, so did the most important and highly valued assets of the company.

But it's not just bodies that matter when calculating Human Capital. Human Capital is greatly bolstered by Response Ability—the workforce's individual and collective ability to respond effectively to whatever comes its way. Without Response Ability, most skill and potential are wasted and Human Capital goes unrealized.

In the New Economy, any training that a person receives should directly and *measurably* contribute to the market value of the organization, regardless of his or her position, tenure, or potential excuses; it is more than a profit-driven business strategy. All organizations, including not-for-profits, have market value, which is calculated beyond their financial statements in the form of the contribution they make to society and their ability to leverage their resources to achieve the greatest potential impact and fulfillment of their mission.

Linking the development of Human Capital with the market value of the organization not only strengthens but also *ensures* the significance of every person. Each person can discern his or her place in the overall value equation. As you look at your company's market value, you should see where and to what extent you add value, *and* what you can do to grow it further.

Training is an important means of helping each person matter more and more by enhancing his or her impact on the true and meaningful calculation of the organization's value—its Human Capital. Climbers are compelled by this level of significance and become actively engaged in training. This helps them further develop their capacity to contribute and grow. They like to see where, how, and to what degree they matter.

The lower a person's AQ, the more likely he or she is to feel overburdened by the increased accountability and demands that come with being included in the Human Capital calculation. As a result, the individual is less likely to rise to the challenge of delivering and growing his or her value. Each person's quest to grow his or her value is rife with adversities. Therefore, people with lower Response Ability are more likely to be intimidated by such a cold assessment of their efforts.

Another reason training fails is that it often lacks relevance and timeliness. As a result, most of it quickly disappears from each person's short-term memory bank as the memory is cleared to take on the demands of each new day. Few ever go back to the three-ring binder to access what they learned weeks before.

Given the powers of the Internet and the enlightenment of many training professionals, more and more organizations have turned to *just-in-time* training, which is done at the time and place that allows it to be immediately put to use. While this helps mitigate some learning fallout, a lack of Response Ability can still hinder the value and implementation of the training in the ways described above.

We have found that training works best when it addresses some unanswered and gnawing pain. If your computer crashed every time you tried to access E-mail and someone could train you to stop this, you would be *hungry* for this knowledge and would not forget the process. If your competition repeatedly wins business from you through competitive sales presentations, you would likely attend a presentation skills training session. The greater the pain, the more burning the need, the more likely the training is to take hold.

To optimize training, it must be made timely and relevant; it must link to and enhance the value of the organization through the development of Human Capital. First and foremost, it must be undergirded by AQ.

Four reasons why traditional training often fails:
1. Overtaxing the human operating system
2. Running competing programs
3. No apparent training-value link
4. Lack of relevance and/or timeliness

UPGRADING AQ FOR THE NEW ECONOMY

Climbing School is about upgrading the human operating system by helping each individual permanently strengthen his or her AQ and Response Ability. Once the human operating system is upgraded, you will be able to adopt new software, programs, and applications that will enable you to achieve meaningful improvements in speed, capacity, and capability.

Climbing School can also replace old, outdated programs with new, more effective ones. Based on new research and more agile methods for growing capacity, the skills taught in Climbing School help a person jump tracks from old pathways to new ones that are based on Response Ability. After that occurs, Response Ability tends to dominate, if not eliminate, many older programs acquired from your earlier years and upbringing. It will not clear the slate, however; we all have our baggage. But even so, this training can go a long way toward fundamentally rewiring and restoring the programs within.

Climbing School addresses the training-value link required to increase Human Capital by going beyond the fact that AQ bolsters the bottom line. Yes, high-AQ individuals sell more and tend to be visionary, bold, agile, and persistent. They are also more tenacious, resilient, hardy, and focused. However, much of the true value of Climbing School comes in the qualitative, or less tangible, improvements in morale, problem solving, and decision making—as well as the less definable effect on your organization's climate.

Any training that bolsters AQ and Response Ability adds both financial and intellectual value. It updates the Human Capital, enlarging its capacity, performance, innovation, agility, decision making, determination, and optimism—all of which meaningfully contribute to Intellectual Capital and market value. A company's financial valuation is increasingly based on these ingredients.

Last, Climbing School is generally greeted with a profound sense of urgency. Once people understand the nature of AQ and Response Ability and can see its predictive power, they perceive training as addressing an immediate and pressing need. Climbing School can help people raise their AQs and become more Response-Able. The moment these skills are learned, they can be applied to the next challenge, difficulty, or annoyance people might face. Climbing School starts at this very practical level, providing *ultimate relevance*. It achieves this by equipping you, your team, and your organization with Climbing skills that will help you overcome and learn from difficulties as they arise.

There is also evidence from earlier research that those with higher AQs learn better and more than those with lower AQs. It makes logical sense that an upgraded operating system can absorb and utilize more information with greater speed and effectiveness. This can help every organization rethink its training strategy and dramatically enhance the value of *all* learning.

The important point about problem solving is not that some people are better at it than others. Instead, the important point is that problem solving can be learned. It frequently isn't learned because it isn't taught.

—John D. Bransford and Barry Stein, *The Ideal Problem Solver . . .*

THREE LEVELS OF CLIMBING SCHOOL

The focus of Climbing School is to improve one's AQ, one's Response Ability, and the overall culture. Level One of Climbing School focuses on gaining a greater understanding of—and improving—your CORE. It involves measuring and graphing your AQ and CORE, as you did in Chapters 3 and 4, as well as some new methods for strengthening your CORE.

Level Two of the Climbing School curriculum teaches an abbreviated approach to the LEAD Sequence. Within this level you are presented with three elevations, or Base Camps, each of greater difficulty and value. The idea is to provide you with a path and a set of goals for increasing your level of expertise in using the LEAD Sequence. Additionally, Levels One and Two are employed again in later chapters, where we apply them to coaching and leading Climbers and developing Climbing Teams.

There is also widenee from a third level, Level Three, which is beyond the scope of this chapter and focuses on formally assessing and then creating a high-AQ culture that nurtures Climbers and climbing behavior. It is equivalent to creating the environment where the new operating system can be fully utilized and will flourish. This is the focus of Chapter 10.

The Origins of Climbing School

The Climbing School model has evolved over the past ten years and has been implemented with tens of thousands of people worldwide.

Around seven years ago we stumbled upon some research from the

University of Pennsylvania that caught our attention. Lisa Jaycox and her team of researchers had taken on a formidable task—immunizing teenagers against depression. We were impressed with her 50 percent success rate. More important, further studies revealed that the improvements apparently lasted and became stronger long after the training was over. Jaycox and her team had devised and employed a special method called "cognitive disputation," which involves keen awareness, disputation, and rewiring of one's response to a given event. This implied that people were hardwiring the new lessons and experiencing fundamental and enduring improvements.

The PEAK team put forth a model and method for improving AQ that was based on this research and appeared to create similar results and improvements. We had three criteria for declaring victory. Improvement had to be *measurable, meaningful,* and *sustainable.* At first, we could see some inkling of all three criteria but were unimpressed by the magnitude of improvement. It was not good enough, and we knew we could do better, so we worked to devise the next level of improvement.

We have since refined all three levels to the degree that the training can reliably create meaningful increases in individual, relational, and team AQ. With Level One, we see a 5 to 15 percent improvement in AQ. That rises to an average of 20 to 25 percent improvement in a given team as we implement Level Two. Level Three sustains the improvements. You will find that Climbing School follows a natural progression from Level One to Level Three.

We went through all three levels with members of a sales team at ADC Telecommunications. Their results are indicative of what you might expect. Initially, they performed moderately well as a team; they were responsible for the AT&T account. Though not a major customer at the time, AT&T is now one of ADC's top clients. Phil Styrlund, their lead Climber and divisional vice president of sales for the Global AT&T account, embraces AQ as "the sustainer and enhancer of all the other coaching and learning. It enhances and extends the impact of all other development initiatives. It creates staying power." AQ is now required learning for ADC's entire sales force. Top executives view AQ as essential for growing from $3 billion to $10 billion in annual revenue.

Overall, Climbing School impacts their bottom line. In 1998, our first year with the people on this team, they implemented Levels One and Two and surpassed their financial goal by 203 percent. The goal was then doubled.

In their second year of Climbing School, when we focused on Levels Two and Three, the team exceeded this higher goal by 170 percent. These are the results you can get from embracing and completing Climbing School.

Today more than 100,000 people have completed AQ training and enjoyed measurable improvements in their AQs and Response Ability, as well as significant enhancements of their operating systems. As this book goes to print, new leaders, organizations, and communities from various parts of the globe are taking on the Climbing School challenge to address their emerging challenges and needs. You can, too. Ultimately, AQ will upgrade your people and add substantial value to your organization.

CLIMBING SCHOOL—LEVEL ONE: CORE AWARENESS

The brain operates in some elegant and powerful ways. In Chapter 2 you learned how the brain hardwires patterns of behavior and thought. I believe a person's AQ is mostly hardwired by age twelve, becoming quite firm by age sixteen. These patterns do not fully mature until the brain is completely developed around age twenty-three. For improvement to occur in AQ, a person must be made keenly aware of his or her AQ and CORE pattern of response to adversity. In other words, we must know the current configuration of our operating system before we can implement the proper upgrade.

CORE Dimensions of AQ

C = Control

O = Ownership

R = Reach

E = Endurance

Through the initial measure, a person gains new insights into how he or she responds to life's events. Given the importance of these patterns, most people want to learn all they can about their AQs.

To jar loose these embedded patterns requires awareness and desire. Simply by becoming more aware of adversity when it strikes and understanding your CORE response to any given adversity, you can already experience some change at Level One. Awareness also alters the physiology of your responses, opening a gateway to improvement. The deeper your awareness of AQ and CORE, the more profound the shift can be. You will also find it valuable to improve your AQ radar by learning to pinpoint the CORE dimensions from the stream of information in the world around you. Below are some tips to sharpen your skills. Level One builds on what you learned in Chapters 3 (your measure of AQ and CORE) and 4 (the detail of your CORE) and provides some specific methods for becoming a CORE expert.

Six Ways to Improve Your AQ Radar

The first step to improving your AQ is to find and read the four CORE dimensions. You began by measuring your own AQ and graphing your CORE. That provides you with initial awareness of your own pattern of response. It is highly worthwhile to deepen your expertise in listening to the CORE in yourself and others. Here are six ways to sharpen skills that serve as both exercises and homework for those attending AQ Climbing School.

1. *AQ on television.* As you watch a television drama or sitcom, listen to what the characters say when faced with adversity or even a minor challenge. Listen for each of the CORE dimensions of AQ. Does the response indicate a low, moderate, or high AQ?

    How does their response affect how the other characters respond?

    Does their response make you like them more or less?

    Based on their response, what behavior would you expect from these characters?

2. *AQ on radio.* As you listen to talk shows and the news, pay close attention to what people say in describing or responding to disasters, setbacks, or crises. Listen for the four CORE dimensions in their language. Does the response indicate a low, moderate, or high AQ?

    What is the range of responses from people confronting the same issue?

    How is their AQ communicated in their tone of voice?

    How does the CORE response affect how others respond to them?

3. *AQ in conversation.* Turn on your AQ radar during meetings, phone calls, and casual conversations. Pay attention to how people describe the challenges of their day, as well as what they think, say, and do about difficulties of all sizes. Pick out the CORE dimensions in their words. Does the response indicate a low, moderate, or high AQ?

   How do facial expression, posture, and demeanor reflect people's AQ?

   What effect does their CORE response have on their hope, motivation, performance, and likelihood of resolving the situation?

4. *Reading for AQ.* As you read newspapers, magazines, and books, look for specific quotations indicating what different people say when faced with adversity. Notice the CORE dimensions in their words.

   To what extent does their CORE response shape their reality?

   Is everyone responding in the same way?

   How do different responses to adversity affect the outcome of the story?

5. *AQ in art.* As you watch dance, examine paintings, scrutinize sculptures, and view performances, look for any indications of what is being communicated about the CORE dimensions of AQ. Notice how the heroes and villains handle adversity. Look for the role adversity plays in the underlying message.

   In paintings and in sculpture, how does the use of light, color, expression, setting, and angles affect your perception of hope? What is the mood created in the work? What story would you assume it is trying to tell?

   In a performance, what role does adversity play in the development of certain characters? What range of responses to the adversity is being demonstrated? Who has a lower or higher AQ? Who fares the best?

   In dance, what story is being told? What setbacks or challenges are being faced?

   How is AQ communicated with the body? Which performers have higher or lower AQs?

6. *AQ on the Net.* As you surf the Internet, explore advertisements and analyze the language people use to explain their businesses and them-

selves. Pay attention to how certain Web sites grant you control and ownership, and how some provide ways to deal with any adversities that may arise.

Which Web sites do you find most inspiring? What about them inspires you?

Which Web sites give you the most control in getting to the information you seek?

When something goes wrong, do the companies take Ownership for the glitch, or do they blame the technology? What do they do to own the adversity? When something goes wrong with a search or a purchase, how do different companies and individuals deal with it? Do they have a built-in mechanism for limiting the Reach and Endurance of the adversity? Or are you stuck trying to figure it out for yourself?

Learning your CORE and heightening your awareness of CORE is what Level One of Climbing School is all about. Becoming a CORE expert can be of substantial and measurable benefit. You can extend this improvement through some additional methods the PEAK team has designed for building awareness and further strengthening your CORE (see Exhibit 5.2). These roles provide useful language and valuable lenses through which you can assess the CORE of the world around you. They are useful within yourself and in coaching others.

Now that you are becoming a CORE expert, you are ready to further strengthen your AQ, CORE, and Response Ability with Level Two of the Climbing School curriculum. Try to ascend through all three Base Camps, which represent increasing levels of expertise.

1) **Be a Detective.** As difficult situations arise, immediately pinpoint at least one facet of the situation that you can influence, if not control.

2) **Be a Lawyer.** Silently or vocally question people who say, "Well, there's nothing we can do about it." Find specific ways to prove them wrong. Prove your case with real evidence.

3) **Be a Judge.** Impartially consider the evidence that supports any conclusions indicating that in a given situation you *have to* lack

control or the adversity *must* extend into other areas and/or endure. Issue your judgment based only on facts.

4) **Be a Pioneer.** Be the first to take Ownership of difficult situations, whether or not you were the cause. Pick your moment and step into the wilderness of responsibility by declaring your accountability and intended action.

5) **Be an Opportunist.** Ask yourself what will *for sure* happen as a result of a given situation within the next 24 to 48 hours. Pick those outcomes for which you feel most compelled to take Ownership and action.

6) **Be a Firefighter.** When adversity strikes, immediately contain the blaze by acting with urgency to prevent it from affecting other areas of your life. Hose down emotional brushfires as they pop up.

7) **Be a Surgeon.** As difficulties arise, prevent them from bleeding into other facets of your business, relationships, and life by surgically clamping the damaged artery and operating on or even removing damaged tissue.

8) **Be a Visionary.** No matter how severe a setback may be, imagine life after it has passed. Force yourself to rise above and see beyond the adversity. Paint a mental picture of how life is different now that adversity is history.

9) **Be an Accountant.** Create a balance sheet, indicating on one side the likely result of adversity over which you have no Control, feel no Ownership, and which is far-reaching and long-lasting. On the other side, put the implications of adversity over which you feel a certain amount of Control, strong Ownership, and which you see as limited and short-lived. Apply your analysis to the situation at hand or as difficulties arise.

10) **Be a Catalyst.** Take even the smallest constructive action to regain Control, to take Ownership, or to limit the Reach or Endurance of the adversity, and you will immediately begin to see it shrink.

Exhibit 5.2 **Strengthening Your CORE**

CLIMBING SCHOOL—LEVEL TWO:
THE LEAD SEQUENCE

This level of the Climbing School curriculum focuses on a highly precise, effective, and compassionate problem-solving model called the LEAD Sequence. You will find it useful in a broad range of challenges of all magnitudes. It will help you strengthen focus, clarity, and decision making. At each elevation, or Base Camp, you will be presented with a higher-level challenge.

Before we explore how to deal with adversity, consider your current pattern of response. You may have any number of typical reactions. With the first reaction, your AQ triggers a specific CORE response, which unleashes all sorts of consequences. These consequences form a Ripple Effect (see Exhibit 5.3). The consequences of your response influence your thinking, creativity, mood, problem solving, decision making, approach, and beliefs, not to mention your attitude and health. Your response is the epicenter from which everything else emanates.

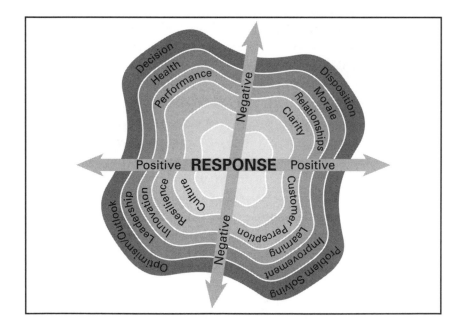

Exhibit 5.3 The Ripple Effect

Usually, your CORE creates an instant reality, which you immediately accept and then react to accordingly. It forms the "truth" that you unquestioningly allow to pervade your world. So, if you have a less-than-ideal AQ, you may see the adversity as far-reaching and beyond your control. This response determines your actions, causing you to throw up your hands, ruminate over the impending fallout, and make sure other people understand how terrible the situation *really* is.

Most training tries to get you to alter the consequences, but it doesn't ask you to consider why you reacted as you did. The standard call to arms demands that you "be bold, take more risks, never give up, think positive, and dig deep to find new solutions." These slogans make better wall hangings than strategies for change. You can no sooner expect to make a difference by telling someone who is depressed to "cheer up" than you can by telling a moderate- or low-AQ person to "give it your all" and "deliver relentless perfection every time."

Let's explore a way to first strip-search the response so that this Ripple Effect is altered. Each step of the LEAD Sequence has distinct Base Camps, or elevations, of expertise. You may begin at the lower elevations and strive toward the upper levels of expertise.

L=Listen to Your CORE Response

Listen—Base Camp 1: Elevation 3,000 meters. This is the most basic application of listening to your CORE. It involves simply listening for your AQ response. You get a quick gut-level read of your CORE, without assessing each dimension. You became an expert at this when you completed Level One. You can pick out the CORE in the response. "This is a real disaster (Reach). We'll never pull out of this mess (Endurance). Well, there's nothing we can do about it now (Control). I hope upper management knows what it's doing (Ownership)."

It is easy to underestimate this apparently simple step. However, just by listening to your response, you alert your brain to shine a light directly on your AQ and CORE, interrupting the pattern of response. You also create a biochemical change, which allows the brain to consciously alter what takes place. This is like switching your garage door from automatic to manual, so you can adjust the track.

Listen—Base Camp 2: Elevation 4,000 meters. To ascend to this second level, you need to tune in to each CORE dimension more precisely. With the help of Chapters 3 and 4 and the above exercises, you know enough to do this immediately. The questions in Exhibit 5.4 will help. These are devices for jogging your brain to step out of a lifelong pattern and analyze it with the cold eyes of an objective observer. This opens the door for effective problem solving and renewed perspective.

You need not go through this list of questions to listen to your CORE. Quite the contrary: with minimal practice and keen focus, you will be able to sense your AQ *instantly.* You can sense it at a level much deeper than words, which are formed to explain what has occurred inside of you. Once you have listened to this whole-body response, you are ready for the second step in the LEAD Sequence as you continue with Level Two of Climbing School.

The following questions are designed to help you listen effectively to your own CORE response to adversity. This is the first step in the LEAD Sequence, or Level Two of Climbing School.

When adversity strikes
- Do you hear a low or high AQ (based on the CORE)?
- How much Control to better the situation does your response indicate?
- To what extent do you take it upon yourself to better the situation?
- How far-reaching and long-lasting is the adversity, based on your response?
- As you feel your response course through your body, how does it feel? Does it strengthen or weaken you? Why?
- What CORE dimensions are playing the most significant role?
- If others were to read your nonverbal expression (facial expressions, gestures, posture, eye movement, etc.), how would they characterize your AQ?

Exhibit 5.4 **Listen to Your CORE**

E = Establish Accountability

This step has the power to help you rise to meet the adversity. It is an internal call to arms, a noble request for doing what is right. You know when something feels right, and any progress in this step of the LEAD Sequence is a positive move for all involved.

Let's assume that a major customer calls because he is upset about delays in getting something he asked for. This is the response:

"This is such a mess. We're sure to lose this customer; he has obviously already made up his mind. And, when word gets out, heads are going to roll. I am sure I'll be the first to get cut. It will destroy me financially, with both kids in college, after all those years of scrimping and saving too. Well, there's nothing I can do about it. We will never hit our performance targets now!"

To establish accountability, your goal is the opposite of what you might assume. You might guess that this step requires that you take it upon yourself to solve or deal with the entire problem. In fact, such a response can backfire and, depending on the magnitude of the adversity, can be genuinely overwhelming. This is where many well-intentioned leaders and managers go awry. Knowing that accountability is sacred, they feel it is incumbent upon them to guide their people to shoulder the problems of the world. Climbers may thrive under the added weight, or they may end up like the world's top Sherpa, who died under the added burden placed upon him by his leaders.

Rather than accepting the entire problem, your goal is to determine which part of the situation you are responsible for improving to even a minor degree, *no matter how small*. The magnitude of accountability is less important than *taking* some because the simple act of stepping up and saying "I own this part" strengthens Control and creates an inward momentum toward action. How big "this" is does not measurably determine the benefit.

The moment you pinpoint your accountability, you establish an inner pact and noble quest to "better this particular facet of the situation to the best of my ability." It is hard to imagine a problem that cannot be conquered by such a pact. Surely whatever adversities you face can be influenced when you take accountability to better even a small fraction of the overall challenge.

Establish Accountability—Base Camp 1: Elevation 3,000 meters. At its most basic level, you might consider these questions:

> Of the entire situation you just described, if you were to pick one small facet of it to improve, even in the tiniest way, what would it be? Or you can draw a huge circle and ask, If this represents the whole situation, what sliver of it would you most want to help improve?

This cracks open the door to Ownership.

Establish Accountability—Base Camp 2: Elevation 4,000 meters. If you prefer a more formulaic approach to establishing accountability, here are some questions to consider. Starting with the response to the customer, ask:

> 1. Of all the things you just mentioned that will happen, what do you know will happen *for sure* in the *next twenty-four to forty-eight hours*?

This question is designed to force you to limit your thinking to a specific time and to focus on a much smaller puddle of *for sures*. This causes you to shed a huge portion of the initial burden and allows you to concentrate on those parts of the situation that you want to hold yourself accountable to improve.

> 2. Of those things you decided are *sure* to happen, which ones do you feel the least bit accountable for improving? Or, of the items on your list, which one do you most want to work on?

In this way, you discipline yourself to pick a specific, reality-based facet of the problem to improve. As you take on accountability, you create an inner momentum, which is easily contagious. It makes you feel both responsible and Response-Able.

When others see you rise up to deal with the problem, they are much more likely to do the same, making a real solution all the more imminent. Leadership starts with yourself, and this step of the LEAD Sequence can help you lead more effectively. You also create and strengthen your sense of control to positively impact the event, no matter how serious. This is simply an alternative strategy for the more visually oriented learner to help work through establishing some initial accountability so you can move on to the third step of the LEAD Sequence.

A = Analyze the Evidence

This is potentially the most powerful step of the LEAD Sequence. It plainly separates facts from the assumptions that make up any low-AQ response and clears away all barriers to meaningful action. The good news is that even in your first attempt to use this step, you will most likely enjoy some real benefits. However, it is through focus and repeated effort that you turn this step into an art form. As you rise to the higher elevations of skill, you can develop a rhythm between the response and the evidence, which gently shakes loose all of the damaging *assumptions* of a lower-than-ideal AQ. It also makes the LEAD Sequence feel as natural as casual conversation, when, in fact, it is an extremely precise method for disputing and raising your AQ. But let's start with Base Camp 1, using the same situation and response described previously.

Analyze the Evidence—Base Camp 1: Elevation 3,000 meters. This level involves the most basic and generic questions. It is easy to remember and use.

1. What evidence suggests that this *has to* be out of my Control?

2. What evidence suggests that this *has to* be far-reaching?

3. What evidence suggests that this *has to* last a long time?

Step 2 (E) of the LEAD Sequence addressed Ownership. Now in Step 3 (A—Analyze the Evidence), we address the remaining CORE dimensions, Control, Reach, and Endurance. The most basic strategy is to ask questions on each dimension. This is highly effective but may feel stilted in comparison with the natural flow you'll experience when you activate the more advanced elevations.

One of the most powerful facets of the questions in this part of the LEAD Sequence is that each answer is always "none."

Analyze the Evidence—Base Camp 2: Elevation 4,000 meters. Begin and work with your response. Here is the example, once again:

"This is such a mess. We're sure to lose this customer, he has obviously already made up his mind. And, when word gets out, heads are going to roll. I am sure I'll be the first to get cut. It will destroy me financially, with both kids in college, after all those years of scrimping and saving too. Well, there's nothing I can do about it. We will never hit our performance targets now!"

1. What evidence suggests that this has to spell the end to your function or role in this organization?

2. You said this is a huge mess. What evidence suggests that this has to be a huge mess?

3. You said that this will destroy you financially. What evidence suggests that this has to destroy you financially?

4. You said there is nothing you can do about this. What evidence is there that any effort to improve the situation would have to fail?

These questions carry the power of Base Camp 1 and a lot more. And, of course, the answer is always "none." They reflect superior inner-listening skills followed by questions customized for the actual response. When used within yourself, they force you to examine the precise wording of your response before it escapes through your fast-sparking neuropathways. In the chapters ahead, you will explore further uses of this as a leader, team member, coach, and mentor.

Analyze the Evidence—Base Camp 3: Elevation 5,000 meters. This level takes all of the advantages learned at Base Camp 2 and adds an important tool: the ability to refocus the question to get the right answer. This level prevents you from going astray by misunderstanding the questions above, or responding to them other than the way they are so precisely worded. These skills are applicable in many settings, both intrapersonal and interpersonal. For example, when you ask yourself:

1. What evidence suggests that this *has to* spell the end of your function or role in this organization?

You may respond by thinking, *There are a lot of reasons this could spell the end. It happened last time we went through one of these, and my boss said it looks really bad, and* . . .

2. Yes, you are right. It certainly *could* end up like that again, but what evidence indicates that this *has to* be the end of your role at this time? Or, I know that is how it happened *before*, but what evidence is there that it *has to* happen that way *this time?*

None.

3. You are right, this *could* lead to financial ruin. But what evidence suggests that it *has to* destroy you monetarily?

None.

This higher-level cognitive disputation method has a rhythm like aikido, the ancient martial art. In aikido, you take in your opponent's energy and return it to him without it hurting you. So a punch becomes a throw, or a kick becomes a roll. In this level of the LEAD Sequence, you take in the response—all the reasons that things could be horrible, long-lasting, and out of your Control. You then return them with a slight wording change, altering the *coulds* to *have tos*, so that your brain can readily grasp the difference.

In a sense you are forcing your brain to hear the same question differently the second time. This can unleash higher Response Ability. In your initial responses to these questions you are releasing the programming that could otherwise prohibit you from moving past this adversity. This higher elevation of the LEAD Sequence enables you to clear out the old programming so that you can speak directly to the CORE of your operating system.

D = Do Something!

This step is designed to go beyond a primitive and often overwhelming list of actions to specific steps you must take to address the facets of the adversity that most concern you.

Begin with the basics. After completing the first three steps of the LEAD Sequence, try these questions.

Do Something!—Base Camp 1: Elevation 3,000 meters. This basic level helps you ask CORE-specific questions that force you to list specific actions related to each dimension.

1. Specifically, what could you do to have more Control?

2. Specifically, what could you do to limit how far this adversity reaches?

3. Specifically, what could you do to get past this adversity?

Do Something!—Base Camp 2: Elevation 4,000 meters. Consider the example once again as you ascend to the next Base Camp:

"This is such a mess. We're sure to lose this customer, he has obviously already made up his mind. And, when word gets out, heads are going to roll. I am sure I'll be the first to get cut. It will destroy me financially, with both kids in college, after all those years of scrimping and saving too. Well, there's nothing I can do about it. We will never hit our performance targets now!"

Your job is to ask precise questions that will jar your thinking and acuity.

1. Specifically, what could you do to reduce the chance that you will lose your job?

2. Specifically, what could you do to make this less of a mess?

3. Specifically, what could you do to make sure you do not get destroyed financially?

4. Specifically, what could you do to keep on track with your performance targets?

This level goes beyond generic CORE questions and ties directly to your words and concerns, enhancing the likelihood that you will come up with actions that are a good fit with the situation and contribute meaningfully to its improvement.

Do Something!—Base Camp 3: Elevation 5,000 meters. At this level you force the actions you write down to be more precise and specific. Here's how the inner coaching might work.

"Specifically, what could you do to reduce your chances of losing your job?"

"I guess I could talk to Julia, my boss."

"Specifically, what would you talk to her about? What would be the goal of the conversation?"

"I would want to find out all I could about what is really happening so I can figure out the best plan of attack."

"Specifically, what questions would you want to ask?"

"I would ask her, 'What do we know for sure about this situation, and what do you predict will happen based on the facts you have so far?' And I would ask her if she recommends that I start looking for another job."

"Specifically, what could you do to make this less of a mess?"

"I probably could do something to help make sure we don't lose other valued customers in the process."

"Specifically, how would you do that? What specific actions would be most likely to help keep your valued customers in place?"

"I would need to call them and make them feel okay about what is happening so they don't react adversely when they read about it in the paper or hear it on the news."

"Specifically, whom would you call first? What would you say? How would you imagine wording your message to accomplish that goal?" And so on.

The point of the higher-elevation expertise is to work with great precision within yourself to make sure you are not shortcutting the process with vague answers that sound good but can be difficult to apply when the moment of truth comes. People can be masters at this evasion. It requires inner discipline to force yourself to follow this kind of precise action, but if you do, you end up with a clearer, generally superior strategy for taking on the adversity.

L—Listen to Your CORE Response

1. Was it high or low AQ?
2. What CORE dimensions did you hear in the response?

E—Establish Accountability

1. Of the entire situation you just described, if you were to pick one small facet of it to improve, even in the tiniest way, what would it be?
2. Of all the things you just mentioned that will happen, what do you know will happen *for sure* in the *next twenty-four to forty-eight hours?*
3. Of those things you decided are *sure* to happen, which ones do you feel the least bit accountable for improving? Or, of the items on your list, which one do you most want to work on?

A—Analyze the Evidence

1. What evidence is there that this *has to* be out of your Control?
2. What evidence is there that this *has to* be far-reaching?
3. What evidence is there that this *has to* last a long time?

D—Do Something!

1. Specifically, what could you do to have more Control?
2. Specifically, what could you do to limit how far this adversity reaches?
3. Specifically, what could you do to get past this adversity?

Exhibit 5.5 The LEAD Sequence Base Camp 1

THE ACTION FUNNEL

In *Adversity Quotient: Turning Obstacles into Opportunities,* I introduced a method of funneling actions from the D = Do Something! step of the LEAD Sequence down to a precise plan of attack. This refined version is called the Action Funnel (see Exhibit 5.6). It is best used by people who simply like to list their possible actions as they answer the questions in the final step of the LEAD Sequence. It may also help you dodge many traditional action-planning pitfalls, and so it will enable you to dive into the action you are most compelled to take.

Beginning with your list of potential actions, consider these basic questions:

1. Of these possible actions, which one are you most compelled to take? Or, *specifically*, which action do you want to *commit* to taking first?

2. Specifically, by when will you have completed that action? Or, if you were to set an absolute deadline for completing this action, what specific day/time would you set? This means a *specific* day and time, not "next week."

3. What resources might you seek to assist you in completing this action?

Now you have completed the LEAD Sequence, which has helped tens of thousands of people to rewire their responses to adversity. This is not only a scientifically grounded method for upgrading your operating system but also a very efficient, effective, and compassionate problem-solving model.

Initially, it will take you five to fifteen minutes to complete this process, but over time, it will become second nature and you will discover how to draw out those facets of the LEAD Sequence that best address any given challenge or setback.

Clients have reported that using the LEAD Sequence has given them greater inner agility, allowing them to be resilient when adversity strikes. Leaders find that this strengthens the respect and trust of their followers.

You can create your own route by plotting out a 90-Day Trek made of weekly trail markers that will remind you to stop and assess how you are progressing in the LEAD Sequence. You can plot your trek within your own scheduling system or by using something like the form provided in Exhibit 5.7. The main components include (1) planning for and reflecting upon specific situations where you use the LEAD Sequence to strengthen others' Response Ability, (2) pinpointing what elevation of the LEAD Sequence you employ, and (3) pinpointing what specific alterations you can make to strengthen your ability to LEAD others. This will increase your understanding of CORE when adversity strikes. The 90-Day Trek is more self-reliant and low-tech than the Web-based program we currently employ with our clients to reinforce the lessons and track individual progress. And the 90-Day Trek puts you in charge of your reinforcement so

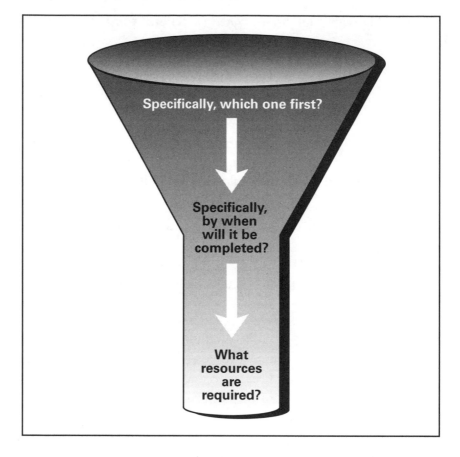

Specifically, which one first?

Specifically, by when will it be completed?

What resources are required?

Exhibit 5.6 **The Action Funnel**

you can begin to use Level One and Level Two methods as a coach, mentor, and team leader in the chapters that follow. You will learn about the additional strategic level of improving AQ—Level Three—for strengthening Cultural AQ in Chapter 10.

LEADing Others

Consider specific situations where you can use the LEAD Sequence to grow Response-Able Climbers. Specify and track your progress by completing the blanks below as shown in the example.

Example

Situation:	Person/People involved:	Date:	Next time I will improve by:
Presenting ideas to boss.	My boss.	2/8	Remembering that the LEAD Sequence is about asking questions, not giving answers. I need to reach the next elevation.

Reflections:

When you allow lower-AQ people to vent and let in their response, it diffuses their anger. People don't want to be burdened by negative assumptions. The wording of the LEAD Sequence is precise, and the more I stick to the way it is presented, the better I do.

Week One:

Situation:	Person/People involved:	Date:	Next time I will improve by:

Reflections:

Week Two:

Situation:	Person/People involved:	Date:	Next time I will improve by:

Reflections:

Week Three:

Situation:	Person/People involved:	Date:	Next time I will improve by:

Reflections:

And so on. At certain times stop and ask these questions:

How can I apply the LEAD Sequence in the future?
How has the LEAD Sequence been most useful?
What have I learned so far?

***Exhibit 5.7* LEADing Others**

Topographical Map of Chapter 5

Developing Response-Able Climbers

Human Capital (knowledge, skills, aptitudes, talents) is the most important factor in an organization's market value. Training should enhance the value of Human Capital.

Four reasons why traditional training often fails:
1) Overtaxing the human operating system
2) Running competing programs
3) No apparent training-value link
4) Lack of relevance and/or timeliness

Climbing School at all levels will help you optimize your training investment.

Level One of Climbing School involves deepening CORE Awareness.

Level Two of Climbing School involves the three elevations (Base Camps) of expertise in the LEAD Sequence.

The LEAD Sequence
L = Listen to Your CORE Response
• Did it indicate a higher or lower AQ?
• What aspects of the CORE were strongest? Weakest?
E = Establish Accountability
• Of all the facets of the situation, which one would you want to improve first, even in the smallest way?
• Which one do you feel most accountable for improving?
A = Analyze the Evidence
• What evidence is there that this *has to* be out of your Control, far-reaching, or long-lasting?
• What evidence is there that any of these assumptions *have to* come true?
D = Do Something!
• *Specifically,* what could you do to have more Control?
• *Specifically,* what could you do to limit the Reach of this adversity?

- *Specifically,* what could you do to limit how long this adversity endures?
1) Of this list of actions, which one do you commit to taking first?
2) Specifically, by when will this be completed or begun?
3) What help is required?

CHAPTER 6

COACHING AND MENTORING CLIMBERS

L IKE MOST LEADERS, you are probably convinced that the people around you possess tremendous potential. Do you wonder how much potential gets tapped each day, particularly when adversity strikes? Coaching people to expand all forms of their potential and to be high-AQ, Response-Able Climbers is easier than you may think! This chapter will show you how to coach, mentor, and lead others using the Level One and Level Two AQ-strengthening skills. You will help people ascend through a sequence of elevations, or Base Camps, each with greater promise for strengthening AQ.

For those who are naturally gifted coaches, mentors, and leaders, this chapter will provide new tools to strengthen, guide, and inspire others. For those less gifted in these roles but enacting them nonetheless, this chapter will provide a structured process you can follow to guide others toward greater Response Ability.

CAN ANYONE BE A COACH?

Coaches, mentors, and leaders are people who seek to guide and inspire others to a higher and more meaningful ascent. In broad terms, *anyone* can serve in one or more of these roles. However, managers are often promoted or selected for their positions because of their expertise with processes, not people. They are often thrust into the coaching role without the tools to do it effectively.

Ideally, leaders help match people's jobs with their strengths, so they can leverage their gifts for the benefit of all. Dick Leider, the bestselling author of *The Power of Purpose,* calls the resulting sense of flow in one's work "natural productivity."

It does not require brilliant interpersonal savvy to help others strengthen their operating systems. It only requires an authentic concern for others and a modicum of dedication to the process about to unfold in the pages that follow.

I am often asked, Can a Camper coach a Climber? I generally answer, "Yes, with the same credibility as the morbidly obese doctor who advises you to be more disciplined in your exercise and diet regimen." Leadership begins with *self-leadership.* This involves working through your own questions, purpose, and challenges. You must use the Climbing School tools provided in Chapter 5 to strengthen your own Response Ability in order to have authentic credibility as you coach, mentor, or lead anyone else. Sometimes the culture does not support Response-Able behavior. The culture serves as an overhang, hindering the ascent.

Within us all there are wells of thought and dynamos of energy which are not suspected until emergencies arise. Then, oftentimes we find that it is comparatively simple to double or treble our former capacities and to amaze ourselves by the results achieved. Quotas, when set up for us by others, are challenges which goad us on to surpass ourselves. The outstanding leaders of every age are those who set their own quotas and constantly achieve them.

—Thomas J. Watson Sr.

USING AQ TO MENTOR, COACH, AND LEAD

To be an effective AQ mentor, coach, or leader, you must consider certain criteria. Many of these can be applied to anyone trying to assist others in their ascent. These are particularly important if you are to play a vital role in helping others strengthen their Response Ability and overall capacity for challenge.

Mentoring relationships may be formally assigned or arranged either within or outside of one's organization. Some of our clients have formal mentoring programs in which certain people are carefully selected and paired. In other instances, an individual may seek out someone in particular and ask him or her to serve as a mentor. Or you may even serve as a mentor without ever being asked. In these instances, mentors simply provide the guidance, wisdom, feedback, and investment to help others grow and improve.

Although approaches vary, coaching is often a more directive role. Coaches generally provide more direct guidance and are more prescriptive than mentors. They may also play the role of motivator. Coaches often have a specific area of expertise, such as selling, which is the focus of their skill coaching. Others can be life coaches, providing broader and deeper guidance on life-scale choices and development.

Leaders can be coaches, mentors, or simply people who help you do something you otherwise might not attempt. They help you draw forth the discretionary effort that helps you go from good to outstanding. The leader can be designated formally or informally.

For the purposes of AQ, these terms are interchangeable. All three describe people who are invested in others' ascent and can play a vital role in strengthening others' AQs. Just as you hope to learn the violin from a skilled virtuoso, people who serve these roles ideally should have at least moderately high AQs, because this influences their perspective and approach in developing others. You may also want your mountain guide to have the capacity and skills to help others take on a sometimes formidable route.

Effective AQ mentors, coaches, and leaders:

- Help others grow their sense of significance
- Focus on asking more than telling
- Are committed to the ascent of others
- Are working on strengthening their own AQs
- Understand the CORE and AQ principles
- Help guide others to reach their own conclusions and decisions
- Are open about their purpose (mountain) and struggles
- Find significance in helping others
- Are willing to invest time in LEADing others
- Are supportive and nonjudgmental
- Are solution-oriented
- Follow up with others to help them stay on track
- Are dedicated to helping people grow all three forms of capacity (Accessed, Existing, and Required)

BRIDGING THE GAP IN POTENTIAL

To successfully coach or mentor anyone, you must consider all three forms of capacity introduced in Chapter 1: Required Capacity, Existing Capacity, and Accessed Capacity. You may recall that Required Capacity is what a person needs in order to meet the demands of the day. Whatever a person is capable of contributing at any point determines his or her Existing Capacity. However, what he or she actually draws forth is Accessed Capacity.

Chances are most of your coworkers (and maybe you, too) are experiencing two gaps in potential. First, the gap between their Existing and Accessed Capacities is most likely significant, especially when adversity becomes a powerful intervening force. The second, and for many the most destructive, gap occurs when their Required Capacity continually outpaces their Existing and Accessed Capacities—both what they can and do contribute. These gaps stress and demoralize people, causing many would-be Climbers to camp. The end result is frustration and consternation not only for you but also for all involved.

The growing gap between what is required and what a person possesses—and what is ultimately delivered—is caused when expectations interact with reality. According to the Law of Adversity: "The greater the complexity of the systems we operate within, the more adversity we must face in our endeavors."

Simply put, as the weather on the mountain intensifies, greater chaos, uncertainty, and challenges require more of us. In other words, our Required Capacity expands at an accelerated rate at the same time that most individuals' operating systems force their Existing and Accessed Capacities to shrink. Sadly, most people's operating systems (AQ) literally *prevent* them from rising to the challenge of these expanding forms of potential. An overloaded system is not able to tap or expand skills, knowledge, and capacity. Therefore, defining and improving AQ clearly plays a central role in expanding all forms of capacity.

Most people lack the AQ and related Response Ability to meet these demands. When they are faced with adversity, their patterns of response cause their capacities to shrink, just at the moment when those capacities most need to expand. We see it in the store clerk who is bombarded with questions, requests, and demands, all of which he fails to meet satisfactorily. Or, we see it in the middle manager who becomes unable to demonstrate the coolheaded decisiveness she once possessed.

As our world becomes more challenging, the standards for an "ideal AQ" are likely to rise. Like having one foot on a dock and the other on a drifting boat, the wider the gap, the greater the pain.

One reason why coaching, mentoring, and leading are such powerful roles is that they can reach people and influence them at multiple levels. This is a vital part of a comprehensive approach to upgrading the individual and collective operating systems. In this chapter we will specifically focus on the first two levels of strengthening AQ.

BEGIN WITH THE MOUNTAIN

Before measuring anyone's AQ, you must address the basic elements of human motivation and endeavor, both of which can elevate who a person is and what he or she does. They define the mountain, giving them *purpose* or *significance*. Effective AQ coaches, mentors, and leaders are dedicated to growing others' significance in their work and lives.

The thread of significance is woven throughout this book, because it strikes at the essence of a Climber's motivation and quest. It plays a vital role in coaching, mentoring, and leading others, as well as in synchronizing all forms of potential so that one's natural productivity can be fully optimized. Great coaches, mentors, and leaders help draw out, strengthen, and sustain significance and purpose in others. This is one of their distinguishing traits.

Life coaching expert Dick Leider explained, "Many people perceive their work as their mountain, which they climb for strictly financial ends. Or they have a sense of purpose that is not aligned with the purpose of the organization for which they work. In short, many people do not connect deeply with the mountain they're climbing in their work. There is a deep hunger to connect 'who I am' as a person with 'what I do' to make a living."

Purpose goes beyond crafting an eloquent personal mission statement and framing it as a reminder of your life's quest. In practical terms, purpose is about the higher "why" inside each of us. It is why we do what we do and, ultimately, why each of us is here. We are often asked questions like "Why did you take this job over that one?" "Why do you live there?" "Why are you in this business?" "Why does this matter to you?" The answers are highly individual and will reveal one's values. This leads to the ultimate essence of their purpose. Purpose is the final "why."

Purpose defines your mountain and how far you move forward and up along its slope; it is the extent to which you ultimately succeed. In one's final breath, it defines what really matters. No other measure of success can compare in clarity and truth.

Related to purpose, significance is about mattering. Significance is the experience of being purposeful. It is the feeling and reality that who you are and what you do matter. Beyond our primal needs, *significance is the strongest human drive.* So deep is the drive to feel significant that *it motivates all of our major life decisions.* Although seemingly ethereal, significance is made practical every single day. Our choice of careers, bosses, projects, spouses, communities, lifestyles, even material goods, is based on their contribution to our sense of significance. This quest for significance fuels the ascent.

Given the power of significance, it is alarming to see how little attention it receives from many leaders and how many people unnecessarily suffer from a feeling of insignificance in their work. What do you believe your coworkers would say, assuming they were to be completely honest, if asked, "On a scale of one to ten, how significant do you feel here on a daily basis in your work?" Or, "Since you started working here, when did you feel most significant?"

When people experience high or strong significance, they tend to be vibrant, healthy, focused, and strong. We are deeply inspired by significance and by those who have it coursing through their veins. We see it in their eyes, their work, their relationships, and their everyday decisions. Significance elevates profoundly and authentically.

In contrast, insignificance is an insidious and potent virus that, once it spreads, can crash your operating system. It can also spawn all sorts of horrid consequences. Those who lack significance can become irritable, resentful, and, in extreme cases, violent. They may become physically ill and depressed, apathetic and dysfunctional. Some completely check out. Insignificance is like climbing through quicksand. It saps vital energy, productivity, and the sense of engagement. A sense of insignificance can metastasize throughout a culture, becoming dangerously rooted in its norms, assumptions, and beliefs. Insignificance kills the ability to tap and grow anyone's potential.

In the United States, as in many countries, most governmental agencies are going through a fundamental transformation to become more agile, cost-effective, and customer-focused. The U.S. Forest Service is no exception. When I was asked to work with the staff of the Kaibab National Forest, which surrounds the Grand Canyon in Arizona and Utah, the service had just hired a new forest supervisor, Connie Frisch. It was clear to Connie and me that people were severely jaded by their many years of past experience with less-than-effective leaders. Changes and initiatives had come and gone, and like a small forest fire, they had eventually burned out before they could do much damage.

People at all levels were skeptical that a government agency subject to congressional whims could enact meaningful change. My first action was to do a significance check. I asked leaders and people at all ranks what happens when they offered up suggestions and ideas. Most made snide remarks or laughed dryly. They consistently reported that they felt their additional effort, ideas, initiative, creativity, and commitment were for naught. They felt insignificant. As a result, the Kaibab National Forest was riddled with infighting, formal complaints, people falling ill, and a sense of learned helplessness. One leader summed it up by comparing it to a "ship lost at sea without a rudder. Why paddle?" he asked rhetorically, "when the tide is stronger than your stroke?"

Connie worked hard to prove she was different and that she intended to influence their empowerment and effectiveness to the fullest extent without breaking the law. She used many strategies, including putting the entire workforce through AQ training, beginning with her leadership team. But her day-to-day strategy was to establish a sense of significance within the group by clarifying each role and articulating the group members' contribution to their vision and mission.

Significance is also one of the primary predictors of employee turnover. The less significance people feel in their work, the less likely they are to stick around. Most turnover stems from a dearth of significance. Many members of the Kaibab National Forest put in their time, but little else. Over time, as their sense of significance became clear, they became more engaged.

Three years later, the Kaibab National Forest is considered a model of agility and innovation. Connie Frisch's investment in establishing, communicating, and honoring the significance of each person and his or her role in the Kaibab ascent has paid off.

If It's Not Significant, Why Climb It?

Climbers are *repulsed* by insignificance and consider it an unacceptable state. Campers, however, may trade significance for stability and security.

Whatever the perspective, the more significant people feel, the more likely they are to give their ultimate effort to their work, drawing upon their Existing Capacity. This is why a coach cannot overestimate *the significance of significance* in hiring, coaching, and leading.

I regularly ask people in a wide range of industries: "How many of you took and keep this job primarily because you believe that who you are and what you do here matter?" All hands are raised. "How many of you would stay if the significance of what you do was doubled, but your pay was cut by 25 percent?" All hands remain raised. "How many of you would stay for long if your pay was doubled, but within six months it became convincingly clear that who you are and what you do here do not matter, and probably never will?" All hands drop.

Money matters, but not for the reasons you might think. Money is a currency of significance. It symbolizes how important you are perceived to be within an organization. Look at money through the lens of significance, and its symbolic value becomes readily clear. For example, take a recent conversation I overheard among a group of MBA students.

"Hey, I hear you took the offer!"

"Yeah, I couldn't turn down that kind of starting pay. They even give you a car!"

"I hear you walk in earning over 140K. Is that true?"

"Even more, if you negotiate well!" (Delivered with a smile and wink.)

"Wow, they must have *really* wanted you!"

"That's what I figured. That's why I said yes!"

This person's life will not be meaningfully improved with an income of $140,000 versus $120,000. The number represents the *intensity* with which she was sought and wanted, and that was the deciding factor in her decision. By offering $140,000 to this student, the company said, "You *really* matter." It communicates how much the person is valued and quantifies the significance of her contribution.

The good news is that money is not the only currency of significance. Since as a leader you seek to unleash all forms of potential, you can gauge your words and actions by the Significance Scale (see Exhibit 6.1).

Either side of this scale represents those things that contribute to your sense of significance or insignificance. Which way and how decidedly the scale tips for each person is determined by how one interprets what he or she hears, sees, and experiences each moment and over time.

A common mistake is for a leader to pay no attention to this scale until he wants something from his people. Any deposits of significance are then likely to be perceived as inauthentic, and this may backfire. Significance is increased by daily deposits, not last-minute displays. Because significance is so powerful as a motivator and tapper of potential, it is often used to manipulate the goodwill and effort of others. This may work in the short term but is sure to backfire in the long term. If you want to tap, grow, and sustain the highest potential of your people, you must grant them deposits of significance on a regular basis, and it must be done with authenticity, or it will mean less than nothing.

Exhibit 6.1 **The Significance Scale**

Significance defines what we call the "good boss" or "effective leader." I remember the day Phil Styrlund left US West to join ADC Telecommunications. It was as if someone had died. I exited the elevator onto his floor at US West for one last visit and met a receptionist who was beside herself, unable to speak. Styrland's assistant's eyes revealed many tears and deep loss. Men and women alike openly cried and hugged. I asked why, who died, what tragedy had struck? "I can't believe he is really leaving. I mean, it's good for him, of course, but it's *so* sad to see him go," his assistant explained. "We will *never* find another one like *him*. He just had this unique ability to make everyone here *matter* so much. It was *never* about title or rank, but about you as a *person*. I sure will miss that. We will *all* miss that."

After seeing Phil interact with people, I understood their tears. No matter what the situation, he found some way to point out a person's value. I remember one time when we went to grab some dinner after a long meeting. After the waiter went to great lengths to provide exceptional service, Phil handed him the bill and said, "The food was great, but the service was *really* memorable." The waiter smiled. Phil continued, "I mean it. This place was packed and you could have ignored us, but you didn't. There aren't many people who work so hard to delight their customers. You really seem to love your job. Thanks. You'll be seeing us again soon!" Phil never makes insincere deposits of significance, but he is always on the lookout for the way each person can and does matter.

As a coach, mentor, and leader, you too can dramatically influence another's Significance Scale. And in so doing, you influence his or her loyalty, drive, and potential. Well beyond such tangibles as money or benefits, the *intangibles* tip the scale.

To start, leaders need to be completely honest with themselves and determine how significant each position is within their organization. If you determine that a given position is not terribly significant, it should be eliminated to preserve the integrity of the person in that role and the people who interact with that role. Every position should have clear significance to the mission and success of the organization. It should be important to the ascent. This is essential for whoever fills the role.

Next, leaders need to determine each person's *currency of significance*. To some, it may be an authentic thank-you, but to others it may be specific resources or seeing ideas put to good use.

My team does extensive work in this area of significance. We ask a lot of people, "What do people do, say, or offer to you here that helps you matter?" Or, "How do people let you know how much you matter here?" The answers show us that there are some standard approaches to growing significance.

Ultimately, if you spend your day helping people matter, you and they will reap rich rewards (see Exhibit 6.2). Significance expands potential and furthers the ascent. Strong significance combined with AQ can be a formidable force.

To help individuals sustain their sense of significance and strengthen their Response Ability, you should lead them through the two levels of Climbing School from Chapter 5, applied here in a one-on-one approach. Therefore, your next step is to help others strengthen their CORE awareness so that they have an understanding and starting point from which they can build and grow.

The following are ways to enhance or communicate a person's significance:
- Showing appreciation
- Providing resources
- Demonstrating respect
- Remaining fair
- Listening
- Granting authority to make decisions and mistakes
- Providing support, especially when the person fails
- Providing time to connect, talk, learn
- Demonstrating thoughtfulness
- Granting credit for the person's contribution
- Having faith that the person can handle highly important responsibilities
- Rewarding with money
- Providing benefits
- Granting freedoms that matter to the person
- Focusing on results over rules
- Surrounding the person with good people
- Caring about the person's life
- Investing in the person's growth and improvement
- Providing opportunities
- Investing in the person beyond the workplace
- Telling the person that he or she matters

- Pointing out the person's contribution
- Openly acknowledging the person and his or her accomplishments
- Caring when you have nothing to gain

Exhibit 6.2 **Significance Deposits**

LEVEL ONE RESPONSE ABILITY— BUILDING A CORE AWARENESS

Leaders beware: awareness creates a powerful physiological change in the human brain. In the previous chapters you learned that the moment you become aware of a pattern like your AQ, it can be rewired, creating systemic changes. Rewiring your AQ requires both awareness of the current response pattern and some viable options for a more effective replacement. The ability to respond effectively to whatever may arise starts with an awareness of your AQ and CORE Profile. Once exposed, your AQ can be upgraded. Of course, to respond effectively, you have to know the menu of possible responses to a given event. Ideally, your menu will be filled with only the healthiest fare, the most constructive, high-AQ assortment of possible responses.

As a coach, your job is to help others go beyond a superficial measure of AQ and quick-fix techniques for being more courageous in the face of adversity. Start by letting others assess their AQs. Your goal is to get them to understand the implications of the feedback and let it sink in. You can teach them what AQ means and the fundamental role it plays in unleashing their natural productivity. Point out the role AQ plays in whatever they consider important. Go beyond the feedback and your knowledge of AQ and CORE to link their results to specific past behaviors so that they can experience how their AQ affects their Response Ability and ultimate effectiveness. Help them get a deep understanding of the role AQ plays in their lives, and the role it could play in where they are trying to go. The time you spend providing these insights is time well invested. Ultimately, these insights should create a sonic boom within others, as they realize how their AQ-based operating systems have been affecting many facets of their lives.

AQ is not the only hardwired pattern we carry around. You may recall that another is laughter, or more precisely our individual patterns of laughter. Therefore, equating people's AQ and CORE with laughter is a good way of getting them to understand how something can be both hardwired and changeable. If your life depended on how you laughed, you'd change your laugh pattern. Understanding that patterns are changeable also reduces the stigma of having a low score, which is not meant as a tattoo but merely as a starting point, almost like graphing a laughter pattern.

You can help individuals further enhance their CORE awareness by employing some of the CORE-sensitizing methods from Chapter 5. In addition, the CORE-specific actions offered in Exhibit 6.3 will begin to shake loose and move their CORE pattern, or AQ. This can provide some early encouraging and enlightening gains in Response Ability. Having provided the awareness, you are now ready to assist with Level Two of AQ coaching, the LEAD Sequence. You will find that this process can prove particularly powerful when used in the leader-follower or mentor-mentee relationship.

As you become more of an expert at using the LEAD Sequence, you will want to ascend to the higher-level Base Camps provided within each step. While slightly more challenging, these higher-altitude skills are enriching and rewarding as you help others in their ascent.

The list includes some initial steps for strengthening others' CORE response to any given challenge. Provide this list of possible steps for improving upon a person's initial CORE profile.

C = Control

How much Control do you have over your own response to events?
To what extent are you able to positively influence the current events?

1. Focus on your CORE response, especially in intense, difficult moments.
2. Control your response, words, nonverbals, and tone.
3. Take a breath, step back from the situation, and focus on what *can* be done to better the situation.
4. What facets of the situation can you influence positively?

O = Ownership

To what extent do you take accountability for improving the situation?

To what extent do you take Ownership of difficulties you did not cause?

1. Regardless of who or what caused the current difficulty, what part of the situation are you willing to own and work to improve?
2. Make it a habit to say "I own this" when something goes wrong, or "I may not have caused it, but I still own it."
3. Help others take Ownership for bettering difficult situations. It's contagious!

R = Reach

To what extent does this difficulty reach over into other areas of your life?

1. Keep adversity in its box. Become adamant about not letting an event in one area bleed over into other areas.
2. Nip catastrophizing in the bud. Refuse worst-case scenarios except when your life is at stake and it is essential to consider them.
3. Categorize adversity. Keep your categories separate.
4. Step back from the adversity, distract yourself, and revisit the adversity when you are refreshed and strengthened.

E = Endurance

To what extent will this situation endure?
How long do you let the difficulty drag on or persist?

1. Force yourself to see past the adversity. Envision the other side of the problem.
2. Get accustomed to saying and thinking "This will pass" or "It can't last forever."
3. Take specific action to limit how long the adversity endures.
4. Creatively solve problems with others to get past the adversity as quickly as possible.

Exhibit 6.3 Strengthening Their CORE

LEVEL TWO RESPONSE ABILITY— LEADING OTHERS

LEADing others requires taking the LEAD Sequence that you learned to apply intrapersonally in Chapter 5 and applying it *interpersonally* in your interactions with your people. The LEAD Sequence is a powerful tool for solving problems, clarifying thinking, deciding on meaningful action, and preserving dignity. Properly used, it can bring out substantial and measurable improvements in AQ.

You will want to use the LEAD Sequence every time another's concern, negative assumption, or worry threatens to pollute momentum and meaningful action. Regardless of your title or assigned role, you can be the one to coach and lead others to higher Response Ability. The LEAD Sequence can be used in nearly every challenge where assumptions potentially cloud action or sap a person's energy. Once you properly employ the LEAD Sequence, those you coach, mentor, and lead will be grateful for the incisive guidance.

Each step of the LEAD Sequence has two or three Base Camps at increasingly more difficult elevations. Your goal is to start at the lower elevations and ascend to the higher ones as you master the subtleties of the methods that follow.

L = Listen to the Response

Listen to the Response—Base Camp 1: Elevation 3,000 meters. The most basic application is to listen to a person's responses to determine whether you hear indications of a predominantly high or low AQ. This provides an instant starting point for the second step in the LEAD Sequence. It also creates a fundamental shift in the brain, enabling rewiring to occur.

Listen to the Response—Base Camp 2: Elevation 4,000 meters. To ascend to Base Camp 2, you tune in to each CORE dimension. Try to pick out Control, Ownership, Reach, and Endurance within the person's response. As you become more skilled at this, you will be able to determine the facets of a person's CORE that come through in his or her response. And you will see which CORE dimensions are likely to enhance or detract from his or her Response Ability.

Next, you have the option of leveraging the lessons of Level One to help that person enhance the awareness of his or her own response. Again, I refer you to the lists of tools provided in Chapter 5. One of the most profound gifts you can grant any follower or team member is the keen awareness of his or her own response to adversity. With this awareness comes change. It is the growth formula for potential and resilience. Having provided the overview of the person's AQ and CORE, you can then ask him or her helpful questions, such as:

1. As you respond to this adversity, how do you see your AQ coming through?

2. How is your AQ influencing this situation? What is the potential Ripple Effect?

3. Which CORE dimensions do you hear or notice?

4. Which CORE dimensions are enhancing you or making you stronger? Which ones might be weakening you?

5. What effect is each of these CORE dimensions having on the people and tasks with which you are involved?

6. If you could do it over, how would you ideally want to respond to this situation?

7. Why would that be a superior response? How does the Ripple Effect from that response compare with the one caused by your original response?

The purpose of these questions is not to have people start scripting themselves like newly programmed robots, but rather to help them recognize that with awareness comes choice. It is hard to overestimate the potential benefits of response awareness. Through your coaching they also start considering their responses more closely, and that is a positive first step in strengthening AQ and Response Ability.

E = Establish Accountability

Your goal here is the opposite of what you might suspect. Rather than heaping the responsibility for the whole situation onto people's shoulders, your goal is to get them to accept even the most minor Ownership for bettering the situation. As they step up and take ownership, they strengthen their sense of control. This leads to more Response-Able action and deeper commitment to solving the challenges at hand.

There are a variety of approaches to establishing accountability. After practicing these, you may develop your own. Although multiple approaches are offered, my advice is to pick the one or two questions that work best for you. You should use them, refine them, and stick to them. There is no need to complicate the process.

Establish Accountability—Base Camp 1: Elevation 3,000 meters. One of my favorite approaches is getting the other person to pick the part of the situation that he or she first wants to better. Here are some useful questions:

1. If you could draw a picture of this whole situation, what part of it would you most want to work on to improve?

2. You indicated that this is a really big problem (challenge, disaster, etc.). Obviously, it would be overwhelming, if not impossible, to take it all upon yourself to solve. But if you were to work on even one small piece to make it better, which piece would that be?

3. If you could choose where to invest your energies, which facet of this situation would you most want to help improve?

4. If everyone had to play a role in salvaging this situation, what role would you want to play?

Establish Accountability—Base Camp 2: Elevation 4,000 meters. You will recall that the other approach is to focus on the facts and derive accountabilities from those things you know will happen for sure in the short term versus the assumptions of what will happen over time. This helps people shrink the situation down to a more manageable window of time. Here are some options for doing this:

1. What do you know will happen *for sure* in the next twenty-four to forty-eight hours? What else?

2. Of those things you mentioned, which one(s) do you feel most accountable for helping to improve or solve?

3. For which ones do you at least share accountability for improving the situation? You said that the whole project will be killed and we will never get another chance like this one. And you may be right.

That is *certainly* possible. But let's break this down and start with the next day or so. What do you know will happen *for sure* in the next twenty-four to forty-eight hours?

You will recall from our earlier discussion of Ownership in Chapter 4 that it is *not* about blame. However, the person may begin by talking in terms of blame. Or he may misunderstand your questions and think you are trying to find out who is at fault. Often low-AQ people internalize bad events, seeing themselves as the sole cause of what will surely be some disastrous and enduring fallout. They feel like the epicenter of blame. This focus can be highly destructive to both them and the process of fixing the problem.

Blame compromises agility, trust, and interdependence, often at a time when these virtues are most needed. Blame can also be highly demoralizing, embarrassing, and demotivating.

Your job is to help keep the person within the Learning Zone, which is that level of blame from which she learns. Beyond that level any blame she takes on is completely unnecessary and often destructive. Again, certain questions can help you get there:

1. Most events have multiple causes. List the ones you can think of for this situation.

2. You have listed (*insert number*) causes here. Together they make up 100 percent of the blame. What percentage of that applies to you?

3. In terms of their impact or importance in bringing about this event, what order would you put them in, from most to least important?

4. You are obviously upset by what could be a very serious situation. What would you want to do differently to prevent this from ever happening again?

5. If you had a friend who was about to get into the exact same situation, what advice would you give to make sure he or she could prevent as much of this as possible?

The point here is to coach efficiently and incisively to derive practical lessons, not to let a person get mired in shame, embarrassment, or blame.

Questions like "How could you do such a thing?" or "Why do you think you did that?" are not necessary. Nor are emotional probes like "You are obviously feeling really bad (guilty, ashamed) over this. Why do you think you feel that way?" or "It must be terribly hard for you having caused all of these disastrous consequences." Although compassionate, these sorts of questions and probes can inadvertently deepen and solidify a person's low-AQ assumptions. They fan the flames.

Establish Accountability—Base Camp 3: Elevation 5,000 meters. The higher-level skill to Establish Accountability is reserved for when a person feels as though he or she has no accountability whatsoever. The method is to blow the situation up to its largest possible size so that having zero accountability becomes nearly impossible. It is used to enhance either of the lower elevations of E (Establish Accountability). Here's how it works.

> "Of the entire situation just described, if you were to pick one small facet of it, which would you want to commit to improving, even in the tiniest way?"
>
> *"None. It's not my job."*
>
> "So you have *no* accountability for anything that happens?"
>
> *"That's right. How can I? They're the ones making all the decisions."*
>
> "So as you look at all of the customers and this entire business, you have no responsibility or role in making any facet of what we do successful?"
>
> *"Well, I guess I play some role."*
>
> "Oh really? What role do you play, no matter how minor?"
>
> *"Well, I guess I play a role in serving some of our customers."*
>
> "Okay. So, knowing you can't do it all yourself, it sounds as if you have at least *some* accountability with your customers?"
>
> *"Yeah, I guess so."*

I have found that few people, when confronted with all facets of the entire situation, will reject having any responsibility for making it better.

It is also important to note that the word "accountability" can turn off some people; they become defensive about what sounds like someone trying to get them to solve the entire problem. That is why I used words and terms like "what *role* might you play" and "do you have any *responsibility* for improving." These are useful alternatives to "accountability" and can help you achieve your goal of getting another person to recognize his or her role in improving the situation.

Notice that it is sufficient for the person to accept accountability unenthusiastically, even reluctantly. It is unrealistic for you to expect him to shoulder the entire situation and eagerly salute the cause as he moves forward. More often than not, you will help the person realize that he plays at least *some* role in improving the situation.

Once you have selected from and used the above tools to establish some initial accountability, you are ready to separate fact from assumptions, freeing a person to take meaningful action.

A = Analyze the Evidence

This step has far-reaching utility. You can apply it to any number of situations from dealing with frustrated customers or an upset staff member to guiding the person you are coaching, leading, and/or mentoring. It will create many "ahas" and deepen genuine empowerment.

There are several ways to Analyze the Evidence. A common mistake people make in applying the LEAD Sequence is to step outside this tightly honed approach and start to freewheel it on their own. Be careful. Even subtle word changes can produce dramatically different results. My advice is to stick with the formula for quite some time before you alter the approach.

Analyze the Evidence—Base Camp 1: Elevation 3,000 meters. Here are a few questions you can use to Analyze the Evidence:

1. What evidence is there that this *has to* be out of your Control?

2. What evidence is there that this *has to* be far-reaching?

3. What evidence is there that this *has to* last a long time?

The most basic strategy is to ask questions on each dimension, with the exception of O, or Ownership, which was addressed in the previous step. Using this basic application can be highly effective, but it may feel stilted in comparison to the natural flow of the higher Base Camps. The higher you go, the more natural and fluid the strategy becomes.

Analyze the Evidence—Base Camp 2: Elevation 4,000 meters. To reach Base Camp 2, begin with the person's response. Here is an example:

"Well, there goes the whole project. We will never have another chance like this one. It was nice while it lasted. I hope upper management figures out something here, because there is obviously nothing we can do about it now."

1. What evidence is there that this *has to* kill the project?

2. You said that you will never get another chance like this one. What evidence indicates that this *has to* be true?

3. You said there is nothing you can do about it now. What evidence is there that this *has to* be completely out of your control?

The advantage gained by graduating to Base Camp 2 is that it includes strong listening skills, which build respect and strengthen the relationship. At this elevation you customize the questions to each statement the person makes, which is like lining up each assumption and shooting it down. And the person holds the smoking gun—not you.

Analyze the Evidence—Base Camp 3: Elevation 5,000 meters. This elevation goes beyond the previous lessons. At Base Camp 3 the flow becomes more natural as you employ additional strategies for overcoming potential misunderstandings while refocusing the interaction. Given the same example, see how you can coach someone to Analyze the Evidence and handle his or her adversities more effectively. Consider this sample interaction:

In response to your first question, "What evidence is there that this *has to* kill the project?" the person may say, *"The last time this happened all of our projects were killed on the spot."*

You respond by saying, "So, it clearly *could* kill the project again, right?"

"Right."

"Okay. Given that it *could* be killed again, what evidence is there that it *has to* be killed this time?"

"I guess none, but it probably will be."

"So, you think it will, but there's no evidence that says it *has to?"*

"Yeah, that's right."

"Okay, let me ask you this. You said that you will never get another chance like this one. What evidence is there that this *has to* be true?"

"This is a one-time deal. Terry even said that this was a special project. And people worked so hard to make this one go. There's no way anyone will want to go through this again."

"So there are a lot of good reasons why you might not see another project like this one, right?"

"Definitely!"

"Good point. Now tell me, given these reasons why it *could* be a one-shot deal, what evidence is there that it *has to* be that way?"

"Well, nothing says it has to."

"Okay, that is a good clarification. But you said there is nothing you can do about it now. What evidence is there that this *has to* be completely out of your Control?"

"Hey, I'm not the one who makes all the decisions on these projects around here. I just do the technical stuff. I have no say on what happens next."

"So you have no authority over the project whatsoever?"

"None."

"So you cannot Control the decision, right?"

"That's the idea."

"Okay, given that to be true, what evidence is there that you have utterly zero influence over even the smallest facet of this project and its future?"

"Well, I guess it's not zero."

"Great. That really helps me better understand the situation. It appears that there is no evidence that the project has to be killed, or that this has to be the last one. And you feel as though there must be some facet of the situation you can influence, in at least some small way. Is that correct?"

"Yeah, I guess that's all true."

"Excellent."

Now you are ready to immediately transition that person toward meaningful action by employing the fourth step of the LEAD Sequence.

D = Do Something!

The point of this step is to use precision and clarity to avoid many of the classic pitfalls that may arise in coaching a person toward action. These pitfalls include vague actions that sound meaningful but are difficult to implement, as well as vague or nonexistent deadlines, no backup plans, a list of too many actions, or an unrealistic plan. These pitfalls can be overcome with some precise language and focus.

Your goal in this stage of the LEAD Sequence is to help the person create a list of potential actions from which he or she selects what to do and when to do it. Ideally, there will also be a backup plan. There are three Base Camps with increasing levels of expertise, each demanding and offering greater precision and clarity.

Do Something!—Base Camp 1: Elevation 3,000 meters. Base Camp 1 is based on CORE-level questions, such as:

1. Specifically, what could you do to have more Control?

2. Specifically, what could you do to limit how far the adversity reaches?

3. Specifically, what could you do to get past this adversity?

Given the coaching you provided in the Level One CORE awareness steps above, the person should have some fairly specific answers to these questions. Even at Base Camp 1, he or she should be able to list some valuable ideas. These ideas can be enhanced at the next base camp.

Do Something!—Base Camp 2: Elevation 4,000 meters. This level addresses the specific words people use in responding to adversity. It ties actions to their precise concerns and assumptions; therefore, it is a meaningful improvement over Base Camp 1. Go back to the example:

"Well, there goes the whole project. We will never have another chance like this one. It was nice while it lasted. I hope upper management figures out something here, because there is obviously nothing we can do about it now."

Here are more precise questions that can help draw out meaningful action:

1. Specifically, what could you do to reduce the chances that the project falls apart? What else?

2. Specifically, what could you do to increase your chances of being on another project equivalent to this one, or better? What else?

3. Specifically, what could you do to better the situation, even in the smallest way? What else?

The point is to gather a complete list of possible actions, all of which *the person* dreams up. It is important to know that some people have trouble with this step and need your help to unclog their flow of ideas.

CLEARING THE TRAIL

Occasionally, people simply cannot come up with solutions that will better a situation and allow them to keep climbing. To get them past these rocks in the trail, you might ask one of the following questions:

1. If someone you really cared about was in this identical situation, what specific action would you suggest that person take?

2. What specific actions *might* you take to prevent this project from being killed?

3. I understand that you don't know what to add to this list of actions. If you *did* know, what sorts of things do you think you might suggest?

4. What would the most effective problem solver you know specifically do to better this situation and help make sure these concerns do not come true?

5. Since you cannot think of any answers right now, what do you want to do to feel at least some positive momentum in this situation?

Base Camp 2 allows you greater flexibility and is more likely to create a meaningful list, despite potential clogs in the flow of the process. But it's up in the rarefied air of Base Camp 3 that you will find the greatest rewards and results.

Do Something!—Base Camp 3: Elevation 5,000 meters. To achieve the greatest flexibility and consistency in the LEAD Sequence, you should strive toward Base Camp 3. To reach this elevation you must listen carefully and ask precise questions. It has many applications for helping people choose meaningful action when faced with all sorts of challenges. Here's how it might work, drawing from the previous example.

"Specifically, what could you do to reduce the chance that this project will be killed?" you ask.

"Well, I guess I could talk to my boss."

"Good thought! Do you mind if I make a note of that idea?"

"No, go ahead." (Write it down.)

"What else could you do to keep this project alive?"

"I could try to better understand why past projects have been killed and see if we can avoid the same problems."

"Would you like me to add that to the list?"

"Sure, why not."

"Specifically, how would you gather that information?"

"I guess I would ask some of the people who were around when that happened."

"Like who?"

"Like Lorenzo, and maybe Tanya. They will probably have some ideas."

"Want those on your list?"

"Sure, go ahead."

"Specifically, how could you increase the chances of having another project as good or better than this one?"

"I have no idea."

"If you were coaching someone reasonably bright and capable like yourself, and he was in the same position, what specific advice would you offer? Specifically, what would you suggest he do to make sure this is not a last-chance situation?"

"I guess I would tell him to go create the opportunity."

"What specific action could he take to make that happen?"

"I guess he could talk to the tech-trends folks about what is on the horizon."

"Exactly what would he ask?"

"Questions like 'As you look six to twelve months out, what projects are going to emerge and shape our company for the next couple of years?' And, um, 'If you could give birth to only one of these ideas, which one would it be, and why?' "

"Okay, and then specifically what would you do with the information?"

"Focus on the one that is most compelling. Create a sketch plan and take it to their team to begin crafting a proposed project."

"Has that worked for others?"

"Yes, in fact, that's how most of our projects are decided."

"Great! Would you like to add those questions to your list too?"

> **Advice is the weak substitute we resort to when we cannot help a person help him- or herself.**
> —Anonymous

The Action Funnel

The Action Funnel (see Exhibit 5.6) gives you a precise method for moving people from a potentially overwhelming list of actions to one specific action they feel deeply compelled to take by a specific deadline. Without restating its subtleties here, the basic steps are:

1. Of these possible actions, which one are you most compelled to take? Or: *Specifically*, which action do you want to *commit* to taking first?

2. When will you complete that action? Or: If you were to set an absolute deadline for completing this action, *specifically* what day/time would you want to set for yourself?

3. What resources do you need to complete this action? Or: Within reason, how can I help?

As a coach, you will want to carefully review and work through this process with your people, to make sure their actions are specific, clear, and within a precise deadline. Lacking any one of these elements can lead to failure. You may also wish to establish a backup plan. You can accomplish this simply by asking some basic questions; for example:

"So, you are committed to talking to Lorenzo by the end of Monday. Is that correct?"

"Yes, by end of business Monday."

"Great. If he's unable to give you the information you need, specifically what would you want as a backup plan?"

"I guess I would have to get Tanya involved, maybe even download case histories from our Intranet."

"And when do you want to commit to having the information you need?"

"By the twelfth at the latest."

"So, in other words, if Lorenzo does not come through, you are going to talk to Tanya and download case histories from the Intranet by no later than the twelfth to make sure you have the information you need?"

"That's right!"

LEADing others can help people tap and expand their potential by growing their Response Ability. That is why this method is gaining popularity as a source of competitive advantage in some of the most dynamic industries on the planet.

At Cypress Semiconductor, the LEAD Sequence is being used by sales managers as the coaching model to guide their salespeople. It is also the problem-solving and mind-training template for a more formal mentoring program. Cypress has to be able to instill even greater agility and focus in its high-performing superstars. Darryl Carson, director of marketing development, and Marie Schilly, manager of training, view Response Ability as the CORE competency for anyone selling in their highly competitive and rapidly changing industry.

Carson believes that "one key to success in our industry is the swiftness with which we assess market shifts, make decisions, and implement new product development initiatives or systemic changes to the company's business processes. It's vital that our employees take Response Ability in order to execute those changes. That's why we assess, interpret, and teach AQ at Cypress Semiconductor. It strengthens the CORE of our top-performing employees and is the cornerstone of our formal mentoring program. AQ is a vital source of competitive advantage for not just our top performers but our workforce at large."

Clearly, the LEAD Sequence provides immediate value and results. It will help you guide your people from their worries and assumptions to meaningful action. And the more you use it, the more advanced and natural it will become. You will quickly learn to appreciate its clarity, efficiency, compassion, and consistent results. As you get better and more comfortable using this process, you will find that it is also virtually bulletproof, and you will enjoy its unique power to make sure people are compelled to help themselves. It will help them expand their Available and Realized Potential to meet the expanding requirements of the day. Before long, the LEAD Sequence will become your coaching tool of choice.

It is one of the most beautiful compensations of this life that no man can sincerely try to help another without helping himself.

—Ralph Waldo Emerson

Assessing Your Success—When to Measure AQ

It is highly gratifying to see yourself improve and also to see that the gains you are making are real. Chances are that the people you coach through Levels One and Two will see significant gains. And since the ascent never ends, you will want to help your Climbers to be ever stronger. As Campers begin to climb, they will reignite their inner relentlessness and that will fuel their curiosity and their quest to improve. For these reasons, you will want to remeasure each person's AQ a few months after the initial assessment. A third measure can be timed another six months out.

When you measure AQ for a second or third time, the focus should be on the overall gain as well as the specific CORE-related changes. Acknowledge the gains and help each person recognize the areas that need additional improvement.

These lessons can be deepened by linking the lessons to actual behavior or to specific situations, such as what a person said or did in a specific meeting, or how he or she handled a specific challenge.

The Validity of Repeated Measures

I am often asked to what extent a second measure is valid. The PEAK team and the independent statisticians we hire have examined this issue carefully and found that repeated measures are statistically sound. Years ago, we crafted a complex post-test version of the ARP to measure AQ weeks, months, and years after the initial measure. When we compared results of the convoluted measure with those from using the same instrument twice, we found no statistical difference between the two. Using the same instrument proved to be an equally valid remeasure of AQ. We were quite surprised by this result, since we thought people might "cheat" by simply circling what they thought they *should* circle rather than their genuine response. However, as thousands of people complete the ARP for the second, third, or fourth time, we begin to see why these additional measures are valid.

If you can respond to adversity effectively on paper, you should be able to monitor your CORE equally well when real adversity arises. If you still feel uncomfortable using the same instrument repeatedly, we also employ alternative versions for measuring improvement.

Extended Coaching

Regardless of your role, you are coaching people to expand their capacity every day; otherwise, you would not be reading this chapter. Most of us think of coaching and mentoring as a formal or informal process targeted at people who work for you. However, I encourage you to expand your thinking, whether for altruistic or purely business reasons.

Think of those who influence your success. Consider each customer, vendor, stakeholder, coworker, and competitor. What if you simply roamed the planet employing the Significance Scale and LEAD Sequence every day? In each interaction, you would focus on and authentically offer a significance deposit—something that helps the people you're dealing with feel as though who they are and what they do matter. Whenever a concern, worry, or negative assumption arises, you draw from and employ the LEAD Sequence, using the parts of it that most artfully address the issue at hand. The impact would be tremendous. First, like Phil Styrlund (the significance-enhancing leader formerly with US West), you gain fiercely loyal followers and coworkers who would go way beyond their job descriptions to help you get things done. Second, turnover plummets. Who would want to leave a place where they are listened to, dignified, and coached with such skill and compassion? Who would abandon a place where they learn to solve their *own* problems, and where they benefit from your wise guidance with the LEAD Sequence? My surveys of people around the world tell me that most individuals would readily take less pay for a job that makes them feel more significant. But they would *never* stay long term in their current job if the formula were reversed. Challenges are far easier to find than a workplace community where one is fully valued. True climbing teams are still rare. These models will help you begin to create your own.

Third, as others' operating systems are strengthened by their growing AQs, they are likely to grow and realize greater potential. They will also experience the natural exhilaration of surmounting ever-greater obstacles. Your people will then be able to access more of their "software," which puts more of their training, learning, experiences, and talents to good use.

What about you? How would *your* day change after employing these two models consistently and authentically? Significance begets significance.

Dr. Ronda Beaman is a maverick professor of education at Northern Arizona University, who has been awarded the first National Education Association Art of Teaching Award. She also has multiple sclerosis. She uses the LEAD Sequence and her knowledge of AQ to keep herself strong and continue her own ascent. She focuses on those facets of her disease she can control and takes Ownership for doing all she can to limit the Reach and Endurance of each episode. She now views her workouts as physical therapy. At worst, she has only "occasional bad days," and ten years after being diagnosed, her disease remains imperceptible.

As an educational entrepreneur, Dr. Beaman coaches her future teachers with the LEAD Sequence and uses the Significance Scale to help them see past obstacles and elevate their sense of purpose. A Climber herself, Dr. Beaman has become nationally known for using innovative new methods within a stodgy bureaucracy. Dr. Beaman knows that bureaucracy motivates many potentially gifted teachers to Camp. Her students have the lowest initial AQs of any major on campus. However, by instilling significance she achieves her goal of graduating teachers who inspire others and climb to meet the challenges of the new millennium. While her subject is education, her currency is *significance*.

"It's so true that you get what you give. My life and work are made much more significant by helping others matter. I know what I do is important for these young teachers and the legions of students they will someday influence. How they deal with each adversity will determine their tenacity to stick with the most noble job one can have—teaching. It just fills my heart."

Every interaction involves deposits of mattering. Dr. Beaman starts by videotaping each student as he or she departs on day one so that she can memorize all 350 students' names by day two. If you doubt the power of significance, you should see day two. People are utterly stunned, some moved to tears. "I've been here four *years*," one moist-eyed student explained, "and I don't think *any* of my professors ever bothered with my name. Ronda did it in a day, and this is the biggest class on campus! She just makes you feel so *important*. It makes everyone work their hardest, give their best, and learn, learn, learn."

But Dr. Beaman knows that these teachers-to-be will face unprecedented challenges along the way. Therefore, she equips them with AQ early in the semester. She takes them through Levels One and Two, as described in this chapter. All students measure and graph their AQ. They learn some CORE-level skills, and she employs the LEAD Sequence to get beyond whining and blame into agile problem solving and toward meaningful action. Throughout the semester she employs these methods to help Campers become Climbers.

The return for Dr. Beaman goes beyond the hundreds of heartfelt letters, notes, and gifts she receives each year from students and their parents thanking her for changing their lives and making them matter. In every class she stretches students' potential, and she enjoys seeing them dig deep and draw forth their greatest efforts. At night, she puts her head on the pillow knowing that the lives of hundreds of teachers and tens of thousands of children will be improved and will matter more as a result of what she has done.

Growing potential, significance, and AQ strengthens the human operating system and results in natural productivity. These are the rewards you will enjoy as you take on the mantle of "Lead Climber." Being Lead Climber does not always mean going first. It means inspiring people to go further on the mountain than they might otherwise go.

> While walking across the hills above his village some years back,
> Nelson Mandela recalled a lesson from his youth. . . .
> "When you want to get a herd to move in a certain direction," he said, "you stand at the
> back. . . . A few of the more energetic cattle move to the front and the rest of the cattle follow.
> You are really guiding them from behind." With a smile he added, "This is how a leader should
> do his [her] work."
>
> —Richard Stengel, "The Making of a Leader," *Time*

Topographical Map of Chapter 6
Coaching and Mentoring Climbers

Coaches, mentors, and leaders are people who seek to guide and inspire others to a higher and more meaningful ascent.
- Focus on asking more than telling.
- Understand the CORE and AQ principles.

- Help guide others to reach their own conclusions and decisions.
- Be supportive and nonjudgmental.
- Be solution-oriented.
- Follow up to make sure actions are taken and improvements made.

Existing and Accessed Capacity must be expanded to meet **Required Capacity.** By improving others' AQs you help them grow their capacities.

Begin with the Mountain.
- Explore elements of significance or purpose.
- Significance is one of the primary predictors of employee turnover.
- Make significance deposits daily by:
  —Showing appreciation
  —Providing resources
  —Demonstrating respect
  —Granting authority to make decisions and mistakes
  —Providing support, especially when people fail
  —Providing time to connect, talk, learn
  —Granting credit for others' contributions
  —Having faith in others to handle highly important responsibilities
  —Rewarding with money
  —Granting freedoms that matter
  —Focusing on results over rules
  —Investing in others' growth and improvement

Build a CORE awareness of AQ and CORE for each person.

Use the LEAD Sequence to solve problems, clarify thinking, decide on meaningful action, and preserve another's dignity.

CHAPTER 7

DEFINING AND
FINDING CLIMBERS

Dig where the gold is . . . unless you just need some exercise.
—John M. Capozzo, *Why Climb the Corporate Ladder*
When You Can Take the Elevator?

A LARGE, WEATHERED, stubble-faced fisherman stepped off his small boat with an enviable stringer bulging with trophy-sized fish. As he passed by the locals, you could see the silent respect in their eyes for this sage of the sea. They nodded reverently as he lumbered down the wide-planked dock that creaked loudly beneath his sizable mass. As he passed, I leaned toward him, gestured toward his bountiful catch, and gently inquired, "Excuse me, but I would like to know—what *is* your secret?" He stopped, slowly craned his large neck, and said in a deep, raspy voice, "The secret to fishing . . ."— he paused so everyone could grasp his profound insight—". . . is to sink your line where the greatest number of fish can be found." His face cracked into a broad grin, and with a confirming nod and a sparkling wink, he strolled off to clean his catch. It was hard to argue with *that* sort of logic.

Perhaps the fisherman's wisdom can be applied to your quest for Climbers, because now that you have seen the advantages of climbing, you need to learn how to find these relentless, high-AQ, Response-Able types.

It is not enough to fish long and hard, with the right technique and the right equipment. You must fish in the right place, and the kind of fish you want to catch must be there—hopefully a lot of them!

This chapter reveals where and how to hook potential Climbers. Standard hiring practice can breed mediocrity and expand the number of Campers you have. Therefore, this chapter goes beyond conventional wisdom on how to define and where to find a potential candidate, so that you attract *more* than just skilled, competent people. Your first step is to decide what makes a Climber. Then you create a cadre of Climbers from whom you can then choose to invite "on rope."

The challenge is to help you figure out the composition of a Climber, where to seek out Climbers for any position, and how to attract the highest number of them to apply for your climbing team. Next, Chapter 6 tells you how to hire the best people for your ascent.

These suggestions will not guarantee success, but, taken as a whole, they can dramatically increase the likelihood of finding the people you need to strengthen your climbing team.

LIMITATIONS OF OLD METHODS IN THE NEW ECONOMY

In the entrepreneurial, networked, globalized New Economy, yesterday's best is today's mediocrity. As one client put it, "Here's the quandary. We spent months in research to learn and implement *best-in-class hiring processes.* Yet we invest all this time and money, and some of our most promising people are out the door by year one. These people pass all the hiring hurdles, including scoring well on our assessments. After we assess candidates so thoroughly, they are *certainly* competent and apparently good fits. Most start out very strong.

"However, most are not able to sustain high performance in our culture. The fact is, we are still chewing them up and spitting them out. Even though we pay top dollar and have the best benefits package in the industry, turnover is still at an all-time high." She threw up her hands. "It is just harder and harder to find people who can make the grade, let alone stick around and stay ignited!"

Best is no longer good enough, and that applies to both people and practices. The best used to be logically defined as the most talented, best-educated people with the most successful track records.

Best practices can live up to their name only if they accurately define and get Climbers. The rules have changed, rendering many practices impotent. In the New Economy, yesterday's definitions and practices fall flat.

THE BEST PEOPLE FOR THE NEW ECONOMY

Competence only buys you the chance to play; it does not make you win. Today, you need Response-Able, Response-Based, purpose-driven, high-AQ Climbers—those with the fundamental operating systems that function effectively in a demanding environment. Unfortunately, Climbers are often confused with their neurotic siblings—the human flares—who ignite brilliantly, then burn out.

At most companies the top performers are not the type A, high-powered java junkies who fly from challenge to challenge as a way to escape their mortality or fulfill some mutated need to please! In fact, Climbers exude admirable vitality and clarity.

Nor do we find that Climbers are the classic workaholics. Rather, they intentionally, often vigilantly, lead relatively balanced lives and seem to do an amazing job of keeping things in perspective.

Unlike some of the shooting stars, most Climbers do not equate their identity with their work. When asked, they describe their mountain as something greater than, but clearly *linked* with, their jobs. Work is either an outlet for their purpose or a conduit to it.

And, as you have seen in so many organizations, from family-run retail shops to giant multinationals, the Climbers are creating all of the breakthroughs and joyfully shouldering a smaller share of the burden. They somehow accomplish five times the work with one-twentieth of the complaints. *Climbers redefine the best.* Before you can find and hire them, there are certain Climber traits you must understand.

Wanted: Response-Able Person to Handle Adversity

Shed yesterday's preconceptions. Not only are good, competent, qualified people harder and harder to find; *they no longer suffice.* Expensive improvements in hiring processes often fail to yield the expected results. Competence and qualifications do not guarantee success, and most leaders we encounter are severely perplexed. They are groping to understand why, like Superman in the presence of kryptonite, such superpeople can be so weakened in their quests. If they were so effective before, why are they not as "super" today? Whatever powers they had on planet Stability prove meaningless on planet Adversity.

It has been predicted that the silicon chip's days are numbered because of its natural limitations, which will become barriers within the next twenty years. As demands for greater speed, agility, fluidity, and capacity increase, molecular computing will likely replace the silicon chip. This new breed of computing will allow microscopic computers to enter the human body and perform miraculous functions. They will transcend today's natural limitations on size, heat, and speed. This represents an entirely new paradigm in computing.

Like the silicon chip, we are all programmed to be *source-based thinkers*—people who focus on the source of a problem. Yet we have reached the natural limitations of this mind-set, and this creates the opportunity and need for the next evolution of mental processing—*response-based thinking*.

There are some fundamental differences between source- and response-based mind-sets, which can lend some vital insight into the candidates you consider and eventually screen for employment. These differences become apparent in how a person views the origin of the adversity.

In Chapter 4, we defined the O dimension of your AQ CORE as *Ownership*. However, in my first book, *Adversity Quotient: Turning Obstacles into Opportunities,* I split the O dimension into two parts, Ownership and *Origin*—both of which were originally taken into account as part of the AQ calculation. Origin is about who or what caused the adversity—its *source*. For example, let's say you've bought a new camera from your local department store. You follow all the directions, but the camera does not work. The fact that it was dropped in shipping might be the *Origin* of this adversity, while *Ownership* is about the extent to which the person behind the customer service desk solves your problem. One of the important evolutions of AQ is that, based on our research, Origin is no longer factored into the quantitative calculation of AQ. Nonetheless, you can gain some insights into the people you hire by exploring their mind-set in this area.

In particular, you might ask people to assess who or what is to blame for different difficulties they have faced. In reference checks, ask how likely a person was to blame others. In selection scenarios, give people an opportunity to blame others for mishaps under pressure, and see if they do— and to what extent.

There are two types of source-based thinking: *internal* and *external*. Those who see themselves as the cause of the adversity have an internal mind-set. Those with an external mind-set perceive something or someone else as the cause.

The research in explanatory style described in Chapter 2 suggests that those with an internal mind-set may, over time, suffer from poor self-esteem and are likely to be more pessimistic than those who externalize adverse events. Because these internalizing individuals perceive themselves as the cause of the adversity, they may become demoralized, sometimes severely depressed. If unchecked, internalizers are haunted by thoughts such as "I blew it again. I really let everyone down. My boss is going to be so mad. I should have known better. It's obviously my fault. If I had only . . . I can be so stupid. . . ."

Internalizing adversity, in the proper dose, has its purpose, but if taken too far it can be cancerous. Most of us have friends who need constant consoling because they become so upset with themselves. This is unfortunate and can be burdensome if they are unwilling to get over their self-flagellation.

Another damaging consequence of internalizing happens when a leader internalizes the cause so definitively that it prohibits others from sharing the Ownership to better the situation. For example, the self-made entrepreneur's seemingly noble stance of "The buck stops here" ignores the multiple causes of most adversities and prevents others from growing their accountability and problem-solving skills. Ultimately, neither self-blame nor hoarding Ownership will lead to positive outcomes.

Interestingly, the pool of research in cognitive psychology clearly suggests that an external mind-set is superior to an internal one when it comes to optimism, resilience, and performance. Those who perceive adversity as originating from or caused by something outside themselves are typically more upbeat and quick to rebound. Theoretically, this may appear sound; however, these conclusions are dangerously incomplete. In reality, such externalizing often equates with deflecting responsibility or assigning blame. Externalizing can be superior to internalizing when it comes to personal resilience, but not without a price.

As a result, I challenge this strand of cognitive psychology research on two fronts. First, I have yet to meet a single leader who supports hiring and developing people who externalize blame when adversity strikes! Can you imagine the repercussions? Intuitively, we know that deflecting blame compromises learning, trust, and accountability. Who would intentionally hire a person with such an embedded pattern of blaming others? Few behaviors will make one's blood boil more than when someone refuses to acknowledge his or her role in something that went awry. Blaming others only exacerbates the situation and depletes accountability.

Chances are you have worked hard to engender trust and accountability among your team. Given how easily this can be dismantled, people who deflect Ownership or externalize blame probably do not fit your definition of the best people to hire or have on your Climbing Team. However, there is one way in which source-based thinking can be of particular value.

Getting to the Learning Zone

In Chapter 6 I introduced a facet of internal source-based thinking that I call the *Learning Zone*. The Learning Zone was defined as the level of blame from which one can learn. The goal is to pinpoint exactly what to change in order to avoid similar mistakes in the future. However, it is important to note that any additional blame is unnecessary, if not destructive.

If an important multinational video conference call fails to connect, those involved might be quick to assign blame:

"Those corporate video folks blew it again."

"Actually, I think it was our data-link provider."

"I wouldn't bet on it. I think the German group never pretested the lines, as instructed."

"All I know is I arranged my whole schedule around this and stayed up half the night preparing. I want to know who is responsible for this embarrassing mess."

"Find out who is at fault. I want them to know how severely they endangered this whole project."

Within each seemingly innocuous, if not understandable, statement of blame lay some damaging effects. Vital relationships with vendors and coworkers were denigrated by such words. People were put on the defensive. Accountability was deflected out of hand. Never considered was each individual's opportunity to step up and take Ownership for making it better. People became so focused on blame that they never explored alternative plans or technologies, which could have sufficed. Nor was there any sign of response management—exemplifying and coaching toward a high-AQ response—the imperative of the Lead Climber.

Ideally, one undertakes just the right level of self-analysis to eliminate a blind spot and emerge bettered by the adversity. Imagine if the video conference attendees had responded with comments like "I don't know exactly what went wrong, but I know I did put a lot of pressure on these folks by springing this on them at the last minute."

"I can see that asking the Germans to be the hub, given their current relocation, might have been unfair. Next time I won't put them in such a tough spot."

"I didn't stop to consider the importance of this call. Although I am not on the connection team, I could have called in early to make sure everything was pretested prior to the scheduled hookup. Well, I, for one, learned some vital lessons about international video conferences!"

"We can find out what went wrong later. I will do some digging and let you know what I find out by Friday, so we can avoid this sort of mishap in the future. For now, how about cell phones, landlines, and fax machines?"

Unfortunately, most of us fall short of the ideal. Most people, as illustrated above, will externalize to such a degree that they miss the point as well as upset several people in the process. Others may internalize so much that they damage their self-esteem, become depressed, or appear apathetic and self-absorbed. Both approaches are taking blame beyond the Learning Zone.

When you lose, don't lose the lesson.
–The Dalai Lama

Thick Versus Porous Skin

Externalizing can be an act of self-defense, or for those of frail self-concept, an act of self-preservation. Like putting on an emotional flak jacket, externalizing is the human way of inoculating yourself against what is perceived to be impending injury. For example, if a report is misplaced, rather than recognizing why others are making snide remarks about your being disorganized, you externalize the problem. You deflect those messages by assuming "they are just trying to avoid looking at their own faults" or "no one told *me* I was supposed to be the caretaker of this report." Even constructive feedback can be misconstrued as incoming missiles and shot down as such. This is an all-too-common pattern in the people you hire. Those with strong self-esteem might also be unwilling to look inward to discover their own weaknesses and mistakes. Externalizing even coincides nicely with what we fondly refer to as "having a thick skin," which, contrary to popular belief, is not *always* a positive attribute.

The same thick skin that can protect a new employee's fragile ego may also prevent her from learning, reacting, problem solving, and improving at the speed you mandate for success.

Improvement takes a *porous* skin. A thick skin chooses protection over self-awareness, without which there is no growth. A person with a porous skin undertakes the proper level of self-analysis. This rare ability can be useful for learning how to handle similar situations in the future. This is the Climber's habit—to constantly assess and make ego-free adjustments in his or her actions to further the ascent. In short, to whatever extent possible, you must seek porous-skinned candidates who welcome feedback and use their source-based training to optimize the Learning Zone.

Source-based thinking poses additional dangers, such as leaving one ill-equipped for how adversity really strikes. Think of adversity as a falling rock. In source-based thinking you assess and recover from each rock as it strikes you in the forehead; you may dodge the next one with greater aplomb—a sensible strategy for the occasional pebble. But often challenges, setbacks, and annoyances take the form of an avalanche of rocks, pebbles, and boulders from all directions. When you operate from a source-based mind-set, you are constantly off center and can be buried in adversity. You may be virtually stymied by the bewildering barrage of adversity, unable to mentally dodge each falling rock.

Even when expertly executed, source-based thinking takes time and good footing, which are in increasingly short supply. Since more often than not we hire source-based thinkers, it's not any surprise that they lack the agility, resilience, and sustainability we seek.

Skiing Atop the Avalanche

In contrast to source-based thinkers, those who ski atop the avalanches of adversities are *response-based*. When adversity strikes, they first look to their own response. This does not mean that they ignore or fail to learn from the situation—quite the contrary. For response-focused individuals, each situation provides rich and constant opportunity for adjustments and improvement. Learning is fluid, and reactions appear intuitive.

Response-Based individuals recognize that their response to any situation is the single greatest factor in all that follows. Ideally, they try to leverage their response for the betterment of all. Response-based thinking correlates nicely with high AQ. It reflects a person's individual control over his or her reactions and behavior, as well as accountability for dealing with the situation at hand, *regardless* of cause.

It is in response-based thinking that we identify, manage, and separate out many of the lower human traits that can pull one off the rope and back into the campground. It is the intentional quieting of the louder and more developed primitive brain so that the quieter music of the civilized brain can be heard.

Misplaced but natural human motives such as envy, greed, retribution, selfishness, pettiness, anger, and malice can be collared before they are able to perform their distasteful displays. Like a misbehaving pet, they may at times escape and offend, but response-based individuals are quick to rein them in and apologize for their behavior. Ideally, these base motives remain leashed, despite their incessant tugs.

Rather than resorting to excuses, response-based people own their behavior, avoid the pit of self-blame or pity, and move on to solutions. They are often generally able to move toward meaningful action much faster than source-based individuals, who may remain insistent on addressing the causes in more depth before moving on. "Learn, fix it, and move on" is the unspoken mantra of the response-based individual, often to the frustration of the less-enlightened masses.

At the highest level, response-based thinkers avoid causing most interpersonal damage by demonstrating spontaneous, even quick, response control. The AQ Hierarchy of Control presented in Chapter 4 (Exhibit 4.1) describes the upper-level skills and tendencies of response-based individuals. By weeding out or preventing damaging thoughts, words, nonverbal indicators, and behaviors, response-based people contribute powerfully to the well-being of others and the organization. Their restraint, discipline, respect, and positive focus inspire others to emulate this higher-order mind-set.

In our work we hear leaders word the same challenge in different ways. They used words like "staying power," "fortitude," "guts," "gumption," "chutzpah," "energy," "relentlessness," and "can-do spirit" as a way of defining the elusive element they seek in their new hires. In addition to—and sometimes instead of—the most competent people, they seek those most impervious to adversity. Most have simply lacked the clarity, words, and technology to describe and pinpoint such individuals. Exhibit 7.1 provides a review of source-based *internal* and *external* characteristics.

Source-Based *External*
- "Thick-skinned" response
- Associated with defensiveness
- Promotes blame
- Compromises learning

- Compromises agility by getting caught up in the event
- Compromises trust
- Can reveal the source and solution
- Preserves one's sense of self

Source-Based *Internal*
- Threatens self-esteem
- Triggers depression
- Legitimizes blame
- Strengthens learning if self-esteem is strong
- Others may take advantage

- Can be perceived as humble
- Can pinpoint one's errors

- Can engender trust

Exhibit 7.1 Overview of Source-Based Thinking

SIX FATAL FLAWS IN FINDING CLIMBERS

When looking for Climbers, it's as important to know what steps to *avoid* as it is to know what steps to take. Though the Six Fatal Flaws in Exhibit 7.2 are key, this list of pitfalls is far from exhaustive.

Actively avoid these flaws to keep your hiring process alive. Based on the wisdom of professional recruiters, you want to be sure not to:

1) Compromise Your Criteria Before You Begin
Be careful not to:
- Fold under pressure
- Hire based on "fit" or intuition
- Hire your clone

2) Confuse Attitude with Altitude
- Desperation hires lead to regrets

3) Use the Road Most Traveled
- Search in places that your competition is overlooking

4) Search for a Sherpa on the Internet

- Match the technology to the position
- Internet searches draw applicants from many countries
- Only use Internet searches when you want a high diversity of applicants

5) Cut Short the Climb

Beware these common reasons for shortcutting the process

- Hiring your clone—you found one like you, so . . .
- Nepotism—hiring those you know instead of those who may be best
- Connections—hiring for their network instead of AQ
- Urgency—making a long-term commitment/decision based on pressing, current need

6) Put Pedigree Over Performance

Exhibit 7.2 Six Fatal Flaws in Hiring

Fatal Flaw #1: Compromising Your Criteria Before You Begin

There are any number of ways you can compromise what *really* matters. One is folding under pressure and inverting your priorities by looking for someone based solely on skills or personality instead of AQ or other climbing criteria. Paul Schween, a successful entrepreneur and cofounder of Sales Teknologies, admits he struggles to stay on task in the hiring process. He warns, "If you do not go into a job search with the line clearly drawn between what you will and will not accept, you will almost *always* compromise your standards with the good intent of giving the potential applicant the benefit of the doubt. You are likely to hire under the same compromise. In the long run this always proves to be a costly mistake."

When the pressure is on, it is tempting to sacrifice the seemingly less tangible factors of AQ and Response Ability for the readily documented skills, such as computer programming, that you *know* you need for the job. You may be thinking, "The heck with hiring a Climber, I need a marketing manager!" In other words, why mess with the deeper psychological traits when the basics are obviously there? Hiring skilled people is difficult enough, especially in tight job markets—why bother with AQ? Isn't it a luxury? Won't it scare away potential candidates who can get jobs elsewhere without such folderol? On this issue, the PEAK team has witnessed a fundamental shift toward more resources and effort being put into being *sure* of hiring the "right people."

As you know, highly skilled people with lower AQs never fully optimize their talents. They are also less likely to grow their skills at the pace required for our dynamic and demanding world. Higher-AQ individuals, on the other hand, are likely to download information needed to meet and surpass the challenges and demands of their jobs. Given this and many other AQ-related differences, can you really afford to overlook this factor any longer?

Given the real costs of hiring and retention, it is imperative not only to your customers but also to your future that you find and hire people who can and will thrive under the pressures of the day. It is the ultimate win-win. Customers enjoy more of a can-do spirit of service and innovation, along with greater consistency in their personal contacts with your company, and you reap the rewards that loyalty, retention, and high performance can bring. Accountability becomes an authentic pillar of your culture when you form a critical mass of individuals who take Ownership for problems regardless of their cause. Change becomes a game of artfully managing the transition from where you are to where you are going for optimal agility and gain. Climbing teams are energizing and inspiring; therefore, you avoid many costly pitfalls.

Beyond skills or competence, the second way in which you can compromise your original prospecting criteria is finding someone who "just feels right" for the job. You have instant rapport and really connect. You cannot believe your luck. This often happens in a chance meeting on the train, at a coffeeshop, or while waiting for the elevator. Magically, the right person for the job appears right next to you. You hand him or her your card and say, "Give me a call. I would like to have a chat." Or maybe you ask for his or her card. Your instant reaction may be elation: "If we can hire this person, I will have saved thousands of dollars and countless hours." Maybe, but maybe not.

While fit is highly important, it is rarely sufficient. When you hire an ill-equipped person, regardless of the interpersonal connection, everyone loses. You especially lose if he or she lacks Response Ability, porosity, and a sufficiently high AQ. Yet these mistakes are regularly made under the guise of "smart business" decisions. Never underestimate the human powers of rationalization!

Every time I have fallen into the fit trap in the past, I have been sorely disappointed that I did not check my assumptions by measuring and assessing that person's AQ—now standard practice in my firm. The world is filled with upbeat people who are devastated by adversity, as well as even-keeled, seemingly unenthusiastic people with a quiet, relentless optimism. It is easy to abandon the discipline of a good search by hiring in the name of fit. Don't be fooled!

The third way you might compromise your search standards is in an effort to clone yourself. There can be much comfort in finding someone who seems to be just like you. There is even some evidence that we are most comfortable with people who look similar to us. This can dangerously and subconsciously translate into any of the various "isms," including racism, ageism, and sexism. Or we may attract and hire people who have the same blind spots and weaknesses we possess.

John Giovale, a longtime leader and associate at W. L. Gore and Associates, actively avoids what he terms searching and "hiring in your own image." Selecting candidates because they remind you of you is called the "like-you syndrome" by Vanessa Cornelius, a human resources manager for Deloitte & Touche, LLP.

While you and that person might have certain values or attributes in common, there are two dangers. First, you are likely to assign all your qualities to that person, proven or not. Second, even if you are right, and that person is a semiclone, you assume that more of the same is the best choice. As good as you may be, your company may need something or someone *different*. It is easy to inadvertently sacrifice the rich value of diversity.

One of the most dangerous facets of this is that people often fast-track those they think make a good fit. They compromise or usurp a well-thought-out hiring process because they "just know this is the right person." One compromise begets another, which ends up as nothing but headaches and a bulging campground.

Fatal Flaw #2: Confusing Attitude with Altitude

In polling my clients, the most common and painful error they cited was hiring when desperate. To a person in this state of mind every Camper becomes a potential Climber, no matter how meager his or her past ascents.

The dangers of this flaw are numerous. Chief among them is sacrificing the careful search to bring in the greatest proportion of Climbers.
Desperation-based hiring currently occurs with the new generation of
employees. At its extreme are employers in Silicon Valley and other upstart
areas who snatch up stereotypes, grabbing anyone with a goatee, body
piercing, or a tattoo. However, this flaw is certainly not limited to Gen-X!
Desperation hiring happens in all age groups, and while it may be most
obvious in the applicant-scarce high-tech industry, its practices and pitfalls can apply to any job in any industry. There are two problems with this
approach.

First, you must be careful—you might just get what you asked for! In
other words, you may get all of the attitude and no performance. Many
young workers represent a classic values clash with the established corporate culture. A recent article in *Fast Company* magazine warns of the
demands and expectations of workers entering the New Economy. These
people don't like being told what to do and are akin to self-sufficient
hunters: they constantly scan for new challenges and become easily bored
with anything routine. They do not want to farm; they want the quick kill
and instant gratification.

They are drawn to companies with dramatic performance, quick
growth, a relaxed environment, and, yes, stock options. They want to be
part of a place that is on the move and making an impact in the market—
and maybe the world.

Well *some* of them do. Today's workforce comprises four generations,
each with its own version of *attitude*. Each generational version may be
different, but each is challenging in its own way. Even though Gen-Xers
and Millennials (post-Gen-X recruits) have been part of the workforce for
years, managers are still bewildered by the different values they see in
young people. They perceive a poor work ethic, complete lack of loyalty,
impatience, and a lot of attitude. Somewhere between *Fast Company* and
these managers lies the truth. The reality is that these people represent the
future of your workforce.

Therefore, the second reason why hiring the attitude of Gen-Xers or
Millennials out of desperation can be a serious problem is that not all of
them are purpose-driven Climbers or "hunters." As with any group of
folks, many *pose* as Climbers. The test is the incessant flow of everyday
adversity.

During a recent visit to a Silicon Valley E-commerce upstart, the twenty-something president took me around the facility. It had all the right stuff, including basketball hoop, nearby mountain bike trails, skateboarding in the hallway, and "cool toys," as one twenty-four-year-old referred to the pile of technology covering his desk and the nearby floor space. The decor, if you can call it that, looked like a dorm room after a beer bash.

They were experiencing Silicon Valley Fever. They had an inflow of new venture capital, were growing at outrageous rates, and were working sixteen-hour days to make it all happen. Certainly, you would expect nothing but Climbers. "Maybe, *maybe* 60 percent Climbers, and all the rest are camping," the president reported. "They are here to look and be cool, so they can tell their friends they work here. They just are not on fire like the rest of us. They are betting on us going public, so they can score on everyone else's hard work!"

I asked him what types of people were applying to work there. He responded, "It's about the same ratio [about 60 percent Climbers]. But we can't hire people fast enough. We are picking people off everywhere we can find them, just like everyone else! We hire people on the spot. It's 'sign now, or never see them again.' Sometimes I think all they need to do is have a pulse and a mountain bike to work here! And when we're out there meeting them, there is no way to tell who will really crank out for us and who will lie back and do the basics while the rest of us drive the growth of this company!"

Regardless of what age group you are recruiting, a desperation hire, whether it is based on false assumptions, a cool attitude, or the need for a warm body, is always a mistake.

Desperation of the kind of experience by our E-commerce upstart comes from the urgency to meet backlogged demands, staff a fast-track project, and fulfill the requirements of growth. Once the urgency to hire people has passed, you are stuck with the often unfortunate result of your impulses. Confusing attitude with those capable of altitude may result in a lot of empty pizza boxes, frustration, delayed projects, and an expanded campground.

Fatal Flaw #3: Taking the Road Most Traveled

One of the timeless errors in searching for the best people is expecting to find them in the same places where your competitors are searching. Job postings, classified advertisements, campus recruiting, job fairs, Internet postings—these equate to hiking the same most popular, overcrowded, and less scenic mountain trail as everybody else.

I have several clients who all compete for the top MBAs or top undergraduates in the United States. Some put on huge recruiting conferences at high-end resorts, complete with extravagant cuisine and various activities for hundreds of prospects. The costs are enormous. They do this as a way of getting mutually acquainted and luring more bright, capable, poised Climbers to apply. And that is who they get. At least they get people who *appear* to be Climbers. So do their competitors who are putting on their best show to get the *same* people, all under the assumption that they are the only ones searching the trail.

Yet employers remain perplexed when only a small handful of these "top people" thrive over the ensuing years within the increasingly demanding environment of the New Economy. They are perplexed as good people wilt on the vine or leave for greener pastures. This is a matter of AQ.

Approximately 80 percent of those bright, capable people get slowly eaten alive once they are hired. This is the silent toll of adversity. Sure, some last longer than others. Yet for most, the employer and their demanding clients unintentionally suck dry what talents the employee can deliver. Bottom line? Be careful where you hike. IQ does not replace or outweigh AQ. Nor does past success promise future success. If your company requires you to draw from this pool of elites, perhaps you need to gauge your criteria on more than brains and past accomplishments.

There are other popular trails to which many continue to gravitate. You are not going to lure the highest percentage of Climbers through a classified advertisement or standard job posting. This is Hiring 101. Quantity can never supplant quality. Although there are exceptions to this rule, in most cases the best people are employed, or fully engaged in some meaningful pursuit, not sitting at home eating bonbons and scanning the classified ads. The better the economy, the more engaged these people are likely to be. You need to take the trail less traveled.

Fatal Flaw #4: Searching for a Sherpa on the Internet

Sure it's the information superhighway, but some of the most worthy Climbers may be taking alternative transportation! While evolving with revolutionary speed, the Internet is still not a one-stop-shop for hiring or finding candidates for *all* types of positions. If you need a Webmaster or systems analyst, use the Internet, among other tools, to help find the best one. What better place to catch their eye, see their work, and enter their world? If you are hiring a housekeeper to clean rooms for your hotel, there is no indication that the few who might respond to an electronic inquiry are necessarily any more desirable than anyone else in the pool.

Lisa Ashton, a selection consultant in South Africa, reports her continued amazement at the money wasted on Web advertising aimed at people from populations with relatively low Internet use and capability.

Tony Antonucci, a Chicago-area entrepreneur, affirms Lisa's concern. "The Internet is the medium for sure," he reports. "But, in terms of recruiting, it is also very difficult. A majority of responses come from people outside your country, which for us is the United States. Since it's so easy to E-mail your résumé, we tend to get a lot of 'bad fit' résumés."

The larger message is to use job-appropriate technology for finding the pools of Climbers in a given field. With the Internet, you are posting your job for an explosively growing population of on-liners. That may be exactly what you want. If not, prepare for the onslaught!

Fatal Flaw #5: Cutting Short the Climb

I learned a lesson when I was an impetuous young Climber. I was working for the summer in Denali National Park in Alaska, which is dominated by 20,320-foot Mount McKinley. To the frustration of many a tourist, "The Mountain" is shrouded in clouds for sixteen out of every seventeen days. Determined to get the finest view, I awoke early and began my ascent of a much lower peak known to offer a breathtaking panorama. I was supposed to meet up with two fellow Climbers along the trail, so we could enjoy the view together.

I climbed, hiked, and scrambled all day through dismal rain and mud. Finally, after becoming demoralized and utterly convinced that The Mountain would be invisible and that my friends had given up long before, I turned back. That night at dinner, my table was buzzing with excitement. Apparently, my fellow Climbers had been on the same trail and were waiting about a half mile from where I turned back. When it was clear I was not going to show up, they kept going and finally saw the most breathtaking view as a rainbow broke over The Mountain. This was also considered a sacred blessing by the local natives. It was the greatest view I never saw.

There are many mistakes that can lead to coming off the climb prematurely. One mentioned earlier was instant rapport leading to the gut feeling that you've found your person. All of these errors share the same theme of making an emotional decision to stop climbing and start hiring. Big mistake.

Another mistake that short-circuits the process is nepotism. If we expand our definition slightly, nepotism comes in all forms, from skipping the search to hiring those you worked with previously or family members. This latter form of nepotism may seem like a wise shortcut, but it is based on the assumption that they will thrive in this new position and are the *best* for the job, which, as you know, is not always the case.

"Connections" can be another search buster, according to Dr. Shirley Lim, president of Research Communication International Pte Ltd, and a respected consultant and researcher based in Singapore. Whether we admit it or not, hiring can be highly political. We all work and live in communities, and some are tighter than others. In some places in Asia, your reputation can precede you, and you may be assessed, even hired, on the basis of who you know or have been working with previously. Dr. Lim explains that many people make the mistake of cutting their search process short because they find someone who claims to have the right connections with either significant people or corporations.

Other reasons we cut our climbing trip short may be quite practical but ultimately costly. These include an urgency to fill the job now, shortage of staff to continue the process, "no bites" or interest from the right people, the need to move on and address other pressing concerns, a loss of focus on this position or search, and sheer disappointment. All of these open you to compromising your choice of whom you ultimately hire.

Fatal Flaw #6: Putting Pedigree Over Performance

Many organizations base their reputation on how many pedigreed people they have from highly regarded institutions. Professional service firms, venture capital firms, law firms, medical practices, and universities commonly position for boasting rights for the most esteemed partners or faculty. Though understandable from a marketing standpoint, this approach can make you blind to the merits of real top performers. Dr. George Collier, a professor at Southeastern Oklahoma State University, believes academic institutions are notorious for this. "One ridiculous thing is searching and hiring driven by accreditation standards. One example is needing to hire completed Ph.D.s with publications in order to meet accreditation standards that preclude hiring great instructors with practical experience and expertise in specific areas [because they don't have the 'letters']."

In searching for Climbers, do not assume that they come from traditional settings, backgrounds, and career paths. They often do not. In fact, they may come from the fringes. Bill Gates is not the only entrepreneur who dropped out of school (in his case, Harvard) in order to pursue his dreams!

Do not let the rules of pedigree blind you, preventing you from finding the best people. It takes some real introspection and courage to blast away old norms of getting people to fill the job and to adopt new ways of getting the *right* people to grow the job.

AQ-BASED HIRING STRATEGIES

Now that we have clarified what *not* to do, it is time to consider some new approaches to finding the best. As you read these ideas, you may squirm at the thought of using them, or wish to reject many of them out of hand. Instead, allow yourself to step outside the hiring norms and explore new territory for getting the best.

Proportionally, most Climbers do not really climb rocks. They are found in all walks of life. So look beyond the literal mountain to the figurative one. You will recall that the mountain represents one's purpose in life. Climbers are those who demonstrate the fortitude, courage, and tenacity to keep their purpose alive and growing no matter what obstacles may arise.

It therefore makes great sense to seek out people who are engaged in purposeful pursuits. There are several strategies you can employ.

Begin with Significance

Remember, we all seek to work in places where we believe who we are and what we do matter. This is part of our Core Human Drive to Ascend. Climbers are simply less compromising and more adamant about this central facet of their work choice. Given a choice, they will not take a job that doesn't have a strong sense of significance.

There are many ways that you can express the significance of the job and their potential role. If a job has strong significance, even a Climber who chooses not to apply will likely tell others. Word spreads.

ADP has enjoyed 150-plus straight quarters of double-digit growth. It has unusually low turnover, even among the highly sought-after information technology folks, and it is seeking to double again within five years. John Hogan, its Brokerage Services Division president, cites its motto: "Each Client Counts, Each Associate Counts, Each Deed Counts." When asked to what extent this is put into action, John pointed out that there is virtually zero client turnover! "Actually, one client left a couple of years ago," he explained, "but they came back." ADP enjoys equally impressive low employee turnover. Clearly, ADP creates the kind of significance that helps it get and retain good people and clients.

Whenever you write a job posting, do a significance check. Make sure it effectively communicates why this job matters, or at least implies the deeper part of why it matters. I learned long ago that this single strategy can go far to capture the interest of Climbers. They scan ads and opportunities looking for ones that help further their ascent and offer a chance for meaningful work.

Passion, energy, challenge, aspiration, purpose, meaning, mission, values, deeper, higher, further, strive, vision, future, achieve, determination, persevere, fortitude, dig deep, together, freedom, uncommon, agile, distinctive, risky, best, legacy, difficult, uncertain, not for everyone, special, influence, change, difference, optimistic

---

Exhibit 7.3 Sample Climber Words

The ultimate measure of a man is not where he stands in moments of comfort and convenience, but where he stands at times of challenge and controversy.

—Martin Luther King Jr.

You must do this with authenticity. If you employ these strategies as quick-fix, superficial tricks, they will be perceived as exactly that, and you will pollute the marketplace with more slick maneuvers. Only promise meaningful work if you have it to offer.

Other significance-enhancing facets that will attract Climbers to come forth and apply include:

- Writing personal notes, especially in the Internet age. This says, "You matter, and I am taking the time to demonstrate my commitment to your interest, and my interest in you as a person." Climbers hate being a number (insignificance!) and love being special, not out of a needy ego, but out of a drive to contribute. One genuine note may be all it takes to make a Climber say, "Now this is a place where I could really see myself."

- While you are in the search process, respond quickly to everything Climbers ask for, *especially* when you are busy. If they ask for information, provide more than they ask for, immediately. Climbers notice when someone really on the go makes the world stop for them; it is a great way of communicating significance even well after they are hired.

- In your exploratory conversations, talk in Climber terms—speak of contribution, the higher purpose, why this job and they will matter. Do not shy away from this. Climbers seek these higher levels to elevate themselves and others.

- As you are meeting them, have key members of your staff meet them also, invest their time, even go out of their way to do so. All Climbers keep the question "So, who did you meet?" in mind when they informally visit a potential employer. This influences their likelihood of applying and how important they think they will be once hired. Again, Climbers are not high-maintenance. They are simply examining their potential for impact.

- As you talk about your organization, make it clear that, if they apply and are hired, someone mission-critical will conduct the orientation, *not* some flunky who got stuck with the task. This will communicate the Lead Climbers' level of commitment.

- Point out resources that will help them innovate, think, learn, interact, and climb. Educational benefits, libraries, Intranets, special networks, knowledge banks, computers, and special designations for entrepreneurial projects are all examples of what Climbers appreciate.

- Explain how ideas are handled and how decisions are made. Point out how, if they should apply and join the team, they can contribute their ideas and influence important decisions quickly and meaningfully.

- As they check you out, give them a way to contact other Climbers and, ideally, *only* other Climbers. Let them see how other Climbers make a difference so that they are convinced they can also. Exposing potential applicants to Climbers is likely to assist you in weeding out those who come to camp from those who come to ascend—the former are intimidated, the latter inspired.

1) Write personal notes.

2) Respond quickly, especially when you are busy.

3) Talk in Climber terms.

4) Have someone "important" invest his or her time.

5) Have someone mission-critical conduct the orientation.

6) Point out the climbing resources.

7) Explain how decisions are handled.

8) Put them in touch with other Climbers.

Exhibit 7.4 Significance Enhancers for the Search Process

Look for Purpose-Passionate People

Anyone can write a check for a charity or donate discarded clothing to Goodwill. Only a minority of busy professionals put their time where their mouth is, by investing their precious hours in what they believe. Purposeful pursuits, which benefit the greater good, abound. Nonprofit volunteer groups, governing boards of social service organizations, community meetings, community events, school meetings, and editorial pages are but a few places to find people who are passionately contributing to something in which they believe. Typically, these are people who *refuse* to be helpless or to be a de facto part of the problem through nonparticipation. They are typically inwardly empowered to do what they can to contribute to the cause at hand. Undaunted, these unsung heroes actively take on insurmountable problems like education, the environment, and community planning. Sound attractive?

The challenge is separating the résumé-builders and those seeking political gain from the authentic-purpose Climbers. A few simple questions coupled with your best judgment can often suffice, such as "Why are you here? Why do you invest your time on this cause? What do you hope to gain from your effort? How much time do you dedicate to this cause? Why?"

A man of character finds a special attractiveness in difficulty, since it is only by coming to grips with difficulty that he can realize his potentialities.

—Charles de Gaulle

Look for the Fully Engaged

Because of traditional hiring practices, internal talent is often overlooked and underemployed. You might have a Climber in your midst (or in the mist!). Seek out those who are going above and beyond their job descriptions by engaging in some of the company-sponsored purposeful events and campaigns. These are generally people who are willing to invest in the community, another attractive attribute.

Ask leaders throughout the organization who the Climbers seem to be. Ask who deals with adversity the most effectively. Who remains unfazed without becoming disengaged? When discussions of purpose, mission, values, principles, and vision take place, which volunteers contribute? Who takes time away from the day job to define the mountain? Who do others find the most inspiring, engaged, passionate, and elevating? Sadly, these people are generally rare enough that they are no more difficult to find than a sequoia among scrub brush. They stick out!

Look for Who Comes to You

I remember standing in the lobby of the Covey Leadership Center years ago, when the book *Seven Habits of Highly Effective People* was just beginning to catch on. There I witnessed an amazing phenomenon. Every several minutes, someone entered the lobby, purposefully approached the central receptionist, and recited the most passionate appeals. One I remember clearly: a thirty-something gentleman explained, "I do not have an appointment. But I just flew here from the East Coast. I read Dr. Covey's book. I am a marketing manager for IBM, and I know you may not have any job openings. But, by any chance, is there someone I could speak with? I *have to* be a part of what's happening here."

One by one they arrived, driven by their purpose. Many of them were Campers who were now bravely poking their heads out of their tents to rejoin the ascent they now realized they had abandoned. Everyone shares the Core Human Drive to Ascend. It takes a sufficiently high AQ to continue to honor that drive. These people merely recognized the compelling purpose Dr. Covey and his team had created, possessed sufficiently high AQs, and were willing to sacrifice what they had for what could be.

But you don't have to write a best-selling book to create a gravitational pull. Viral marketing is used to help Internet companies expand. It is based on the idea that the customer can spread awareness to other customers better than through traditional means. For example, Hotmail, a prominent E-mail program, was made popular through having a notice at the bottom of each message sent by a Hotmail user inviting others to "click here" and download Hotmail of their own. Although Hotmail enjoys some proprietary technology, the same viral marketing concept can apply to communicating your purpose and attracting Climbers.

If, like many of my clients, you are a large enough business or are growing fast enough to be in constant hiring mode, you could use E-mail in a similar way. What if you embedded the following invitation at the end of E-mail messages sent out by all new hires: "Does your job make you dig deep and draw out your best every day? I recently joined an extraordinary company that taps and grows the best of every person. To learn more about a place to ascend in your work, click here."

"My company is driven by a compelling purpose. (Insert your purpose.) If you think you can contribute to our success, click here."

"Do you feel a deep sense of purpose and significance in your job? If not, click here."

Or you could issue a challenge: "If you are the kind of person who flourishes on uncertainty and doing the impossible perfectly every time, click here to learn where to apply." There are many ways to employ viral marketing. Have you thought of sponsoring a Web site that tracks who clicks on yours? You get the idea. The point is that you can customize your own approach to spreading the word from Climber to Climber.

By hiring, nurturing, and being Climbers, your hiring team will attract Climbers with greater and greater ease. Climbers network. They find one another, and once word gets out, Climbers will be lining up at your door. It's the equivalent of having fish jump into your boat!

You do not need technology to employ viral marketing. Climbers unintentionally employ viral marketing by giving off climbing signals in everything they do and say. Each E-mail, meeting, or chance encounter carries an embedded message, "This company hires Climbers. For more information, click here."

"Does your job make you dig deep and draw out your best every day? I recently joined an extraordinary company that taps and grows the best of every person. To learn more about a place to ascend in your work, click here."

"My company is driven by a compelling purpose. (Insert your purpose.) If you think you can contribute to our success, click here."

"Do you feel a deep sense of purpose and significance in your job? If not, click here."

"If you are the kind of person who flourishes on uncertainty and doing the impossible perfectly every time, click here to learn where to apply."

Exhibit 7.5 **Viral Marketing/E-Mail Appeals**

Never underestimate the power of significance. Who one is and what one does really matter, and people will do almost anything to be a part of a higher cause. Many World War II veterans struggle with the fondness they feel for something as horrible as war. Yet being a part of something with historic importance, such as saving the world from Hitler, made many people feel uniquely vibrant and alive. Significance elevates us above the mundane, even the horrible.

You do not have to be a teacher or a surgeon to experience significance. I recently asked a guy who ran a small air-conditioning repair business why he started his own business. "When I worked for them," he explained, "it was all about how many calls you could turn over in a day. Now, it's about working for *her*," he added, pointing to where an elderly customer was standing by the window watering her houseplants. "Her life is more comfortable, safer, better, and maybe even longer because of what I did for her today. See how happy she is now? That's enough to keep me going for months!"

Often we think that the only way to attract the best people is with expensive programs and initiatives. While these may prove useful, nothing can compare to the genuine sense of significance people feel in your organization. Why do we remember those few truly inspirational teachers? It is because they are so *rare*. The same can be said of workplaces where people universally feel significant. Rest assured, if you build it, they *will* come, and bring others with them.

Before you position significance as a real selling point for your organization, you may wish to honestly assess to what extent you can deliver on your promise.

The Significance Quiz
How ready are you to hire Climbers?

Reflect on and answer the following questions to assess your readiness to hire Climbers. Be honest with yourself.

1. How significant do you feel in *your* work? Why?
2. What do others do or say that enhances your sense of significance?
3. If 10 is ultimate significance and 1 is zero significance, how would most new hires rate your company after their first few weeks? Old hires?
4. How would most people answer this question: "What is most significant about this company and what you do?" What degree of agreement would there be?
5. How does this company rate in the significance people express and feel in comparison with others in your industry?
6. If you hired people today with the promise that who they were and what they did would really matter, how well would that promise be fulfilled?

Follow the Sherpas

The higher one's AQ, the more likely one is to be effective at optimizing adversity. Statistically, the highest AQs are found among entrepreneurs. The international average AQ score is 147.5, with entrepreneurs averaging an impressive 158. Today most organizations seek to build a more entrepreneurial workforce. This Climber's spirit is what drives innovation, risk taking, and possibility thinking. Consider what motivates true entrepreneurs or Climbers from any walk of life.

Entrepreneurs and most Climbers are deeply compelled by freedom and Control. They thrive on the freedom to make their own choices and the ultimate Control of their own destinies. Most have a strong aversion to traditional corporate life and look with disdain on the organizational world that places the masses in mental and physical cubicles. Many view anything with the slightest scent of bureaucracy as a prison for the weak and downtrodden. It is difficult to underestimate the intensity of their drive toward freedom and Control.

You cannot lasso an eagle, nor can you force Climbers into a campground. So, if you are up to the challenge, there are some authentic ways in which you might spark the interest of entrepreneurs to at least consider such a dramatic change in lifestyle as joining your team.

Entrepreneurial/Climber Motivators

- Freedom
- Security
- Control
- Shared accountability
- Compelling vision
- A worthy mission, significance
- Resources for the ascent

Entrepreneurs and Climbers often agonize over sparse resources and the constant headaches of running their own shops. Having ultimate accountability for everything can also get pretty old. Entrepreneurially spirited people will enter your pool of potential candidates if you can genuinely offer these seven factors: freedom, security, Control, shared accountability, a compelling vision, a worthy mission, and resources. Here's a brief definition of each:

1. *Freedom* is like air to Climbers—they cannot live without it. In fact, very often it is freedom that lured them to sacrifice so much to become an entrepreneur in the first place. They seek freedom to decide, achieve, do, and say whatever they want and are willing to bear the consequences. They want freedom to invent, influence, and choose.

2. *Security* is the one thing many entrepreneurs and Climbers lack. It can be very enticing, for as entrepreneurs age, they become increasingly concerned about financial security. Some are simply ready to shed the incessant worry and burden of being a solo or Lead Climber all of the time.

3. *Control* relates to freedom, but it is the single most common word in the vocabulary of entrepreneurs when explaining why they do what

they do. They want Control over their day, lives, and destinies. To the extent you can offer this, do. Entrepreneurs understand the language of Control. This is why they score the highest of any career category on the C, or Control, dimension of AQ.

4. *Shared accountability* is very enticing to entrepreneurs and Climbers because they probably have experienced the opposite. They *despise* poor accountability. Convinced that your organization is truly different, they will be drawn to a team on which accountability is genuinely shared.

5. *A compelling vision* is important to nearly everyone, but it is a sacred requirement for the entrepreneur. Climbers are inherently visionaries, so they readily speak and relate to the language of vision. Be prepared: they are likely to ask you about your vision and will be the first to sniff out any hint of inauthenticity. They are repulsed by empty words on the wall. They want to be convinced that the vision is real and in the bloodstream of everyone on the team.

6. *A worthy mission* is what draws entrepreneurs/Climbers in the first place. They need to know the where (vision) as well as the why (mission). If either one is lacking, they will look for another mountain to climb. Entrepreneurs know they have a lot to offer and are careful to select a worthy mountain.

7. *Resources for the ascent.* Entrepreneurs grow weary of scrapping for resources and are attracted to resource-rich environments. They are less compelled by a bunch of camping equipment and policies that foster comfort and complacency than they are by resources that help them climb. What resources can you offer that would entice a scrappy entrepreneur? They are sure to ask.

If these seven factors are in place in the proper proportions and intensities, some entrepreneurial-spirited Climbers will join your pool of future prospects. But if you are not prepared to deliver on your promise, do not bother inviting these special creatures to join your crew. Hiring Climbers takes the same courage and tenacity that you seek from your Climbing Team.

Look for Purpose-Passionate People

- Charities
- Community service groups
- Boards of nonprofit groups
- Editorial pages
- School board and community meetings

Look for the Fully Engaged

- Internal people who go above and beyond
- Those most engaged in discussions of purpose and vision
- Those most unfazed by change
- Those most emotionally involved in the success of the team
- Those others find most inspiring

Look for Who Comes to You

- Those in alignment with your purpose
- Employ viral marketing to spread the word

Follow the Sherpas

- Consider entrepreneurs
- They have the highest average AQ
- Be prepared to speak to their intense needs and motives

Exhibit 7.6 Where to Find Climbers

I hope this chapter has raised as many questions about how to find Climbers and what you could do to substantially improve your success as it has provided answers. The tough news is that none of this is easy, and Response-Able, Response-Based Climbers are *definitely* the minority. The good news is, once found, they will drive the future of your organization.

Topographical Map of Chapter 7
Defining and Finding Climbers

Hire the Response Able, Response-Based, Porous-Skinned Climbers who ski atop the avalanche of adversity.

Six Fatal Flaws in Finding Climbers are:
1) Compromising Your Criteria Before You Begin
2) Confusing Attitude with Altitude
3) Taking the Road Most Traveled
4) Searching for a Sherpa on the Internet
5) Cutting Short the Climb
6) Putting Pedigree Over Performance

Find Climbers by
- Looking for Purpose-Passionate People
- Looking for the Fully Engaged
- Looking for Who Comes to You
  —Those in alignment with your purpose
  —Employ viral marketing to spread the word
- Following the Sherpas
  —Consider entrepreneurs

Significance is a primary motivator for Climbers.
- How do you communicate significance?
- How do others reinforce your significance?

CHAPTER 8

HIRING CLIMBERS

AFTER YOU HAVE assembled some Climbers who are vying for a position on your Climbing Team, how do you determine which ones to bring on rope? By recognizing and avoiding two types of hiring errors and adhering to the Seven Screen Savers discussed in this chapter, you will be equipped with the tools and strategies required to pinpoint the most summit-worthy candidates.

> **Climber Characteristics**
> • High AQ Response Able
> • Response Based
> • Porous Skinned
> • Solution versus Blame focused
> • Operate in the Learning Zone

I recently talked with a vice president of a prominent Asian electronics manufacturer who shared an all-too-familiar story. We were discussing his screening process, when he said, "I have always been very careful about whom I hire. We hold three interviews from which we select our people. Occasionally I skip the extra interviews, if the first one is excellent. We make sure they spell everything correctly on their résumés and cover letters and that they are punctual for their interviews. I believe that if people make a good impression on me, they will do the same with our customers. I've always felt that my first instincts were pretty good over the years.

"But *now*," he continued, "those instincts seem to fail too often. Our service and adaptability is suffering. I have too many people who are not able to deal with the challenges they must face every day, I don't understand why they do not succeed."

This executive, like many others, discovered that despite his instincts something was clearly *amiss*. He couldn't understand why many of his new hires weren't sticking around or weren't rising to the challenge of the New Economy.

The problem was that his hiring process did not have a mechanism to reveal the true characteristics of Climbers over Campers and Quitters. Nor did anything prevent him from rejecting potential Climbers who simply misspelled a word or failed to charm the interviewers.

The trend is clear. Given the demands placed upon every individual, standard hiring practices, which unfold like a careful dance, no longer reliably predict who will thrive. Both sides try to anticipate and respond to the other's moves. Skilled interviewees can anticipate interview questions and rehearse good answers, and anyone can hire a master résumé writer. Today's employers must go beyond the surface and get inside the human operating system in order to determine who has the greatest capability, speed, and capacity.

> People who take risks are the people you'll lose against.
>
> —John Scully

TWO TYPES OF HIRING ERRORS

The first error is the most obvious: you select individuals for the ascent, but they fail to climb. They have not realized their true potential, nor have they tapped their full capacity. And you are left wondering why. You regret these hires not only because of their shortcomings but even more so because they drag down the Climbers who are "on rope." Every time you bump into them in the hallway, in a meeting, or via E-mail, you are reminded of how negatively they affect the organization and its ascent. We have all made these Type One errors, but have you ever stopped to calculate their *true* cost?

L^4—Type One Hiring Errors

L^4 stands for Lose—Lose—Lose—Lose, which refers to the losses suffered by the customer, workforce, employee, and organization when you commit a Type One hiring error. Each party suffers significantly when AQ is not incorporated into the hiring process.

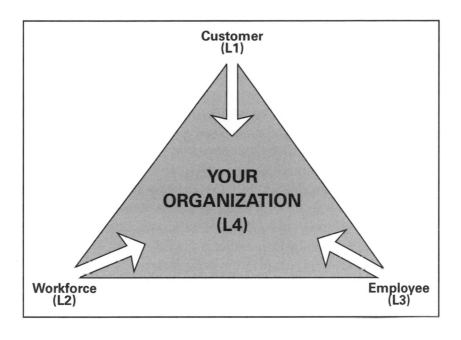

Exhibit 8.1 L^4—**Type One Hiring Errors**
Lose—Lose—Lose—Lose

L1—The Customer: The most costly loss is the one least often understood—the *customer*. First, consider the role of AQ. You hire a "qualified" person with a lower-than-ideal AQ. Adversity strikes: a technological glitch slows the promised delivery of your shipment. Your low-AQ employee mishandles the situation internally, and the damage flows to your customer. The worker perceives the adversity as substantial, out of her control, far-reaching, and likely to endure. She deflects vital Ownership and is unable to solve the problem.

"Oh great," she mutters sarcastically. "We'll *never* get this to them on time. The whole system is *bogged down*, and our customers are going to be *irate*! I can imagine what will happen when the word gets out. I am *sure* to be blamed. Well, there's nothing I can do about it now. I sure hope my boss figures out *something*."

Her response to adversity may bleed over to the customer, and the disease may also permeate her group. "I'm sorry," she tells the customer. "I don't know *what* to tell you. This is a system-wide problem. And it is likely to take us a long time to fix it, assuming we even *can*. They should have known better than to promise this so soon. Well, it's out of *my* hands. I wish I could be more help, but . . ."

She explains to her team, "Well, it finally happened. I *told* them we were over capacity. Now we've got a very upset customer. I mean, he is *miffed*. And what can *we* do? *Nothing*. We just sit here and wait for our marching orders. Oh well. . . ." Soon the whole team is infected, and even some "wanna-be Climbers" may be tempted to Camp!

Perhaps the customer loses respect for your organization because of your inability to show your best during a moment of truth—when adversity strikes. You have let a low-AQ person handle your customer's adversity—a bad call all around, and the customer pays the price.

L1 (the customer) is also adversely impacted by employee turnover. Consider the vendor who constantly introduces you to a new contact person. In the world of client-services relationships this instability can be the deciding factor. If clients trust their business with a particular person, they may move their business if that person leaves to join a competitor. Even if they stay, their loyalty must be re-earned.

Consider the restaurant where you are greeted warmly, referred to by name, and your special needs are usually anticipated. Then consider the high-turnover establishment where you are clearly a burden, and the waitperson rolls his or her eyes and sighs when you ask for something special. Where would *you* rather eat?

Have you ever switched suppliers, stores, or vendors because a key employee has left? Employers usually expect their new salespeople to try to win over some of their old customers unless expressly prohibited from doing so. It is sheer hubris to believe that your customers' approach would be any different.

Employee turnover creates customer turnover. It's that simple. If you are in a relationship-based business, and we *all* are, then having the right people stick around becomes vital. Turnover can be the determining variable in your customer's decision to pick you—or someone else.

L2—The Workforce: A poor hiring decision may also hinder, if not incapacitate, the *workforce*. Pause and consider who among your current workforce was hired as a result of a Type One error? Also think of someone who has met expectations. What is the *real* impact of those individuals on your team, their fellow employees, and your organization's culture? Chances are it is considerable. Early in our work with AQ, we learned never to underestimate the potential impact of one person, regardless of his or her title. That impact can be positive or negative, depending on the person, his or her AQ, and the company's culture. Before moving on to the Type Two error, it is important for you to fully grasp the fallout caused by that one person.

When AT&T broke up and competition began, an upstart firm in Los Angeles set out to win its piece of the long-distance dial-up market. After several months of lackluster sales, the owners hired a new sales manager named Fred who had many years of experience in several related industries. They believed, based on his background and interviews, that he would shake things up and deliver increased market share.

What they did not know was that Fred had always excelled at jobs where the sales were put into his lap. In the highly competitive dial-up long-distance market, Fred was about to face relentless rejection and adversity. It was cutthroat. Every time a customer called with a problem about the service, Fred would say, "There goes another one." Over time, as the company had trouble with its technology, Fred began drinking and missing days of work. When he did show up, he was highly demoralizing to the rest of the sales force. He lied to customers; he would rip the phone away from a salesperson and begin saying anything to win the customer. His behavior swung between depression and desperation. Finally, the company lost all of its top salespeople to a competitor. They just could not stand working for Fred any longer. Sales plummeted, and the startup disappeared.

Like Fred, that mediocre performer you hired affects everyone's morale, performance, productivity, learning, and innovation—as well as everyone's prosperity and happiness. It is as if a virus spreads from the main server into the network of employees, causing a potential crash in the operating system at large. Your team's high hopes for that person's success are now dampened or snuffed out, and will not be resolved by simply placing that employee in a distant cubicle where he or she can no longer do harm.

L3—The Employee: The third loser from the Type One hiring error is the *employee*. Consider the incalculable effect a misguided hiring decision has on the person hired. This impact can go deep, and when the decision is wrong, *everyone loses.*

A poor hiring decision is not just about the obvious botch. More often than not the new hire is nearly sufficient to fill the new position, but he or she does just "okay." The person may be nice, well intentioned, and likable. But personality and intentions do not cover the mistake you made in hiring him or her.

For the employee, the fallout can range from dissatisfaction with how he is spending his prime hours to diminished respect from his coworkers and boss. This person feels insignificant, becomes demoralized, suffers from chronic stress, and so on. These system crashes are a result of an underequipped operating system.

The long-term fallout can challenge the employee's identity. When there is a nagging discrepancy between how a person sees himself ("I am a talented, capable, competent person") and how he is perceived by others ("What a loser!") that person must resolve this discrepancy either by disregarding everyone else's opinion or by reducing his own sense of self. A high-AQ person will find ways to alter that perception, probably by working hard to make his contribution matter; a lower-AQ person may question his worth, abilities, and capacity to contribute. For a low-AQ person, being the wrong person for the job can take a real toll on the soul.

L4—The Organization: The organization also suffers in visions unrealized, goals unmet, and a compromised ascent. The most obvious hiring expense is the cost of compensation and the explicit and implicit benefits. Less obvious costs can include the amount of time and resources your organization devotes to the hiring process. Even the basics of posting job openings, fielding résumés and inquiries, screening candidates, as well as scheduling and conducting interviews, can be a substantial cost. See Exhibit 8.2 to calculate your true costs.

After the person is hired, you shell out for orientation, getting him or her on payroll, office space, technology, resources, and training. These expenses can be substantial. I recently asked the hiring team at one of the big insurance companies if they had ever calculated the true cost of hiring a commission life insurance agent. Their answer was a definite *$200,000!* Your true costs are probably several times higher than you might imagine. Doing a true calculation can provide a powerful wake-up call.

When you commit a Type One hiring error, everyone ultimately loses × 4, especially you.

[(Monthly salary + Benefits) × number of months required before performing at 100%]

+ Hiring personnel's salary divided by the number of hours spent hiring

+ Cost of space required for hiring

+ Orientation training

+ Skill training

+ Customer fallout

+ Drug tests

+ Mistakes and lost opportunities while learning

+ Cost of hiring supplies and materials

+ Cost of lost productivity while searching and post is vacant

+ Cost of lost productivity of search committee members

+ Cost of advertising for the job

+ Cost of headhunters

+ Cost of time not spent doing other things

= True Hiring Cost for One Person

Exhibit 8.2 The Hiring Cost Calculation

Type Two Hiring Errors—The Ones Who Got Away

The second hiring error is subtler and much easier to overlook. This happens every time you fail to recognize a Climber. It's easy to forget this mistake because generally these people disappear right after they are rejected (unless, of course, they are inside your company). They also typically don't have the most obvious qualifications. They may not have the highest academic degree, the most years of experience, or the most perfect career path.

In the past, the only way of knowing how well the "rejects" might have performed was the occasional story of how they were doing with a competitor. But now, with AQ technology, we can document the fact that high-AQ people—who were initially rejected in the hiring process—have outperformed everyone else in their respective areas. Some of the most dramatic examples can be found in sales.

The earliest study of this kind was conducted by Martin Seligman in the mid- to-late 1980s. He and his team attempted to address turnover at Met Life. The study involved more than 15,000 agents. They convinced Met Life to hire 256 "rejects"—people who failed the intense interviews, screening, and other assessments, but who measured strongest among all rejects on their ability to respond to adversity (what we now call AQ). This "special force" of high-AQ rejects *outsold everyone else by two to one!*

With a Type One hiring error everyone loses, while a Type Two error causes everyone to *miss out* on the opportunity to harness and enjoy a high-performance resource and to add another valuable Climber to the team.

Both hiring errors produce tremendous costs and consequences, which are several times greater than the considerable expense of hiring. Since your success is highly dependent on the people who are "on rope," you can't afford such losses.

Experience is not what happens to a man; it is what a man does with what happens to him.

—Aldous Huxley

WHY SCREEN ANYONE?

Five years ago many managers were reluctant to use screening instruments in their hiring processes out of fear that they would scare away some attractive candidates. But today those same managers are using anything that can help them pinpoint Climbers. *What caused this change in perspective?*

The first reason is that turnover is now a major business issue, if not *the* issue. Additionally, you cannot accurately assess turnover without examining the quantity and *quality* of those who leave. In other words, are you losing Climbers, Campers, or Quitters? Losing even a small percentage of Climbers can hobble your organization, whereas cutting bait with Quitters may actually boost efficiency and morale.

Finding people with the "right stuff" is not just a challenge but a business imperative. The question is, What are you screening for and what does your screening instrument tell you? Instruments like the Meyers-Briggs Temperament Indicator and DiSC tools are excellent for assessing issues of style and cultural fit. But your style does not determine or influence your AQ. *AQ is not style, and AQ is not style-dependent.* AQ does not claim to measure everything. It simply provides an essential piece of information that can enhance your overall process and add value to other screening instruments you currently employ.

The question you have to ask is what you want to leave to chance in your hiring decisions and whether you are hiring for the short or long term. Hiring based on skills and experience may address your short-term needs and save short-term training dollars, but it does not address the nagging question of whether or not that person has the staying power to sustain strong performance through adversity-rich times. It's not enough to bring in more warm bodies—you need *Climbers.*

SEVEN SCREEN SAVERS

As we have worked with hundreds of companies representing dozens of industries, the PEAK team has noticed some typical screening blunders, that, if avoided, can put you well on your path to hiring Climbers for your team. Here are Seven Screen Savers to help strengthen your hiring process and get the Response-Able, Response-Based Climbers you seek.

Screen Saver #1: Go Beyond Gut

Even in this age of hypercompetition, when organizations have access to various screening protocols, many people still operate on gut instinct or intuition. The process may have been carefully crafted by human resources or recruiting folks, but a lot of managers simply sidestep it in moments of truth, often with dire consequences.

This can be very tempting when you're screening for AQ. You might say to yourself: if a person has overcome a horrible tragedy and can calmly explain it now, he or she *must* have a high AQ. Not necessarily. This retroactive recounting gives *no* indication of how that person responded when the adversity hit. You have only his much-belated report. He may have been devastated internally and taken years to recover. Or he may have demonstrated admirable resolve and problem solving acuity. Basing your assessment on a story is like assuming I was a great athlete because of my personal accounts of my high school career. That would be a mistake. My family frequently tells me that my recollections of such things are not always 100 percent accurate.

The gut gamble comes in many forms. It is largely an emotional response. It can be based on one thing a person says, or it can be more subtle. Sometimes gut is based on that subconscious lure of "rapport" or connection with a person you hardly know. People base hiring decisions on the oddest assumptions!

One of the best demonstrations of how limited gut instinct can be is dating. How many times have you heard a friend or colleague say, "I just have a *feeling* about this one," only to have it turn comically or tragically wrong within days or months? We all know the stories of Mr. or Ms. Right who turn out to be Mr. or Ms. *Very* Wrong!

We have a natural desire to connect with others and to make snap judgments about them. The first impression is formed within six seconds, much of it at the subconscious level. You get a feel for someone based on his or her similarities to and differences from you and your individual values. Our desire to connect can, therefore, result in our perceiving rapport and assigning similarities in character, values, and other vitals that were never there in the first place!

When dating, many couples go through the integration and differentiation phases. Integration is the "we are *so* much alike" stage. This is when people on both sides of the relationship may compromise who they are in order to enjoy the thrill and closeness of integration. Over time, integration gives way to the reality check—differentiation.

Differentiation occurs when you realize how individual and different you really are. This is the cold wind of reality. Many relationships do not survive differentiation. Some get stronger. The point is that your good intentions may be deluding you into believing there is more there than reality will bear. This may apply to the person's attributes or your ability to work effectively with that person. Besides, screening for and hiring someone highly similar to yourself may not be in the best interest of the organization, with its need for diverse perspectives and capabilities.

Gut instinct has its place: when you are choosing a restaurant, a hiking trail, a vacation spot, or a potential date. It can even be a vital factor in your hiring equation as you try to gauge the cultural fit. It just cannot be the deciding or, worse yet, only factor when choosing your Climbing Team members. Employ Screen Saver #1; stick to your screening protocol. Go beyond gut.

The significant problems we face cannot be resolved at the same level of thinking we were at when we created them.

—Albert Einstein

Screen Saver #2: Be Consistently Consistent

Begin your hiring process with the understanding that *you are a researcher* who has a great deal riding on the results. You start with a question—"Who should I hire?" or "Who is most likely to succeed in this job?"—and you gather information, or data. You then use your data to form conclusions: "I will hire this one." "This one is worth looking at more closely." Or, "This one clearly lacks the right stuff."

One challenge for both the scholar and the recruiter is in the consistency of their data gathering. Inconsistency in data gathering can cause major problems for any researcher. But in hiring the problem is exacerbated by the fact that you will use this data to make a significant decision. Most people are inconsistent data gatherers, and that can skew the hiring decision, if not pollute the whole process.

Researchers know that any variance in who gathers the data or how it is gathered can call into question the validity of the data and the conclusions. For experimental findings to be valid, this variance is tightly controlled. The same is true for hiring.

The process begins. You gather all sorts of hiring data: résumés, applications, cover letters, interviews, references, perhaps psychological assessments, scenarios, others' perceptions. As a researcher you must then consider how consistently your data was gathered by examining it using the criteria and questions set forth in Exhibit 8.3.

Screening Applicants

- Who screens the applications?
- To what extent are the screeners trained?
- What criteria are used to pick applicants worthy of further consideration?
- Do the screeners use standardized checklists or "eyeball it"?

Interviews

- Who conducts the interviews?
- What variance is there in the structure or interview format used by the interviewers?
- To what extent are they trained to conduct interviews?
- Do all interviewers gather identical data?
- What is the standard length of each interview?
- If there is variance among data collected by different interviewers, what is the cause of it?

Reference Checks

- Who conducts the reference checks?
- What structure or format is used?
- How well is that structure adhered to?
- How consistent is the approach?
- How well trained are the people conducting reference checks?
- What strategies are employed to get the most accurate information?
- What strategies are used to cross-check your findings?

First Impressions

- What information about the job and your organization do you provide to your applicants?
- How are interviewees handled upon arrival?
- What variance is there in these items?

Conclusions

- What conclusions did you reach about this candidate?
- Upon what evidence/data are your conclusions based?
- What inconsistencies are there in the conclusions drawn from the same data? Why do these exist?

***Exhibit 8.3* Assessing the Variance in Your Screening Process**

Screen Saver #3: Win the Data Game

After twenty years of research, I have seen just about every distortion and misuse of data imaginable. Some mistakes, such as giving too much credence to a single number and ignoring the data, can spark lawsuits. Others, like using data to legitimize a sloppy hiring process or using just part of the data, are worse than using no quantitative assessments at all.

You must be sure to think through what data you really need and fairly and consistently use what you gather. If you employ the methods listed in Exhibit 8.4, you can enjoy the full value of your investment and effort and win the Data Game.

- Include and consider *all* of your data, not just those that support your point of view.
- *Never* make a hiring decision based on a single number.
- Make sure you use the data to assess what you wanted to know in the first place.
- Be careful not to exaggerate insignificant findings or differences.
- Use the same data to compare different applicants for the same job.
- Make sure that you have people properly trained to make intelligent quantitative assessments.
- Use only measures that pass the statistical and legal tests for no "adverse impact" on a person from any gender or ethnic background.
- Gather only data you intend to use.

Exhibit 8.4 Ways to Win the Data Game

Screen Saver #4: Fog-Proof the Process

Infofog is what happens when you get so much information that it clouds your ability to make a clear decision. As the Internet and the number of publications and resources proliferate, your Infofog is getting thicker. It obfuscates decisions and distances you from wisdom. In the world of assessment, some people assume more is better, which is not always the case. Sometimes *less is more.*

I have discovered companies that conduct *days* of assessments. Unless the position demands special technical information, such extremes are generally a waste of precious time and money. Having more television channels can add confusion and noise to your choice—and so will too many assessments. The tool must match the task. Extra tools do not mean better solutions. Like a Climber, you can carry too much in your backpack, which can weigh you down and hinder your ascent.

A few good tools may be all you need to get accurate, valid insights into each candidate. Knowing a candidate's AQ is a direct insight into her operating system and a good way of assessing her potential capacity to meet the job's demands and her likelihood of tapping into her full capabilities.

So, when screening, if you want to know AQ, measure AQ. If you want problem-solving skills, test problem solving, and so on. To navigate with confidence, be sure to fog-proof your process. Gather only what you need.

Screen Saver #5: Use Mountain Guides

How are your prospects welcomed, greeted, and treated? A common problem is to either have the wrong person show the prospect the ropes or unintentionally have someone communicate Camping terms to a prospective Climber.

When I was first hired as a professor, I was invited to dinner at a veteran faculty member's house. Everyone was certainly welcoming. However, within five minutes the evening turned into a "can you top this" whiners' convention. Faculty told increasingly horrid stories of how the system had messed them up, or how some bureaucrat had treated them unjustly. They were trying to enculturate me into the campground. I found the experience enormously frustrating and left wondering if I had made the right choice.

When potential Climbers visit your company, they want to know certain things. For instance, is this a campground like most places, or is this an agile, innovative, high-performance Climbing Team? If the person showing them around talks in terms of comforts, committees, and compromise, Climbers may go elsewhere. But if that person speaks in climbing terms—urgency, risk, challenge, innovation, independence, leading by competence, values, purpose, significance, and the overall ascent—other Climbers will take note!

Just as the person answering your phones can be the most important person a customer may encounter, so too can be the person who is the point of contact for the job prospect. Climbers hate to waste time and effort with a bunch of Campers and will avoid it whenever possible. Chances are they just left a campground and are scouting out your Base Camp to see if what you say is real.

The first hint of a comfort-driven, slog-through-the-muck, complaining, infighting bureaucracy sends the Climber far away. Letting a Camper escort a Climber can be a huge mistake. If you want Climbers, use guides who will show them the mountain.

Screen Saver #6: Involve the Climbing Team

Just about every position requires some degree of human interface. Beyond interface is interdependence. Climbers find a high nobility in interdependence, placing it high on their list of criteria. Yet prospects are often unclear about "how things really work around here" and who will be on their Climbing Team. Sometimes Climbing Teams are clearly laid out in the organizational chart. More often than not, however, Climbing Teams are informal, requiring an insider's explanation and introduction.

A potential new hire's Climbing Team might include key customers, vendors, internal contacts, and informal advisers. These people may prove inspirational and pivotal to the candidate's interest. It would be a mistake to keep these people out of the hiring process. They can provide invaluable insight into a candidate's fit and nature. Limiting those your prospect meets to the standard list of boss, direct reports, teammates, and human resources is terribly shortsighted and risks losing the person you most seek to hire.

Some of our clients ask their key customers to interview job candidates. As a result, the customers can determine how likely this person will be to meet their demands, concerns, and idiosyncrasies. At the same time, the customer feels a sense of Ownership in the new employee's success. In considering the candidate's AQ, you can tell the customers to ask their toughest questions and ascertain how well this person can meet their needs. This way the customer plays a role in the decision and wants the new hire to succeed. This is an effective strategy, and it can save you a lot of heartache if problems arise on the trail.

Screen Saver #7: Rely on More Than References

The mistakes people make with references come in many forms. First, some people believe they will get *true* insider information through a reference check. Second, most people use reference checks to get the wrong information.

I first realized the potential flaws in reference checks many years ago. I walked into my boss's office as he was on the phone. He waved me to a chair across from him, as he continued with what appeared to be a very important reference check. "You need to know that this person will give anything she does her absolute all," he barked into the phone. "She never does things halfway, she has boundless energy and possesses that rare, gritty determination."

I could not help wondering who in the world he was describing. He continued to extol her virtues. "Dedicated worker . . . yes . . . yes . . . great potential. No, I see no reason Audrey could not work her way into management responsibilities over time. I know she will be remembered here for years to come."

Audrey? That was impossible! He could not possibly be talking about the same Audrey who had become the black hole of the department. Not the Audrey who was referred to as the classic case of big-talk little-do, possessing an ego so gargantuan that people broke out laughing when she spoke of herself in the third person. Certainly not the same person who had achieved the impossible—the lowest performance evaluations in the department's history!

My boss hung up the phone and said smugly, as he wiped his hands, "There, that should get rid of *that* major headache!"

You cannot believe everything you hear. People have different motivations for offering their insights and saying what they say. Without some magic intuition into the reference's true agenda, it is impossible to know why he is telling you what he is. There is also a significant change afoot in people's motivation to offer honest, open references.

Today reference checks have legal implications that threaten what little validity they once provided. References can be sued for defamation or invasion of privacy because of the information and opinions they offer. This relegates references to mere fact-checking missions. You can find out the term of employment and other basics, but it is less and less likely that people will expose themselves legally by giving you their heartfelt opinion. As Mercedes Guzman, vice president of human resources for MP Water Resources, explains, "I don't know why people even agree to offer references anymore. The risk is too great. It's getting harder and harder."

In our original research on AQ we also discovered that people are poor judges of other people's AQs. The primary reason for this is because we so often equate AQ with *attitude,* when it actually runs much deeper. Also, in Chapter 4, you discovered that a low AQ becomes virtually invisible at the mid- to-upper levels of Response Control. And because the AQ response is mostly internal, it can easily be misdiagnosed if it is not measured.

THE FUNNEL: ASSESSING EACH APPLICANT'S AQ

One of the best ways to assess each applicant's AQ is to design an efficient, reliable funnel through which he or she becomes an employee (See Exhibit 8.5). The funnel will be based on your needs; however, you will want to make sure that the measure of AQ is near the very top, simply to prevent a high-AQ person from slipping away.

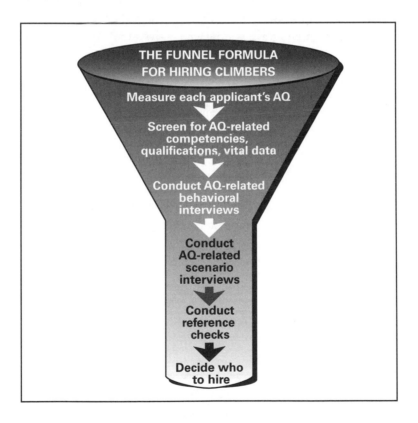

THE FUNNEL FORMULA
FOR HIRING CLIMBERS

Measure each applicant's AQ

Screen for AQ-related
competencies,
qualifications, vital data

Conduct AQ-related
behavioral
interviews

Conduct
AQ-related
scenario
interviews

Conduct
reference
checks

Decide who
to hire

Exhibit 8.5 **Sample Hiring Funnel**

Knowing every applicant's AQ helps you understand the degree to which each of them will be a Climber in your adversity-rich environment. While there are some qualitative indicators of AQ, you will need a quantitative measure. The quantitative measure gives you a more objective means for comparison, with specific statistics against which each candidate can be assessed, based on job and type of industry. Using a substantive and solid measure can also strengthen your legal standing in hiring disputes. For more information on the approved full version of the Adversity Response Profile, see Appendix A.

GETTING AT AQ FROM ALL SIDES

Measuring AQ is the one way to get inside the applicant's operating system and to quantify the vital pattern and predictor of his or her propensity to be a Climber. However, there are more ways to gather secondary or additional data to help further assess how well a given job candidate is likely to deal with challenges.

> Challenges can be like stepping-stones or stumbling blocks.
> It's just a matter of how you view them.
>
> —Anonymous

AQ-Based Screening

Rather than simply reading résumés and cover letters with the traditional mind-set, examine these promotional documents under the lens of AQ. Look for evidence that the person has faced adversities and has overcome them. Or, you may find someone who has had things easy every step of the way. He or she may have a high but untested AQ. This is why the AQ measure is particularly useful when combined with other data. Whatever level of adversity the person has faced, this information can prove useful in assessing that person.

Bruce Merrick, president and CEO of Dant Clayton, a stadium-seating manufacturer, uses the AQ measure and lens in his hiring process. He is adamant about the role adversity and AQ should play. "I try to find three examples of adversity a candidate has faced and successfully overcome before I will even consider hiring that person," he explains.

The danger with this kind of screening is that you can make assumptions based on limited information. Instead, circle or note those items about which you would like additional information.

- What challenges, setbacks, and/or adversities can you find?
- What track record of striving, going beyond the standard rules and expectations, and creating his or her own career does this person have? Or does he or she seem to be following the mainstream formula?
- What, if any, evidence of resilience, fortitude, and/or agility can be found in these documents?
- In what jobs did this person appear to face the most difficulties, setbacks, challenges?
- Are there any jobs in this person's background that most people would shy away from taking on? If so, which ones?

Exhibit 8.6 AQ-Based Screening of Application Materials

Creating a Challenge

Since high-AQ people are typically inspired by a challenge, why not create one for them? I recently did this unintentionally, as I sought to find an office manager who could serve as the operational glue, or Base Camp coordinator, for our Climbing Team. I laid out three challenges.

First, the person had to find us on the Web and learn as much as he or she could about our company. Anyone who did not do this was not considered.

Second, he or she had to find my book, *Adversity Quotient: Turning Obstacles into Opportunities,* which was currently sold out in town and on loan at the library.

Third, I had just recently relocated to a very remote site in San Luis Obispo, California. Our address was not listed anywhere, and I had provided only vague clues in the job description regarding the general area. To learn about us, a potential applicant had to search the Web (intentional), find our address, and somehow locate it, even though it didn't exist on any map. Additionally, our phone number was not yet listed with operator information. Many faxed their résumés, but only a few found our location.

One applicant drove around the area for hours and could not find our street. She called the fire department and the county and searched for our GPS (global positional satellite) coordinates. Nothing. Finally, with assistance from the fire department, she found the street, which matched the address on our Web site. It was gated, so she could not go up the steep hill, but this told her that she would need a four-wheel-drive vehicle if she ever got the interview. In the meantime, she arranged for a private plane and flew over our land to check out the office and setting! She walked into our office with a great story, a stack of research on us and what we do, as well as my book, fully marked and read cover to cover. That is Climbing behavior! Her AQ? 180!

Perhaps you have your own gauntlet that can help you choose which applicant is most determined and undaunted in the face of a challenge.

Scenario Interviewing

Scenario interviewing comes in many forms. The basic premise is to put the applicant in a situation where he or she must face and deal with some adversity. The adversity can come in any form, within obvious bounds. Your intention is to assess how well that person deals with the adversity the moment it strikes.

You want to assess their Response Control and whether they are Source- or Response-Based people. If they are Source-Based, they do a lot of blaming or focus on the source instead of the solution. Response-Based people show strong Response Control, stay cool, and do whatever they can to help the person in need. They will remain largely unfazed—just what you need in the heat of battle!

You can probably create your own scenarios, but here are some examples:

1. The angry-customer scenario can be conducted over the phone, in person, or via the Internet. The intention is to have the person, with very limited information, handle a highly upset, demanding customer. You can "step out for a minute" or ask the applicant to field the call, while you and/or others watch. The situation can be exacerbated by additional calls and angry stakeholders.

2. Have the person deal with a simulated technology failure or crash. Stage a timed Internet search: tell the person to get as much information on a particular subject as possible within the next ten minutes,

then arrange to have the system fail and see how well he or she responds to that adversity.

3. Multitasking on urgent items thrown at them from all sides with little information is a good way to see how people deal with some realistic challenges. Climbers will stay cool and focused, do all they can, respond as if it were a game, ask the necessary questions, and demonstrate uncommon determination and creativity in getting the job done.

These scenarios are not presented as prescriptions, but they may spark your creativity for assessing any applicant's ability to deal with your versions of adversity (see Exhibit 8.7).

Beyond the traditional reference-check questions, consider the following data sources:

- What was the greatest challenge or setback this person faced while under your employment? How did he or she handle it?
- When this person faces adversity, what might he or she typically say or do?
- Compared to the rest of your team, how well did this person deal with the demands, uncertainties, and adversities of the job? If the person who was best at this was rated a 10 and the worst was rated a 1, where does this person fall? Can you give me an example?
- What did you see in this person when some unexpected mishap or setback arose? If he or she faced a different, more difficult setback tomorrow, how would you predict he or she would respond?
- We all say and do things we later regret, especially under pressure. To what extent did this person say and do things he or she might later regret?
- When was this person most overwhelmed? Can you give me an example? How did you know he or she was overwhelmed? Then what happened?
- If 10 is the rating for the most resilient person you employ and 1 is the least resilient, where does this person fall? On what do you base this rating?

Exhibit 8.7 AQ-Based Reference-Check Questions

AQ-Based Behavioral Interviewing

Interviewing to unearth behavioral patterns has been gaining favor over traditional interviewing. Of course, because behavioral interviews are becoming increasingly prevalent, candidates are now skilled at manipulating them. For this reason, behavioral interviewing can be important but of limited value. This is why you should never put full credence in one data-gathering method. Your intent here is to ask behavioral questions about how the person behaved or would behave in specific types of situation. You want to learn how he handles adversity.

- What was the greatest work-related difficulty or challenge you faced this week? What happened? What was the cause? How did you respond?
- What has been the most dramatic failure you have faced in your career so far? What happened? Go through the sequence with me, from the moment it happened. What happened? What was your first thought? What did you say? What did you do? How long did that take? Then what happened . . . ?
- Give me an example of a work-related situation where things totally fell apart, and it was impossible to recover. What happened? How did you feel? What did you do?
- What is the most likely reason for you to terminate your employment in any job?
- When in your career were you most overwhelmed? What contributed to that feeling? How long did it last?
- What sorts of difficulties would you expect to face on this job? On a scale of 1 to 10, with 10 meaning being bombarded with adversity and 1 meaning being adversity-free, what level of adversity have you faced (where and when?) and what level do you feel most comfortable handling? Can you describe a situation where you have handled that level or more before?

Exhibit 8.8 AQ-Based Interview Sample Questions

PROPER USE OF THE ADVERSITY RESPONSE PROFILE

Earlier in the chapter I advised against letting a single number decide a person's fate, whether it is based on AQ or some in-house competency grid. This is unethical and possibly illegal. Although we all want a black-and-white cutoff point, it is unethical to use one.

While AQ is one of the most robust measures available, it should be used as part of the overall hiring formula, along with the Hiring Funnel depicted in Exhibit 8.5.

Since AQ scores fall on a continuum from 40 to 200, the higher a person's score, the more likely he or she is to deal effectively with adversities of all kinds and demonstrate true Response Ability. The lower a person's score, the more of a toll adversity will take on him or her and the less likely he or she is to be a Response-Able, agile, resilient, top performer.

AQ should be used for what it is—a continuum. In other words, if two people look roughly equivalent, let AQ drive your choice. If you have a reasonably high-AQ person who is less than ideal on paper, you should reconsider that person. If you have a uniquely talented person with a low AQ, you may want to hire that person and then use the tools in this book to raise his or her AQ. Over time, you are likely to weigh AQ more and more heavily in your hiring decisions. When it comes to AQ scores, all other factors being moderately close or equal, *hire higher.*

AQs also vary by job classification. Internationally, the average AQ for all job classifications combined is 147.5. For commission salespeople, the average is 157, and I have had some groups of entrepreneurs who average in the low 170s, with an inordinate number of trailblazing top executives scoring in the 170s to 190s! A particular group being honored by *The Business Journal* for their groundbreaking achievements in their respective industries averaged 173. Some government workers, teachers, hospitality workers, and line workers have historically had averages below 147.5.

Full comparative statistics are provided with the ARP, as well as the 1½-day Adversity Response Profile Certification Program (see Appendix B). You can use these statistics to match scores according to the job you are seeking to fill. The certification program is required of all individuals and institutions using the ARP for selection. Its purpose is to make sure each person gets the fullest value and most accurate use of the ARP.

PUTTING THE AQ EQUATION TOGETHER

You will notice that even if you used every suggested method for assessing AQ, the hiring process would take little additional time or hassle. It is simply a matter of wearing an AQ lens throughout the hiring process and gathering as much useful data from as many sides as possible. In this way, you are much more likely to avoid not only experiencing L^4—the Lose-Lose-Lose-Lose resulting from the Type One and Type Two hiring errors of bringing in the wrong person—but also letting the Climber get away.

As an employer, you will want to put on your researcher's spectacles and cross-validate your data; in other words, you should explore which findings come from more than one source and which ones are oddities and therefore suspect and not worthy of further investigation. Imagine a large table onto which you dump somewhere between three and six puzzle pieces. Your job is to see how they fit together and what the final picture looks like. This is precisely what you will do with the information regarding each applicant.

This chapter will convince some employers to rethink their whole hiring equation; for others, it should introduce some meaningful, high-leverage tweaks.

You now know what it takes to define, find, and ultimately hire the best people. You also know how to coach others to improve their AQs and Response Ability. You are now ready for the higher challenge of strengthening your workplace by creating high AQ Climbing Teams and a Climbing Culture.

Topographical Map of Chapter 8
Hiring Climbers

Beware of the Two Types of Hiring Errors.

Type One Hiring Errors—Hiring the wrong person
—L^4 stands for Lose-Lose-Lose-Lose, which refers to the losses suffered by the customer, workforce, employee, and organization.
—Have you calculated the true cost of a hiring mistake?

Type Two Hiring Errors—The Climber that got away.

—Letting go or rejecting candidates who would have been great.

Who are you losing? Climbers, Campers, or Quitters?

The True Cost of hiring a person for your organization (based on Exhibit 8.2) is?

Use Seven Screen Savers

#1 Go Beyond Gut   #5 Use Mountain Guides

#2 Be Consistently Consistent   #6 Involve the Climbing Team

#3 Win the Data Game   #7 Rely on More Than References

#4 Fog-Proof the Process

Use the Funnel Formula to Hire Climbers:

Measure Each Applicant's AQ

Screen for AQ-Related Competencies, Qualifications, Vital Data

Conduct AQ-Related Behavioral Interviews

Conduct AQ-Related Scenario Interviews

Conduct Reference Checks

Decide Who to Hire

CHAPTER 9

BUILDING CLIMBING TEAMS

Adversity has the effect of eliciting talents which in prosperous circumstances would have lain dormant.

—Horace

EVEN AFTER DECADES of getting work done in teams, leaders remain largely mystified about how to bring forth a team's full capacity. They wonder why some teams accomplish extraordinary feats, while most waste time, resources, and capacity. In the following sections, this chapter will: (1) demystify and redefine the high-performance team by seeing it through the lens of AQ; (2) equip you with three ways to assess Team AQ; and (3) help strengthen your team's AQ and Response Ability so that it can *sustain* high performance in adversity-rich times, regardless of your team's function or configuration.

Over the course of this chapter you will complete the Team AQ Process, beginning with a thorough assessment of your Team AQ. Specifically, you will assess and address Team AQ at three levels: Ground Level, which combines individual AQ scores; Mid-Mountain Level, which compiles all the members' assessment of the overall Team AQ; and Sky Level, which includes a panoramic, or 360-degree, view of the team, looking at it through the perceptions of various stakeholders.

Nine members of a medical center leadership team were confronted with new laws that drastically reduced revenue, coupled with wage hikes for nurses and skyrocketing drug costs. These leaders were charged with restructuring their world-class hospitals and medical school. They had to restore profitability and build a new facility that would replace the old one. Their decisions would influence the quality of health care for millions of people in their area.

Many of the members were top experts in their medical specialties who had demonstrated great resolve, resilience, and optimism over the years. But something about how these people worked seemed to squelch their strengths and exacerbate their weaknesses.

They had been gathering data and meeting together for months. But no action had been taken, and the situation was becoming critical. Tom, the provost of the medical school and the leader, said that if they could not resolve their problems and develop a plan of action, he was going to be forced to hire a consulting firm known for its slash-and-burn methods. The threat was looming.

As we chatted informally prior to the meeting, three different people told me how dysfunctional the team was, and how unlikely it was that they could salvage the situation. The stress among the group was palpable.

As people got settled, the body language spoke volumes. Tom arrived early, anxious to get set up and praying for a breakthrough. Then Bob entered, exchanged pleasantries, donned his bifocals, and scanned some of the reams of data piled on the table. Next came Janice, her face tight with tension. "They never listen to me," she said. "And I have a lot of good ideas. I've learned to just sit back and shut up. I just *hate* these meetings!" Mario looked haggard. Ignoring everyone, he turned his chair away from the table and used his cell phone to check his voice mail.

The rest silently took their places. Everyone was either tense or resigned. Tom began the meeting.

TOM (TEAM LEADER): Okay, everybody, as you know, today is a big day. We need to get a lot accomplished and come up with some concrete actions for moving toward our goal. No more sitting on our hands. Now, here's—

BOB: I have to object to this false sense of urgency. We have been gathering data, and we need more data to make the decisions we're being asked to make. Now, I think—

JANICE: Can't you guys see this is impossible? I mean, we're being asked to cut tens of millions from our budgets while preserving the quality of care and the integrity of our academic programs. I think it's time we just admit to ourselves our days of being world-class are over! *(Tom shakes his head slowly from side to side).* And we're going to lose our prized faculty, because this is just the beginning—

JOE: I don't mean to interrupt, but, I'm sorry, I have to disagree with Janice. *(Janice rolls her eyes and slumps back.)* The sky is not falling. We're not the first group of people to face this kind of challenge; we may be the most dysfunctional, but—

MARIO: We can't get this done under this kind of pressure. I think this is the wrong way to go about this whole—

DAVE: In orthopedics we tried this and it failed there, so we need to—

JANICE *(SLAMMING THE TABLE WITH THE PALM OF HER HAND): That's* my point exactly!

And so it went all day, with people talking at, not *with*, each other. The interactions were riddled with attacking, defending, criticizing, complaining, and comparing. Many good ideas were expressed and lost in the same breath. By the end of the day, several team members were resigned, if not despondent. The meeting ended with more conflict and little action. Despite all the pooled talent, brainpower, and experience, they fell far short of their goal and capacity.

Too many teams suffer this fate. Why did a group of talented people fail as a team? How can *your* team avoid such a fate?

As with any group attempting something even mildly ambitious, this team faced some unexpected adversities. New legislation cut its revenue stream. Shortages of nurses threatened care and drove up wages. Delays in getting vital data, not to mention the tremendous hassle of pulling everyone together, all added to its burden and hindered its progress.

As a team the members possessed the software (training, intelligence, aptitudes, talents, knowledge, capacity, and skills) required for the task, but together their operating system lacked the capacity and strength to perform optimally amid their current challenges. The adversity brought out their worst when they needed their best. Their interactions would have been different if they hadn't had impending deadlines, outside obligations, limited resources, or unexpected setbacks. But how many teams operate under such utopian luxury?

What about your team(s) as you gear up for the New Economy? I have discovered that most teams are composed of individuals representing a range of AQs and related levels of optimism, resilience, and Response Ability. Chances are your team is no different.

When you have a team of mixed AQs, the combined effect is often less than the parts, or what we call *negative synergy*. The higher-AQ members may work hard to elevate the team, at least for a while. After facing a wall of frustration, they may focus and dedicate their energies elsewhere. The lower-AQ members dampen team morale, decision making, agility, and problem solving. The moderate-AQ members may get sucked at least partway into the lower-AQ abyss, or they may keep slowly plugging away with uninspired efforts. The result is a team that taps little of its Existing Capacity and is ill equipped for the challenges of the New Economy.

If this describes your team, you will want to invest in each step of the Team AQ Process introduced later in this chapter. Rather than firing anyone who isn't a Climber, you can use the Team AQ Process to expand everyone's capacity and opportunity to play a significant role in the team's success.

The Team AQ Process will provide the baseline of information, understanding, and skills to strengthen your Team AQ. It will enable the higher-AQ members to have a more positive and significant influence on the team's success and allow the lower-AQ members a way to meaningfully contribute to the team's success without having to pretend that they have become optimists overnight. Moderate-AQ individuals will be provided the incentive and means to ratchet up their commitment and investment in the team's success.

Consider the role AQ currently plays in your team dynamics. It's often said that "a team is only as strong as its members." Tom's group made this statement seem like a meaningless cliché.

THE ROLE OF TEAM AQ IN TEAM PERFORMANCE

A team is only as strong as its AQ, regardless of its talents and capacity. To be a true high-performance team it must have a high-performance CORE operating system, one that will sustain agility, innovation, problem solving, and strategic thinking in adversity-rich times. Most teams do not have a high-performance CORE. The key is strengthening your Team CORE.

AQ defines the team's operating system and its ability to tap its wisdom, talents, and capacity with the kind of agility and determination required to prevail through everyday challenges. And the greater the challenges or adversity a team must face, the more important AQ becomes.

When you have a team with mixed AQs, capacity is typically underutilized. The configuration of the team can also influence the role AQ plays.

Teams today are forced to become faster, more agile, and increasingly sophisticated. The Internet has drastically increased globalization and cut product cycles. Virtual teams made up of people at far-flung reaches of the planet connected only by technology abound. Such teams demand increasingly skilled leaders and members. How do you help keep virtual team members fully engaged?

According to Howard Rheingold, author of *The Virtual Community* and founder of the Electronic Minds Web-based community, "It is very easy for people [on virtual teams] to misunderstand one another. People can be ruder to one another than they would be in person. . . . [They must be] committed to painstakingly working through obstacles." Like any network under stress, a virtual team's performance is only as strong as its operating system, or AQ. Mixed-AQ virtual teams are sometimes harder to manage than face-to-face teams, because it is harder to manage the influence of the lower-AQ members.

As adversity mounts, AQ drives everything the team does and how it performs. The classic team activities, such as decision making, problem solving, brainstorming, innovation, listening, trusting, project completion, and information gathering, are *all* heavily influenced by AQ. A team must be able to demonstrate these abilities amid great uncertainty, chaos, and demands, requiring the focus, clarity, resilience, and determination derived from a sufficiently high AQ.

The Team AQ Process forces a deeper analysis of the team climate—its implicit norms, attitudes, conflicts, and strategies—in order to influence how a team approaches continuous improvement and change. No one influences a team's AQ more than its leader. At SunTrust Bank we discovered a direct relationship between the branch leader's AQ and not only the Team AQ but also the branch's financial performance. This is a common pattern. The leader can shrink or enlarge the contribution of team members simply by his or her Response Ability in moments of truth.

Where Capacities Collide

Earlier I introduced you to three forms of capacity—Required, Existing, and Accessed—which can be seen in the example of Tom's group. Existing Team Capacity (what they were capable of doing) exceeded what was asked of them (Required Team Capacity). But, unfortunately, their Accessed Team Capacity (what they tapped) fell shy of the Required Team Capacity, a frustration to all involved. Their Team AQ was insufficient given the adversity of their task and the surrounding conditions. Like many teams with lower-than-ideal AQs, Tom's team was at their worst under adversity, or when it mattered most.

If you have a mixed-AQ team, you probably see this syndrome kick in at the most inopportune times. Regardless of their talent, experience, and perceived capacity (Existing Team Capacity), low-AQ teams rarely deliver to their full abilities (see Exhibit 9.1). When adversity strikes, their sense of Control and Ownership shrinks as the Reach and Endurance of the adversity expand. As a result the team falls into an abyss of blaming, helplessness, criticizing, and frustration.

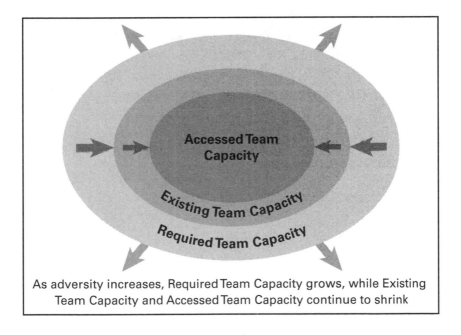

As adversity increases, Required Team Capacity grows, while Existing Team Capacity and Accessed Team Capacity continue to shrink

Exhibit 9.1 **Low-Performance Teams**

In contrast, high-AQ teams exceed expectations by developing and possessing capacity (Existing Team Capacity) and delivering outcomes (Accessed Team Capacity) that go beyond the requirements (Required Team Capacity) (see Exhibit 9.2). Their Response Ability carries the day when adversity strikes. They expand their Control and Ownership while limiting the Reach and Endurance of the adversity, preventing it from seriously hindering their ascent. This is why it is vital to provide the language, understanding, and tools to strengthen Team AQ.

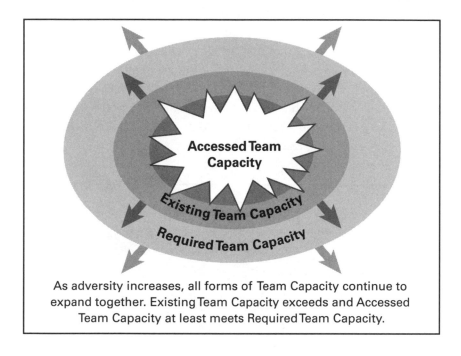

As adversity increases, all forms of Team Capacity continue to expand together. Existing Team Capacity exceeds and Accessed Team Capacity at least meets Required Team Capacity.

Exhibit 9.2 **High-Performance Teams**

Team AQ is more than a collection of individual AQ scores. Each team has a unique AQ-related CORE chemistry that drives everything it does or does *not* accomplish.

THE MYTH AND TRUTH OF HIGH-PERFORMANCE TEAMS

Ironically, most teams that are called *high-performance* are anything but. Simply applying the label "high-performance" or providing "high-performance team training" does not make it so. As Tom's team illustrated, the fact that the individuals possess the knowledge and tools to implement high performance does not guarantee results. Contrary to popular belief, even if a team creates good results within an intended deadline, it's not necessarily a high-performance team. It must *sustain* outstanding results. Creating solid results on time is merely the baseline requirement of any team. Nor does producing exceptional results necessarily define a team as high-performance.

No corporate mandate or newly hatched initiative can guarantee that the promise of high performance will become anything more than another T-shirt logo or phrase in a long list of meaningless verbiage.

What we are really talking about here are the Climbing Teams. Like people, most teams Quit or Camp, while a few forge upward. High-performance Climbing Teams, like high-performance Climbers, are rare—and easy to spot. Exceptional and unnecessarily rare are those who *sustain* high performance through many projects. Yet, as the Required Capacity of coworkers expands, we need these Climbing Teams more than ever.

Climbing Teams' performance extends beyond outputs into the processes by which outputs are achieved to effectively gel and solve problems. They welcome and include opposing opinions or feedback. They build on each member's ideas and are willing to take necessarily bold risks to accomplish their goals. They are compelled by their mission and find it exhilarating to accomplish the impossible. All of these behaviors are essential to a successful ascent. *Campers are left in the dust.*

Therefore, high-performance teams are not about putting a bunch of talented people together, giving them team training, and telling them to accomplish extraordinary things. Nonetheless, most leaders still operate as though they believe that telling or commanding teams to do these things will produce results when, in fact, doing so is no different from telling Campers that they simply need to define their mountain and Climb! Isn't it time you made high-performance Climbing Teams a daily reality rather than a chance occurrence? One proven approach is to measure and strengthen Team AQ using the full Team AQ Process.

> Alone we can do so little, together we can do so much.
>
> —Helen Keller

THE TEAM AQ PROCESS

The most effective way to help your team is to guide it through a very basic AQ-based process (see Exhibit 9.3).

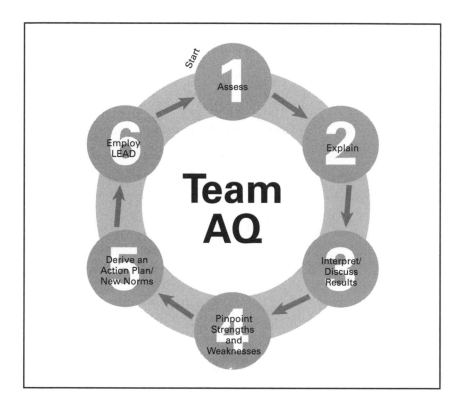

***Exhibit 9.3* The Team AQ Process**

You begin by assessing Team AQ, ideally at all three levels. Each level leads to a different set of insights. Next, you explain or teach your team about AQ so that the members have a baseline of understanding about the concepts, measure, and CORE. Use this book, the assessments, and any other resources you have to assist them in sharing a common language for addressing their AQ and AQ-related behavior. Enlighten them about all three levels of measurement so that they know what they have assessed as well as the data they have gathered and are about to interpret.

Help them interpret their Team AQ measure and CORE Profiles. Dedicate some time with them to discuss the results, what they imply about past behavioral patterns and team dynamics, and how Team AQ is affecting the team. It is useful to make AQ a regular agenda item so that the team can revisit its Response Ability as an ongoing part of its ascent.

At this point in the Team AQ Process it is particularly valuable to compare the results against the team's charge or tasks to see how AQ might be affecting different emphases, such as innovation, problem solving, decision making, listening, multitasking, and competing. This analysis will deepen the value and application of Team AQ.

Pinpoint the team's AQ-related strengths and weaknesses so that you can derive an action plan for improving how your team and its specific members respond to future adversities. You may discover low-AQ norms that hinder your team. You can then consciously choose to select new norms for responding to adversity that are built upon CORE, once you have all three levels of CORE awareness. You will use the LEAD Sequence within and between team meetings to keep the team true to its action plan and to help the team hardwire new patterns of response. Turn the Team AQ Process into an iterative cycle of continuous improvement by reassessing Team AQ periodically and continuing with the process.

As you go through this process, use the exhibits and examples throughout the chapter to generate your own data and wisdom. This chapter is a toolkit of assessments, reports, profiles, charts, and guides. Use what you need. I have provided you with the fully detailed version. You may find it practical to cut to the chase and focus on those levels and facets of assessment, awareness, and action that best fit your current team. Of course, the deeper you go in assessing, explaining, and strengthening Team AQ, the greater and more enduring the benefits your team will enjoy.

You may choose simply to read about the Team AQ Process—culling those tips you wish to keep for future reference. Or you can complete the process—using it as a guide to systematically strengthen your team. To do so, you will want to go step by step. You can even use this process as a template for a series of team meetings. Ideally, you will end up with a complete template for addressing and strengthening Team AQ. (See Exhibit 9.4.1 for the blank template.) You will complete a template for your team throughout this chapter.

The Team AQ Process
Sample Template
Assessment

Ground Level Team AQ_____   Industry Mean_____

Ground Level Team CORE

        C_____   Industry Mean_____

        O_____   Industry Mean_____

        R_____   Industry Mean_____

        E_____   Industry Mean_____

Compile Ground Level Team AQ Report (see Exhibit 9.5.)

Mid-Mountain Team AQ_____   Industry Mean_____

Mid-Mountain Team CORE

        C_____   Industry Mean_____

        O_____   Industry Mean_____

        R_____   Industry Mean_____

        E_____   Industry Mean_____

Compile Mid-Mountain Team AQ Report (see Exhibit 9.12.)

Sky Level Team AQ_____   Industry Mean_____

Sky Level Team CORE

        C_____   Industry Mean_____

        O_____   Industry Mean_____

        R_____   Industry Mean_____

        E_____   Industry Mean_____

Compile Sky Level Team AQ Report (see Exhibit 9.16.)

Exhibit 9.4.1 **Team AQ Process Sample Template**

Steps Two and Three in the Team AQ Process, Explain and Interpret/Discuss Results, respectively, are detailed in Appendix C. Additional insights for Ground Level, Mid-Mountain Level, and Sky Level are outlined in Exhibits 9.4.2, 9.4.3, and 9.4.4 to help you complete Step Four in the Team AQ Process, Pinpoint Strengths and Weaknesses. Exhibit 9.4.5 will help you work through the process of creating an Action Plan/New Norms (Step Five). Finally, Exhibit 9.4.6 will assist you in LEADing the Team (Step Six).

Ground Level Insights

- What does our Team AQ indicate about how we handle challenges and adversities?
- How has our Team AQ affected, and how does it affect, our capacity to innovate, solve problems, make decisions, compete, multitask, and meet ambitious deadlines?
- How do we compare with others in our industry?
- What range do our AQ and specific CORE dimensions fall within?
- What range do we need to be in to perform effectively? (See Appendix C.)
- As you consider the CORE dimensions of AQ, which ones are most important to the success of this team, and why?
- What does our CORE Profile indicate that we do particularly well?
- What does our CORE Profile indicate that we most need to improve?
- What is our range of AQs within this team?
- How are the differences in individual AQs reflected in our team dynamics and decision making?
- How does each of us manifest our AQ and CORE when we face adversity?
- How does each of our AQs impact the team?
- How is our CORE demonstrated in our team interactions?
- What is the real impact or Ripple Effect of our Team AQ and CORE?
- How would we describe our team's overall Response Ability (ability to maintain clarity, focus, and direction regardless of what comes at us)?

Exhibit 9.4.2 Ground Level Insights

Mid-Mountain Insights

- What does our Mid-Mountain Team AQ indicate about how we handle challenges and adversities?
- What new insights can we gain from this level of analysis?

- How do we compare with others in our industry?
- What range do our Mid-Mountain AQ and specific CORE dimensions fall within?
- What range do we need to be in to perform effectively? (See Appendix C.)
- What does our Mid-Mountain CORE Profile indicate that we do particularly well?
- What does our CORE Profile indicate that we most need to improve?
- How does this compare with the Ground Level analysis?
- How do we explain any discrepancies between the Ground Level and Mid-Mountain analyses?
- How is our Team AQ reflected in our team dynamics and decision making?
- How is our CORE demonstrated in our team interactions?
- What is the real impact or Ripple Effect of our Team AQ and CORE?
- What is our team's charge, mission, or objective?
- What would be an acceptable/ideal AQ and CORE, given our team's charge?

Exhibit 9.4.3 Mid-Mountain Insights

Sky Level Insights

- What does our Sky Level Team AQ indicate about how we handle challenges and adversities?
- What new insights can we gain from this level of analysis?
- How do we compare with others in our industry?
- What range do our Sky Level AQ and specific CORE dimensions fall within?
- What range do we need to be in to perform effectively? (See Appendix C.)
- What do different stakeholders perceive? What differences or similarities are there in how each rated our Team AQ?

- What does our Sky Level CORE Profile indicate that we do particularly well?
- What does this CORE Profile indicate that we most need to improve?
- How does this compare with the other levels of analysis?
- How do we explain any discrepancies between the findings at all three levels?
- In what areas do we Climb, Camp, or Quit? (See Exhibit 9.7.)
- How does our Team AQ affect our behavior?
- Where is our Team AQ having the greatest positive impact?
- Where is our Team AQ having the greatest negative impact?
- How does our Team AQ affect our relationships with external stakeholders?
- Where do we need to be on AQ and CORE in order to succeed?

Exhibit 9.4.4 Sky Level Insights

Action Plan/New Norms

- Given what we know about AQ, CORE, and our team, what specific steps can each of us take to improve our Team AQ? (List ideas. Identify specific commitments by individual.)

1)_____

2)_____

- Given what we know about AQ, CORE, and our team, what specific steps can we take and agree to collectively to improve our Team AQ? (List ideas and reach consensus on what the team will do to begin to strengthen how it deals with adversity. Relate it to your specific focus, such as problem solving, decision making, product innovation, etc.)

1)_____

2)_____

- What lower-than-ideal AQ norms does our team currently have? (When we respond to adversity, what low-AQ tendencies or patterns do we demonstrate? See Exhibit 9.7.)

1)_____

2)_____

• If we could write and live by two new, specific, higher-AQ norms for what people say or do when adversity strikes, what would they be? (What new standards of behavior do we want to institutional-ize in this team? See Exhibit 9.7.)

1)_____

_____

2)_____

_____

• What specific steps can we take to deepen our understanding of AQ? (Specify who does what, when. Use the book, tapes, or other resources to learn about AQ and how it applies to your current and looming challenges.)

1)_____

_____

2)_____

_____

Exhibit 9.4.5 Action Plan/New Norms

LEADing the Team

In what specific situations/challenges can we apply the LEAD Sequence to our team interactions? (List looming challenges, meet-ings, situations where you think you can use the LEAD Sequence to strengthen how the team solves problems, makes decisions, and responds to any adversity.)

1)_____

_____

2)_____

_____

Exhibit 9.4.6 LEADing the Team

MEASURING TEAM AQ FROM THREE ELEVATIONS

Perhaps the most powerful step you can take to strengthen Team AQ is to measure it. This is why I have dedicated a significant portion of this chapter to the initial steps of the Team AQ Process. Once team members are provided with the results, an understanding of AQ, and their CORE Profiles, the ensuing discovery and discussion lead to immediate improvements in how team members approach adversity. You will unearth tired, dysfunctional team norms that have hindered team capacity. You will enjoy even greater improvements as you establish new higher-AQ team norms and employ the LEAD Sequence as the central approach to solving problems.

We can *measure* and *strengthen* Team AQ from three elevations. Each elevation provides valuable insights into how your team members deal with adversity, and into their capacity to exceed the expectations by which they measure success. The three elevations are:

- **Ground Level:** Combined individual AQ and CORE scores from the Adversity Response Profile
- **Mid-Mountain:** The Team Adversity Response Profile
- **Sky Level:** The Panoramic Team Adversity Response Profile

Ground Level—Individual AQ Within a Team

The first basic insight into Team AQ starts at Ground Level, which involves measuring the AQ and CORE of each individual. A general team profile can then be compiled by simply adding all the individual scores and dividing by the number of members on your team. This will give you a mean AQ for the team and a mean score for C, O, R, and E. You can then determine which AQ range your team falls within and can graph the mean team CORE Profile. You can compare your results with the standard mean for CORE and AQ (see Exhibit 9.5 for a sample). This Ground Level analysis is valuable for three reasons.

Team AQ — Ground Level Combined Individual AQs and CORE Profiles

Instructions: As you review this printout, consider how your team compares. To progress through the Team AQ Process, construct a simplified report for your team combining the individual AQ and CORE scores, the information in Appendix C, and the information provided in this chapter.

Range of Individual AQs	Mean Individual AQ	Telecom Industry Mean
93–187	147	148

Indications: This broad range of individual AQs is likely to be a source of conflict among the team members, especially when challenges or difficulties arise. Some members are likely to express an urgent desire to tackle a given challenge, while others may feel unable or unwilling to do so. Discrepancies in AQ result in some strongly held beliefs in how serious a given challenge may be and how best to approach it. The team-wide mean is slightly below that of other teams within this industry. Substantial gains can be enjoyed by raising the Team AQ.

Range of Scores on Control	Mean Score on Control	Industry Mean
19–48	36	37

Indications: The range of C scores indicates significant differences in how team members respond to adversity. Some see adverse events as beyond their Control while others are likely to focus on whatever facet of the situation they can influence for the better, no matter how severe the situation may be. The team-wide mean shows an average level of Control, with the opportunity to strengthen the team's resilience and problem solving by focusing more precisely on those facets of a given situation that the team can most readily improve.

Range of Scores on Ownership	Mean Score on Ownership	Industry Mean
21–42	40	40

Indications: The team-wide range of scores on Ownership indicates a moderately low tendency to take accountability for improving situations regardless of their cause. This can degrade team trust, interdependence, and agility. Team members may focus more on blame than resolution. The relatively low team-wide mean shows weaker than normal Ownership, which may be a significant concern. This is the weakest of the four CORE dimensions for the team.

Range of Scores on Reach	Mean Score on Reach	Industry Mean
29–48	37	38

Indications: This is the strongest facet of the Level One measure of team-wide AQ. The team has an above-average capacity to keep adversity in its place. This can help the team maintain perspective when facing a particular setback or series of difficulties. There remain some significant differences in how team members perceive adverse events, which may result in conflict over the size and magnitude of a given problem.

Range of Scores on Endurance	Mean Score on Endurance	Industry Mean
25–46	33	32

Indications: The substantial range of scores on Endurance indicates discrepancies in how long difficulties will endure. As a result team members are likely to disagree on strategies for dealing with problems that some perceive as fleeting and others perceive as enduring. The team-wide mean is slightly above that of similar teams. Responding to adverse events as more enduring than necessary can be a drain on hope and optimism to surmount obstacles as they arise.

Team CORE Profile Based on Individual Scores
Overall, this team has a CORE Profile that indicates moderate resilience, agility, innovation, and problem-solving skills. As difficulties mount and a given project drags on, morale, clarity, focus, and productivity are likely to sag. This team is likely to experience conflict over how different events are perceived, as well as the best strategies for dealing with them as they arise. Given this profile, this team is unlikely to tap the full talents of its members and become a high-performing team.

Exhibit 9.5 Sample Ground Level Team AQ Printout

First, you can compare the team's Response Ability with each individual's results. If shared openly, discrepancies between individual and team AQ should provide insights into specific behavior within the team. For example, the person who is determined, relentless, and optimistic (AQ of 172) is likely to score beyond the Team AQ Profile (Team AQ of 147); this person may also experience and even cause some tension within the team. At the other end, a person with an AQ well below the team average (AQ of 117) might frustrate the team with his or her responses and approach to problems.

The team members must understand the principles of AQ and Response Ability in order to get the full value of their own assessment of what their role is within the team. The rich dialogue that ensues can shed light on the team's behaviors, emotions, and dynamics. If your group possesses a strong foundation of trust, I highly encourage this sort of open discovery of the role AQ plays in what has worked and is not working.

Second, going deeper into the Team CORE will reveal discrepancies between individual and team scores on each dimension. The CORE discrepancies explain why some conflicts arise and what makes them so heated. Getting this out in the open also begins to heal any prior lack of understanding and encourages the empathy and "teamness" that people may experience in moments of truth.

A discrepancy on Control might be reflected in some team members taking a defeatist perspective when adversity strikes, while others try to figure out a way to make things even a little better. For example, this discrepancy in individuals' will to solve a problem might arise if one person scored near the top of the range on C, while some members scored as low as 19.

A discrepancy on Ownership might come to life when lists are made and accountabilities assigned. Those with lower-O scores might say, "Hey, it's not our problem. Let them fix it." Higher-O scorers get past blame and play a role in improving the situation, regardless of its cause. These discrepancies can cause team tension.

A discrepancy on R is apparent when people size up the magnitude of the problem. Those with higher-R scores naturally isolate the adversity. Those with lower-R scores are more likely to fan out on the adversity, spreading its flames to all facets of the situation and beyond, until the wildfire they predicted begins to rage.

Finally, a discrepancy in E shows up in how long a person thinks the adversity will endure. There is a significant difference between those who score in the high range in Endurance and those in the lower range. Lower Es have less faith and hope, while higher Es offer an authentic optimism that flies in the face of lower-AQ assumptions. Those with lower scores may think the higher-AQ individuals are dangerously unrealistic and need to fully appreciate the severity and resulting longevity of the situation. Higher-AQ individuals have little patience for those mired in the muck and often want to scream what a high-AQ team leader recently said to his lower-AQ team: "Hey, build a bridge, and get over it!" Understanding these discrepancies shows us why these conflicts arise and gives us a vocabulary for addressing them constructively.

The third reason that individual AQ scores and CORE Profiles are valuable is that they provide a baseline assessment you can use to compare future measures as you coach individual members to strengthen their AQs. You need to understand where you are now so that you can assess and understand where you need to be in three or six months.

The Ground Level helps a manager see where and how he or she can be most helpful with specific individuals. People scoring low on one or two particular dimensions can be coached using the methods described in Chapter 6. They can even be helped in the midst of team dialogue using the tools given later in this chapter. For example, if their low C and R responses come out, you can help them rewire their response to the current and future adversities. Ideally, as individual AQs rise, you will see their effect in this basic team profile and, more important, in the behavior of specific team members and how they approach difficulties, innovation, and opportunities.

Ground Level Team AQ Ranges and Interpretation

Exhibit 9.5 provided a Sample Ground Level Team AQ Printout. You can begin to compile your own report by graphing your team CORE in Exhibit 9.6 and comparing your team AQ with the ranges provided in Appendix C. You can assess those areas in which your team may be Climbing, Camping, or Quitting.

Insert your four Team CORE totals in the boxes and graph your Team CORE.

	AQ	C	O	R	E
					50
					48
High	200	50		50	46
	190	48		48	44
	180	46	50	46	42
Moderately High	170	44	48	44	40
	165	42	46	42	38
	160	40	44	40	36
Moderate	155	38	42	38	34
MEAN	150	36	40	36	32
	145	34	38	34	30
	140		36	32	28
	135	32	34	30	26
	130	30	32	28	24
Moderately Low	125	28	30	26	22
	120	26	28	24	20
	115	24	26	22	18
	110	22	24	20	16
	105	20	22	18	14
	95	18	20	16	12
Low	85	16	18	14	10
	75	14	16	14	10
	70	12	14	14	
	60	10	12	12	
	50		12	10	
	40		10		
Means:	147.5	36.4	40.4	37.4	33.3

Exhibit 9.6 Graphing Your Team Ground Level CORE

Exhibit 9.7 will further help you assess some of your team tendencies.

Instructions: Based on your team's CORE, AQ, and behavior, assess and discuss which tendencies listed below best describe your team. In what areas do you Climb, Camp, and Quit?

Climbing Tendencies

Your team focuses on what it *can* Control.	People step up and take Ownership for making things better.	Adversity stays in its place.	Adversity is fleeting.
Your teams works to positively influence tough situations.	There is a focus on solutions over blame.	People keep perspective.	Few things endure.
Your team is resilient and tenacious in solving problems.	You enjoy high trust, agility.	Problems are compartmentalized.	The team works hard to get past challenges and remain optimistic.

Camping Tendencies

The team demonstrates a reasonable sense of Control.	People demonstrate a reasonable sense of Ownership.	Some problems bleed into other areas.	Some things drag on.
Some people may get overwhelmed when adversity piles up.	When tired or tense, people may resort to blame.	As adversities mount, it gets harder to separate each one.	Hope and faith are good, except when adversity is high.
Adversity can adversely affect team dynamics.	Ownership could be stronger.	The team often feels burdened.	Realism is valued.

Quitting Tendencies

The team responds as though it has little, if any, Control.	People deflect Ownership.	Problems seem overwhelming.	Difficulties drag on and on.
A sense of learned helplessness may pervade the team.	People resort to blame, pointing fingers.	People catastrophize.	Adversity endures more than necessary.
The team may abandon difficult tasks.	People may become guarded, defensive, or withdrawn.	Little difficulties blow up into major issues.	Hope gives way to cynicism and sarcasm.

Exhibit 9.7 Team CORE Tendencies

Exhibit 9.8 provides an abbreviated list of mean scores for Ground Level Team AQ and CORE by industry to see how your Team's AQ and CORE stack up with those of others in the same or related industries. These provide good initial comparisons. In the long term, the most meaningful comparisons may be with other teams within your organization.

Team AQ: Sample Industry Averages

Compare your Ground Level Team AQ and CORE Scores with these industry averages.

	AQ	C	O	R	E
Aerospace and Defense	143	36	41	35	30
Banking	144	33	41	37	33
Education	149	36	41	38	34
Financial Services	150	37	41	38	33
Government	144	35	39	38	33
Hospitality	144	35	39	36	34
Insurance	151	37	45	36	33
Manufacturing	145	36	40	37	32
Not-for-profit	142	32	40	38	31
Professional Services	157	40	44	39	35
Technology	147	37	40	38	32
Telecommunication	147	37	40	38	32
Training	151	36	42	40	33

Exhibit 9.8 Ground Level Team AQ—Sample Industry Averages

Mid-Mountain—The Team Adversity Response Profile

Mid-Mountain assessment, known as The Team Adversity Response Profile, is designed specifically for team applications. A short version is provided in Exhibit 9.9. It precisely gets at individual members' perceptions of their team's pattern of response to adversity. It shows how well the team deals with challenges and breaks down its CORE response to whatever may arise.

On a sheet of paper list five challenges your team is facing. Next, create an answer grid like the example provided below. Finally, answer these four questions for each challenge in the space provided.

Example — Answer Grid

	Adversity #1	Adversity #2	Adversity #3	Adversity #4	Adversity #5	Total
Question #1 C						➤
Question #2 O						➤
Question #3 R						➤
Question #4 E						➤

Overall Team AQ △ AQ

1) *To what extent does our team feel it can positively influence this event or situation?*
1 2 3 4 5 6 7 8 9 10
Not at all   Completely

2) *To what extent do we step up and take it upon ourselves to improve this situation?*
1 2 3 4 5 6 7 8 9 10
Not at all   100 percent

3) *To what extent does this adversity reach over into other areas of our team's efforts, interactions, and morale?*
1 2 3 4 5 6 7 8 9 10
It affects everything   It has no effect

4) *How long will this specific adversity endure?*
1 2 3 4 5 6 7 8 9 10
Forever   Extremely briefly

Scoring: Total your answers for each row and insert them in the space labeled "Total." Next, add your totals to get your measure of Team AQ. Insert that number in the triangle labeled "AQ."

Average the scores from all team members to get a team-wide measure of your Team AQ and CORE.

Note: This is *not* the full valid and reliable measure of Team AQ. It merely provides a sample snapshot for your initial insights.

Exhibit 9.9 A Condensed Snapshot of Mid-Mountain Team AQ

Once your team has completed the Mid-Mountain Team AQ measure, the score can be graphed using Exhibit 9.10. Then, your Mid-Mountain Team AQ can be interpreted by referring to Appendix C. Additionally, Exhibit 9.11 provides sample industry averages on Mid-Mountain AQ for comparison.

Insert your four Mid-Mountain CORE totals in the boxes and graph your Team CORE	C	O	R	E

AQ

	AQ	C	O	R	E
	200				50
High	190				48
	180			50	46
	170	50	50	48	44
	165	48	48	46	42
	160	44	46	44	40
Moderately	155	42	44	42	38
High	150	40	42	40	36
	145	38	40	38	34
Moderate	140	36	38	36	32
	135	34	36	34	
MEAN	130	32	34	32	30
	125	30	32	30	28
	120	28	30	28	26
Moderately	115	26	28	26	24
Low	110	24	26	24	22
	105	22	24	22	20
	95	20	22	20	18
	85	18	20	18	16
	75	16	18	16	14
Low	70	14	16	14	12
	60	12	14	12	10
	50	10	12	10	
	40		10		
Means:	130.5	32.5	35.0	33.0	30.0

Exhibit 9.10 Graphing Your Team Mid-Mountain CORE

Mid-Mountain Team AQ: Sample Industry Averages
Compare your Mid-Mountain Team AQ and CORE scores with these industry averages.

	AQ	C	O	R	E
Aerospace and Defense	127	30	35	33	29
Banking	129	32	37	32	28
Education	126	32	34	31	29
Financial Services	133	36	37	32	28
Government	129	33	34	31	31
Hospitality	129	32	33	34	30
Insurance	134	37	39	31	27
Manufacturing	130	34	33	31	32
Not-for-profit	128	32	33	32	31
Professional Services	139	38	38	33	30
Technology	131	32	33	34	32
Telecommunication	138	36	39	33	30
Training	137	34	38	33	32

Exhibit 9.11 Mid-Mountain Team AQ—Sample Industry Averages

Assembling a team report using information from the exhibits provided above shows where your team is strongest and weakest when adversity strikes. Based on this information, what adjectives would you use to describe your team? Is the team "resilient, tenacious, and persistent," or "incapacitated, blame-centered, and demoralized?" See Exhibit 9.12 for a sample Mid-Mountain Team AQ report.

Team AQ—Mid-Mountain Team Adversity Response Profile Results
Partial Sample Printout for a Technology Team

Instructions: Use your Mid-Mountain Team AQ results and the information in Appendix C to construct a similar report for your team to progress through the Team AQ Process.

Team AQ   118   **Industry Average   131**

Indications: This team has a moderately low AQ. This indicates a less-than-optimal ability to deal with challenges, difficulties, setbacks, and obstacles. The team's greatest strength is its tendency to keep adversity confined to the situation at hand. The lower scores on Ownership and Endurance indicate relatively weak accountability when the team is faced with difficulties that are often perceived as long-lasting and difficult to control.

Team members are likely to suffer losses in hope, morale, productivity, problem solving, innovation, and energy level as a result of their lower AQ.

Capacity Descriptors: Mediocre performance, blaming, listless, low-energy, unproductive, draining, pessimistic, cynical, and untapped capacity.

When adversities strike, team members need to focus on those facets of the situation that they can influence, take Ownership for improving them, and envision life after the adversity has passed so specific actions can be planned to make the adversity as limited and short-lived as possible.

Team CORE Profile		Sample Industry Averages
Control	30	32
Ownership	22	33
Reach	39	34
Endurance	27	32

Exhibit 9.12 Sample Mid-Mountain Team AQ Printout

The Mid-Mountain measure provides rich insight into a team's Response Ability. It helps explain how the team has behaved in the past and why, and how it can be stronger and more effective in the future. It also reveals the level of synergy by assessing if, and to what extent, Team AQ exceeds individual AQ, or the compilation of individual AQs from the Ground Level measure.

If synergy is strong, Team AQ should exceed the mean of individual AQs, serving as visible evidence for this previously intangible and ideal state of teamness.

If the team has negative synergy (when the sum of its parts is worse than its individuals), this should be apparent in a Team AQ that falls below the mean of individual AQs (as calculated in the Ground Level analysis). Therefore, Mid-Mountain Team AQ will explain specifically how the team behaves and performs under pressure, and to what extent positive or destructive norms rule the day.

The Mid-Mountain analysis also offers ripe opportunity for meta-communication, or communicating about how the team communicates and responds when adversity strikes. Use the exhibits and graphs in this chapter to customize your own Team AQ report, and give every member a printout of the results. Ask for their discoveries. Discussing the words used to describe the team and seeing where and how the team deals with challenges can be one of the most fruitful and powerful conversations your team may ever have. This kind of introspection is precise and hard-hitting because it is directed at the moment when adversity strikes, which then ripples out to everything that follows.

Sky Level—The Panoramic Team Profile

The Sky Level analysis elevates the concept of Team AQ by including the perceptions of those outside the team, such as customers, bosses, and other teams or individuals. This is ideal for teams that are accountable to multiple parties. Their responses (see Exhibit 9.13) are factored into the Team AQ, creating a panoramic view of the team's CORE pattern of response to adversity. You will need both profiles to calculate your Panoramic Team AQ. It's important to note that teams without multiple stakeholders may find the Sky Level analysis of AQ either inappropriate or of limited value.

To score your Sky Level Team AQ, compare your Mid-Mountain scores with the Panoramic scores. You can also graph your panoramic CORE (see Exhibit 9.14) and interpret your results using the information provided in Appendix C. Then you can compare your Panoramic score with those of similar industries using Exhibit 9.15.

You are completing this profile with a specific team in mind. On a sheet of paper list five challenges or adversities you have seen this team face. Next, create an answer grid like the example provided below. Finally, answer these four questions related to each of these adversities by writing down your answers in order under each one.

Example — Answer Grid

		Adversity #1	Adversity #2	Adversity #3	Adversity #4	Adversity #5	Total
Question #1	C					➤	
Question #2	O					➤	
Question #3	R					➤	
Question #4	E					➤	

Overall Team AQ ◁AQ▷

1) *To what extent does our team feel it can positively influence this event or situation?*

   1   2   3   4   5   6   7   8   9   10

Not at all   Completely

2) *To what extent did this team demonstrate commitment and accountability to improve this situation?*

   1   2   3   4   5   6   7   8   9   10

Not at all   100 percent

3) *To what extent did the team let this adversity reach over into other areas of its or your efforts, interactions, organization, or morale?*

   1   2   3   4   5   6   7   8   9   10

It affected everything   The team
                                    contained it

4) *How long did this team let this specific adversity endure?*

   1   2   3   4   5   6   7   8   9   10

Forever   Extremely briefly

Scoring: Total your answers for each row and insert them in the space labeled "Total." Next, add your totals to get a measure of this team's AQ. Insert that number in the triangle labeled "AQ."

Average the scores from all stakeholders to get a panoramic measure of this team's AQ and CORE.

Note: This is *not* the full valid and reliable measure of Team AQ. It merely provides a sample snapshot for your initial insights.

Exhibit 9.13 Sky Level—Panoramic Team AQ

Insert your four Sky Level CORE totals in the boxes and graph your Team CORE

	C	**O**	**R**	**E**
	□	□	□	□

Level	AQ	C	O	R	E
	200				50
High	190	50			48
	180	48		50	46
	170	46	50	48	44
	165	44	48	46	42
Moderately High	160	42	46	44	40
	155	40	44	42	38
	150	38	42	40	36
Moderate	145	36	40	38	34
	140	34	38	36	32
MEAN	135			34	30
	130	32	36	32	28
	125	30	34	30	26
	120	28	32	28	24
Moderately Low	115	26	30	26	22
	110	24	28	24	20
	105	22	26	22	28
	95	20	24	20	16
	85	18	22	18	14
	75	16	20	16	12
Low	70	14	18	14	10
	60	12	16	12	
	50	10	14	10	
	40		12		
Means:	133.5	33.0	36.5	34.0	30.0

Exhibit 9.14 **Graphing Your Team Sky Level CORE**

Sky Level Panoramic Team AQ: Sample Industry Averages
Compare your Panoramic Team AQ and CORE scores with these industry averages.

	AQ	C	O	R	E
Aerospace and Defense	133	33	36	31	29
Banking	130	32	35	32	31
Education	129	30	32	33	34
Financial Services	135	33	37	34	31
Government	128	31	34	33	30
Hospitality	130	31	35	33	32
Insurance	140	36	38	34	32
Manufacturing	131	33	35	33	30
Not-for-profit	129	32	37	33	27
Professional Services	141	36	39	35	31
Technology	133	32	36	34	31
Telecommunication	139	35	38	35	31
Training	137	34	38	33	32

Exhibit 9.15 Sky Level Panoramic
Team AQ—Sample Industry Averages

It is also useful to sit down and discuss the AQ-related level of expectation each group of stakeholders holds for your team. For example, ask the team: If you were to assign a number, what AQ score does each group expect or require of your team? Complete the same discussion on expectations for C, O, R, and E. Then compare the expectations against the real scores (see Exhibit 9.16 for a sample Panoramic report).

Team AQ—Sky Level Panoramic Team Adversity Response Profile Results
Partial Sample Printout for a Financial Services Team

Instructions: Use the following example and the information in Appendix C to construct a report that reflects your Sky Level Panoramic Team AQ to continue with the Team AQ Process.

Measure	Customers	Management	Coworkers	Team Score	Mean
AQ	126	135	141	138	133.5
Expectation	*156*	*165*	*151*		

C	35	37	42	43	33.0
Expectation	39	43	42		
O	23	27	23	24	36.5
Expectation	41	36	32		
R	41	43	41	42	34.0
Expectation	36	44	41		
E	27	28	35	29	30.0
Expectation	40	42	36		

Indications: This team has a moderate AQ that falls below the mean for teams with similar responsibilities within this industry (See Exhibit 9.15.). It also falls significantly below the expectations of its customers (156), management (165), and coworkers (151), on overall AQ and on the C, R, and E of the CORE dimensions.

Of particular concern is the relatively low Ownership score. This indicates the norm of deflecting accountability for improving difficult situations. Indicators show the team is likely to lack the resilience, innovation, persistence, and optimism of a high-performance team. Its members may also get mired in blaming, comparing, and criticizing their teammates. These areas can be strengthened as the team raises its AQ and strengthens its CORE response to adversity.

Exhibit 9.16 Sample Sky Level Panoramic Team AQ Printout

There are some powerful advantages to a 360-degree view. First, it eliminates blind spots by including multiple perspectives. Outside stakeholders may have a different view of the team and how it deals with adversity. This will show if the team has an inflated sense of self or is perhaps underestimating its own Response Ability. With AQ discrepancies of 126 versus 138, it is clear in Exhibit 9.16 that this team's customers do not think it responds to adversity as effectively as the team believes it does.

Second, the team learns how stakeholders rate its ability to deal with adversity in comparison with how they rate other teams. If there were multiple teams serving the same customers, differences in AQ would be likely to correlate to differences in performance and satisfaction. If your team's customers rate its AQ at 126 and another team scores a customer rating of 161, there are likely to be profound differences in how each team handles setbacks with its customers. This Sky Level analysis provides a clearer understanding of what these perceptions really mean. The panoramic view also assesses how the Team AQ translates into actual behavior in dealing with specific challenges. The team in Exhibit 9.16 probably serves its coworkers better than its external customers and management. Or there are differences in standards and expectations, which need to be clarified and dealt with. In any case, this sort of information can be pivotal to a team's success.

As a result, measuring all three elevations of Team AQ is valuable for better understanding your team's past behavior and strategizing specific methods for strengthening the team, its performance, and its contribution to your organization's success. You must decide which of these measures are of greatest value to you and your team. If you want to see discrepancies between individual AQs and Team AQ, you will need Ground Level and Mid-Mountain measures. If you want to broaden your data net to include other stakeholders, Sky Level (Panoramic measure) is required. Equipped with such initial analytical tools, teams can integrate certain AQ practices into their interactions and strengthen their responses to adverse events, which can bolster resilience, Response Ability, and Team AQ

STRENGTHENING TEAM AQ

There are some important differences between the skills you need for strengthening Team AQ and those you learned in the preceding chapters for strengthening individual AQ. Team AQ influences team dynamics, decision making, problem solving, and innovation. As a result the steps you take to improve Team AQ might go beyond awareness and the LEAD Sequence to include task-, situation-, or team-specific actions. To progress through the Team AQ Process, you will need to assess both the generic and the customized steps you can take to strengthen Team AQ. We will begin with the generic steps of awareness and the LEAD Sequence, as applied to teams. You will discover that they have distinct subtleties and applications within a team.

In general, to raise Team AQ, you ascend through the same levels of expertise you employed for CORE awareness and the LEAD Sequence. Mastering these skills for teams is slightly more challenging than it is for individuals, because multiple people are contributing to the team dynamics and Team AQ.

The improvements gained from providing all three levels of CORE awareness of Team AQ typically exceed those experienced when providing similar insights with individual AQ. CORE awareness destroys negative synergy, thus opening the door to higher AQ norms and patterns. It is important, therefore, not to underestimate the power of this step. You will want to invest ample time in providing all three levels of awareness just as you provided three levels of assessment. Invest in meaningful team dialogue about the results; discuss how they relate to current norms and patterns, how they influence team performance (productivity, morale, innovation, decision making, etc.); and explore those that the team can improve upon. Compiling the results into an actual Team AQ report can be the most incisive and comprehensive way of communicating Team AQ so that you can devise new strategies and approaches to adversity.

Level One—Team CORE Awareness

By completing the measures, graphs, and reports for Ground Level, Mid-Mountain, and, perhaps, Sky Level Panoramic Team AQ, you now have vital information and a foundation for your Team CORE awareness. You can go through the same three elevations of awareness as you did in completing the measures. This helps you explain, interpret, deepen, and strengthen your Team AQ as you proceed through the Team AQ process.

Ground Level Awareness: This is meant to provide team members with feedback on their dynamics and the differences in how they respond to adversity and to provide the team with the Ground Level report on Team AQ (a sample was provided in Exhibit 9.5). Each member will gain insight into how his or her AQ and CORE compare with the team's norm, and what that implies in terms of his or her own behavior and contribution to the team's success. It is important that individual scores remain confidential and anonymous. In the Team AQ Process I provided you with some basic questions to establish Ground Level awareness. Exhibit 9.4.2 provides some additional guiding questions for team discussion as part of the Ground Level analysis on Team AQ.

The Ground Level AQ report will also provide team members with the opportunity to view the range of individual scores within the team. This will help them assess where they fall on the team continuum on AQ and each CORE dimension.

This report will give the team the fuel it needs to discuss how the

range of individual CORE responses affects the team's capacity to problem solve, innovate, reach good decisions, meet its objectives, and tap its
full capacity. It provides specific insight into hindrances to becoming a
true high-performance team. Tie the discussion to specific team requirements. If the team's charge is to innovate, then explore how the results
communicated in the Ground Level report might relate to the team's past,
current, and future success with and approach to new products. This discussion and awareness can lead to immediate improvements in how certain individuals respond to adversity and how the team approaches
challenges.

Mid-Mountain Awareness: Some of the most powerful discoveries come
from the results of the Mid-Mountain measure. This measurement provides direct insights into the team's pattern of response to challenges,
annoyances, frustrations, difficulties, problems, setbacks, uncertainties,
and tragedies. This can prove excellent fodder for substantive discussions
about how problems, challenges, and decisions are handled, and how the
way they are handled can be improved.

For example, let's say the medical center team mentioned at the beginning of this chapter discovered that its Mid-Mountain Team AQ was 20
points below the mean and that its CORE Profile revealed low Ownership.
These results and the following discussion would shed light on why these
intelligent, highly competent team members resorted to finger-pointing
and why it had been so difficult to get anyone to follow through on specific
actions. They could review how the team had responded to specific past
challenges and adversities, and how its CORE and AQ had created a Ripple
Effect throughout the organization. Once a team recognizes its role in causing such Ripple Effects, it may take its own Response Ability more seriously.

When the conversation is properly conducted, the insights derived
from the Ground Level report alone can provide some quick and powerful
transformations for your team.

As with the Ground Level report, the same steps can be followed to
assess the Team's CORE as reflected by the Mid-Mountain report you constructed from the preceding Exhibits. This assessment takes on a different
tone, since it is based on the team members' assessment of the team's—not
their own—challenges, and how the team responds to adversity. There is
less discussion about individual differences and more about the overall
team and its hardwired patterns.

People do not argue with their own data. Since they are the ones who assessed their team, they are unlikely to reject the results. The overall AQ will give them a gauge of how their team stacks up against others. The CORE Profile shows which areas of the team's Response Ability are strongest and weakest.

It can also be very useful to compare the results from the Ground Level and Mid-Mountain reports. The team can explore how the combination of individual scores compares with a team-wide measure. Does the team AQ exceed the average of its team members' AQs? In other words, to what extent is synergy just a buzzword? When, and to what extent, do Team AQ and CORE exceed the averages on the Ground Level report? Your answer indicates the degree to which the team is truly greater than the sum of its parts. The inverse is also true. Exhibit 9.4.3 provided some guiding questions for a Mid-Mountain team discussion.

When the Ground Level, individual-based team mean on AQ or specific CORE dimensions is greater than the Mid-Mountain mean, then something bad is afoot. In other words, there is *negative synergy*, or entropy, which means that productivity actually decreases when you form teams! This may sound absurd, but it is frequently true with teams. This is why many team experts argue that, even today, most teams are formed unnecessarily. If synergy is not present, why should the team exist? It takes courage to explore this question.

Sky Level Awareness: Sky Level, or Panoramic, Team AQ is the most comprehensive measure of how your team responds to adversity. By taking into account additional stakeholders, your team members learn how they and their ability to handle adversity are perceived by others. They can see which stakeholders have the strongest and weakest impressions and explore why these perceptions have been formed. They can also compare their profile against the stakeholders' and see if there are any apparent blind spots, or tendencies others perceive to which the team is blind. Sky Level awareness is the final step in Level One of strengthening Team AQ. Once you have the results to consider, talk your team through these questions to heighten awareness, Ownership, and learning.

The discussion phase of the Team AQ Process can be the richest and the most transformational. AQ provides a new framework for considering and exploring team interactions, behavior, successes, and failures. At the Sky Level, the stakeholders' ratings often jar loose even the most stubborn skeptics, since teams are ultimately accountable to others for specific out-puts. It is hard to ignore what others have to say about the team. Again, it is highly worthwhile to include external stakeholders in the discussion, since their insights might prove pivotal when establishing new, higher-AQ norms for how the team solves problems and makes decisions.

Once you have accurately assessed your Team AQ and CORE and have discussed this with your team (and perhaps its stakeholders), it is time to assess your team norms and how they hinder or further your ascent.

> Dependent people need others to get what they want. Independent people can get what they want through their own efforts. Interdependent people combine their own efforts with the efforts of others to achieve their greatest success.
>
> —Stephen Covey

Establishing High-AQ Norms

Part of the Team AQ Process involves taking stock of your current norms or assumed patterns of team conduct. Through frank team dialogue and the three levels of awareness, you can pinpoint your lower-AQ team norms. Examples include:

- Spending inordinate time on the downside of situations
- Blowing ideas out of the water before they have been fully con-sidered
- Making pessimism fashionable
- Assigning Ownership to others
- Pointing fingers, or getting obsessed with blame
- Taking few, if any, leaps of faith
- Being risk averse
- Letting others decide your fate
- Accepting learned helplessness in the face of daunting problems
- Becoming resigned or disengaged when adversity strikes
- Catastrophizing over situations that arise
- Enlarging every problem
- Using low-AQ language like impossible, no way, forever, everything is ruined, the whole project is doomed, etc.

Having members anonymously list what they consider to be any potential low-AQ norms is a good way to get honest input into what can be a politically thorny question. Share the list (no names attached) and have the team discuss and pinpoint the two or three norms that are most threatening and common.

Next, you will want to consider specific higher-AQ norms the team would like to institutionalize as it moves forward. The CORE profiles derived from all three levels of Team AQ are the logical starting points for discussing potential higher-AQ norms. Examples include:

- Focus on and discuss those facets of the situation we can control.
- Monitor our response to anything that arises.
- Include Response Ability as a discussion item on our team agendas.
- Come up with specific strategies to contain the Reach of each adversity.
- Force ourselves to envision life after the adversity has passed.
- Come up with specific strategies for getting past the adversity as quickly as possible.
- Discuss learning points—what we could do better next time to be even more successful.
- Mine the opportunities embedded in any adversity.

Add to your list those actions that are specific to your team and that enhance Team AQ. These actions might be related to limiting the Reach or Endurance of a specific challenge accompanying a specific project. Or, they may be specific strategies for taking more Control and Ownership of a given situation. They may be related to how you are approaching a specific change, person, obstacle, or impending event. Your answers will be a vital part of the Team AQ Process.

You are now ready for Level Two of strengthening Team AQ, through LEADing the team. This takes you to the next step of the Team AQ Process.

Level Two—LEADing the Team

One of the true benefits of the LEAD Sequence is that *anyone* can use it at *any time* within team interactions, with any kind of team. You need not be the designated leader, project head, or team facilitator to put these practical tools to use. They are as useful in your community school board meeting as in the think tank for the next Microsoft.

Team-building expert Chris Roland, Ph.D., of Roland-Diamond Associates, said one of the greatest threats to a team's effectiveness is "an unsafe environment . . . people are not willing to put their critical, sensitive issues on the table." Teams often are hindered, if not crippled, by lack of trust, subversive power struggles, or issues of who controls the interactions, flow, decisions, and outcomes. One of the true benefits of using the LEAD Sequence in a team setting is that it can help create a safe environment and take power issues out of the equation.

For leadership teams on which maintaining respect and power with your peers may be of ultimate importance, the LEAD Sequence is an excellent way to preserve the dignity of all members without coddling, getting distracted, or giving the squeaky wheel all of the grease. It will help members strategize, plan, and solve problems with greater honesty and respect.

The LEAD Sequence will help project or planning teams stay on course and strengthen their Response Ability as they maintain clarity, focus, and direction, regardless of what is thrown at them. Within cross-functional teams, the LEAD Sequence is an effective way to promote effective problem solving, decision making, and fairness among the members, who often represent diverse points of view.

How do your team members currently react when someone offers a response that you now know to be representing a lower-than-ideal AQ? Typically these lower-AQ team members are treated as a source of real irritation. As a result, they are generally confronted or even shunned and discounted. In any case, their dignity is compromised, as is their willingness to contribute at their full capability. Capacity is sapped, talent goes untapped, and destructive dynamics ensue.

These responses, while seemingly justified, are short-term solutions at best, with some long-term consequences. When responded to in such a way, low-AQ team members feel emotionally banished and are likely to withdraw or become increasingly antagonistic. They may begin to undermine the team, because that is the only way they can be perceived as significant. Remember: if a person cannot achieve positive significance, its dark sibling, *negative significance*, often becomes the alternative of choice. Some of the most destructive acts are performed in the name of negative significance.

Sadly, the literature on group communication and team dynamics has yet to offer a feasible strategy for preserving the dignity of all team members and immunizing the team against perceived negativity, while keeping lower-AQ members fully engaged. This is where the LEAD Sequence has unique value.

The LEAD Sequence is best exemplified in a real team's interaction, like the medical center team you read about at the beginning of this chapter, or within your own mixed-AQ team. You may recall that the medical center leadership team was under enormous pressure to restructure their medical center under daunting new budget constraints. In the opening scene, Janice appeared to be dragging down this high-potential team into a low-performance team. Her AQ and the Team AQ were dampening the team's resolve, problem solving, and decision making. Low AQ polluted the dynamics. Once we taught this team about AQ and the LEAD Sequence we saw differences in its interactions (see page 246). Consider how the LEAD Sequence can positively affect the team meeting from the beginning of this chapter. Reread the original interaction on page 207.

This team was behaving normally by confronting and trying to banish Janice for her "negative" comments. But Janice has a lot of wisdom and experience to contribute, which is lost if she's no longer a part of the group. The team's Existing Capacity had been shrunk, and the room was filled with tension. Team members express their discomfort to me privately during the break. Janice was frustrated and later on the verge of tears. She became angry, hurt, and temporarily resigned.

The Ripple Effect of Janice's low-AQ response did not end there. She probably took her negativity home with her that night. What do you think she might have said when her boss asked, "So, how's it going with the rollout plan?" How do you think her intensified pessimism might have affected her coworkers over the course of the ensuing hours and days?

One person can have a dramatic effect, good or bad, on his or her coworkers and organization, regardless of title. Janice was unintentionally and adamantly seeking to validate her low-AQ perspective. If her team banishes her, she will go to others and share her response. She will plant the seeds of her cancer in the fertile soil of people's doubts and concerns, dragging down the chances that the change will be approached or perceived positively. You can see this coming out in her teammates. It is difficult to overestimate the fallout of a low AQ.

Let's take the same interaction and situation and apply the LEAD Sequence. Notice the difference in the dynamics as well as the direction of the team. In this example, we will use different facets of the LEAD Sequence as needed to keep the team on track and focus its energies toward problem solving. We will also add some more team members into the interaction so that you can see how anyone can be a LEADer even with more than one low-AQ individual on the same team. Here is the team scenario with the LEAD Sequence:

> TOM (TEAM LEADER): Okay, everybody, as you know, today is a big day. We need to get a lot accomplished and come up with some concrete actions for moving toward our goal. No more sitting on our hands. Now, here's—.
>
> BOB: I have to object to this false sense of urgency. We have been gathering data, and we need more data to make the decisions we're being asked to make. Now, I think—
>
> JARED: Wait, Bob, you said something important here (**L—Listen to the Response**). You indicated the need to add more data. Now, we're clearly the ones who have to come up with the plan, that's our charge *(others nod)* (**E—Establish Accountability**). Tom, could you clarify the need for the urgency, and what evidence there is that says this *has to* be completed now (**A—Analyze the Evidence**)?
>
> TOM: Thanks, Jared, that's a fair question. If we don't solve this now, we will face another $5 million loss in the next two months, which will make it even harder to pull out later. We also have some mandates from the Board of Regents to have a plan by February 15.
>
> JARED: Okay, so specifically, what can we do to help minimize that loss in the next few months (**Do Something!**)?
>
> JANICE: Can't you guys see this is impossible? I mean we're being asked to cut tens of millions from our budgets while preserving the quality of care and the integrity of our academic programs. I think it's time we just admit to ourselves our days of being world-class are over! *(Tom shakes his head slowly from side to side.)* And we're going to lose our prized faculty, because this is just the beginning—
>
> JOE: I don't mean to interrupt, but, I'm sorry, I have to disagree with Janice. *(Janice rolls her eyes and slumps back.)* The sky is not falling. We're not the first group of people to face this kind of challenge: we may be the most dysfunctional, but—

DENISE: Janice expressed some real concerns that we really need to address (**Listen**). Janice, is it fair to say that if anyone is to take a crack at this, it has to be us (**Establish Accountability**)?

JANICE: I think the Board of Regents are the ones who should fix this, not us. . . .

DENISE: So, even as the leadership team, we have no accountability whatsoever in this entire situation for making it even a little bit better?

JANICE: Well, I guess we have some.

DENISE: That's important to point out. We have at least some, if not the *most*, accountability for finding a way to solve this situation. Now wait. Janice, you said this was impossible. You are right, this is extremely tough. But we need to ask ourselves, what evidence is there that says this *has to* be impossible (**Analyze**)?

JANICE: All the evidence in the world! Name one institution like ours who has been able to pull it off!

DENISE (*TURNING TO THE REST OF THE GROUP*): Janice is right. This *could* be formidable. And no one we know of has done exactly what we are trying to do. So, this is tough. But what evidence is there that it has to be *impossible*?

JANICE: Well, maybe not impossible, but—

DENISE: Good point, Janice. The other point you raised was critical (**Listen**). We could really damage our reputation if we (**Establish Accountability**) don't do this right. But let's look at this. What evidence is there that this *has to* compromise our world-class status (**Analyze**)?

SEVERAL MEMBERS: None.

DENISE: Great! So since this is our charge and we can influence the outcome (**Establish Accountability**), specifically, what could we do to cut costs while maintaining our integrity and quality of care (**Do Something!**)?

TOM: One thing I can do is talk to my friend at the Mayo Clinic and see what they did.

FRIEDA (*MOVING TO FLIP CHART*): Okay, why don't I write that one down under the information category? What other information can we seek to help us speed this up and do it right (**Do Something!**)?

MARIO: Why don't we just wait and see what the Board of Regents is going to do? No matter what we come up with, they're going to chop us to little pieces anyway. They're making the big bucks, why don't we let them fix it?

FRIEDA: Let's consider Mario's suggestion. Mario, we are all charged with this enormous task. You're right, it'd be a lot less of a headache for us to have the Regents handle it. But, before we do, maybe we should consider our accountability. What facet or facets of this situation do we want to shoulder to make sure it gets done right (**Establish Accountability**)? Mario?

MARIO: I guess we're the only ones who can address critical care—

FRIEDA: Good, so you feel some Ownership for that, Mario?

MARIO: Yeah, sure.

FRIEDA: Good. What else do we want to take some Ownership for improving?

And so on.

In this example, there were several instances when the interaction could have stopped the team's momentum. Instead, different members used the LEAD Sequence to preserve the team members' dignity and restore the problem-solving mind-set. Notice that Janice's and Mario's contributions were acknowledged and given real significance because they became the focus of the discussion for a brief while. However, their apparent negativity had no effect on team morale, productivity, or momentum. In fact, in this scenario, unlike the first, Jared, Joe, Frieda, and Denise were able to leverage others' contribution to move the team toward meaningful action. None of them is the designated team leader. They are simply team members who know the LEAD Sequence and want to help their team succeed.

Unnecessary and damaging AQ-related conflict was skillfully avoided, and the team trust was strengthened. Each member is now likely to feel more comfortable voicing concerns, and to do so with a mind-set of *resolving* the situation rather than whining or complaining.

This is an example of how the LEAD Sequence can work when there is more than one low-AQ team member, a situation which creates a low-AQ team climate and hinders problem solving, decision making, and innovation.

Employing the LEAD Sequence with a lower-AQ team requires a gentle relentlessness. Low-AQ people often do not hear questions in the way you intended to ask them, which may require that you repeat them or come at them from a different angle, as Jared, Joe, Janice, and Denise did in the example.

LEADing Teams Out of a Crisis

The LEAD Sequence can be used as the centerpiece of a crisis-resolution model that fosters continuous improvement and agility when they matter most. It involves flushing out the lowest-AQ reality right away so that it can be effectively countered with real evidence and meaningful action. There are five steps to the simple and effective process.

1. *Define the problem.* The team must define the problem as precisely as possible. If, in anticipation of an increased demand for services, a team leader says, "We will be besieged," that statement would elicit a very different response than "We will face double to triple the demand for our services starting tomorrow." That's a precise definition of a problem.

2. *Lay out the worst-case scenario.* This step seemingly goes against the inherent optimism of a high-AQ team. However, there is great value in times of crisis to briefly describing the worst-case scenario so that you have specific words, fears, and assumptions to work with right away. Ask, "What is the worst thing that can happen here?" And keep asking until this low-AQ monster is fully illuminated.

   Example: "We could anger our customers, drop our quality ratings, abandon a lot of shipments, all have heart attacks, and go out of business."

3. *Employ the LEAD Sequence.* In this case, Step 2 above took care of L = Listen to the Response, and sparked a low-AQ response, which you can now dispute.

   E = Establish Accountability by asking,

   Example: "Whose job is it to make this better?" Or, "What facet of this situation are we responsible for improving, even the smallest amount?" (This should take seconds to determine.)

A = Analyze the Evidence that supports each facet of the worst-case scenario.

Example: "If we do not handle this well, the worst-case scenario could come true. Despite all the evidence that we *could* experience this fate, what evidence is there that we *have to* anger our customers? What evidence is there we *have to* drop in quality ratings? What evidence is there that we will go out of business *for sure*?" (This should take one to three minutes.)

D = Do Something!

Example: "Specifically, what could we do to minimize the chance that our customers will be angered? What else? [Make a list.] Specifically, what could we do to sustain our quality ratings? Specifically, what could we do to make sure we not only stay in business but ultimately benefit from this adversity?" (This should take two to five minutes.)

4. *Employ the Action Funnel.* Once you have a complete list of capacity actions, narrow them down using the Action Funnel provided in Chapter 5, or as follows:

   • Of these actions, which one do we want to commit to doing first?
   • Specifically, when do we expect to have this action commenced and/or completed?
   • Specifically, how can each of us help make this first step succeed as quickly as possible?

5. *List the lessons.* Once the avalanche has subsided and the crisis has passed, the final step is to ask:

   • What did we do particularly well?
   • Specifically, what could we do better if we were to face a situation of this nature in the future?
   • If we were to give advice to people about to face the same adversity, what would we offer to help them navigate this challenge as quickly and effectively as possible?

The LEAD Sequence is particularly powerful in guiding a team toward its ascent because the team cannot *help* but move forward. It extricates the members from genuine hopelessness and guides them toward meaningful action even in times of severe crisis. Resistance and initial negativity are accepted as part of the process, because individual and collective buy-in grows as the team moves toward specific actions. But when the team uses these problem-solving methods, pessimism, cynicism, and negativity *cannot* hobble its ascent. Exhibit 9.17 outlines some additional benefits of using the LEAD Sequence within your team.

Consider the following benefits of implementing the LEAD Sequence within your team(s):

1. It preserves the dignity of all team members.
2. It extracts the valuable facets of a member's comments and contribution.
3. It preserves the team's momentum.
4. It is a compassionate problem-solving model.
5. It alters team norms toward a more disciplined and constructive problem-solving mind-set.
6. It eliminates whining, complaining, and negativity.
7. It leads to well-thought-out decisions and precise action.
8. Team members feel significant and energized.
9. It can be customized to work with any problem, challenge, setback, or adversity.
10. It creates a safe environment.
11. It reduces political game playing.

Exhibit 9.17 Using LEAD with Teams

PUTTING IT ALL TOGETHER

Now that you have learned about the steps of the Team AQ Process in detail, you have the opportunity to complete each step within your own team.

In twenty years of studying group and team dynamics, I have found that the Team AQ Process is the most consistently effective method for strengthening team relationships and achieving task-related success. You will find it useful for any kind of team. Teams using AQ and LEAD to enhance their effectiveness today include management teams, leadership teams, functional teams, project teams, cross-functional teams, design teams, sales teams, and planning teams. As you complete the Team AQ Process and employ the LEAD Sequence to rewire teammates' approach to adversity, you will see dramatic and sustainable gains in team performance and morale, as well as experience the deep gratification of helping others to ascend.

These skills and insights will form a natural bridge to your next level of the ascent—assessing and strengthening Cultural AQ.

Topographical Map of Chapter 9
Building Climbing Teams

A team is only as strong as its AQ, regardless of its talents and capacity. Like individual AQ, Team AQ determines the strength and health of the team's operating system and its ability to perform under adverse conditions.

Three Elevations to measure Team AQ:

Ground Level—Individual AQ scores within a Team

Mid-Mountain—The Team Adversity Response Profile

Sky Level—Panoramic view of Team AQ, which includes various stakeholders

Use the LEAD Sequence to
- preserve team members' dignity
- improve team dynamics
- solve problems
- make decisions
- engage everyone
- strengthen Team AQ

A Crisis Resolution Model using The LEAD Sequence includes these steps:
1) Define the problem.
2) Lay out the worst-case scenario.
3) Employ the LEAD Sequence.
4) Employ the Action Funnel.
5) List the lessons.

Our
Ground Level Team AQ is _____(insert score)
Mid-Mountain Team AQ is _____(insert score)
Sky Level Team AQ is _____(insert score)

BUILDING A CLIMBING CULTURE

Character cannot be developed in ease and quiet. Only through experience of trial and suffering can the soul be strengthened, vision cleared, ambition inspired, and success achieved.

—Helen Keller

I WRITE THESE pages on an airplane, sitting next to a suntanned, bespectacled gentleman who had just climbed the Grand Teton after two previous attempts. In addition to being a mountaineer, Arthur Lewis is a senior programmer for Prodigy, a prominent on-line service company. I had noticed Arthur before we became seatmates. Because the passengers on our flight had not been able to board the plane from the gate at Los Angeles International Airport, we were driven several miles in buses to another gate, which caused unforeseen delays and consternation. The first bus was packed to the hinges, forcing many of us onto a second and a third, creating additional delays.

Most people appeared stressed and disconcerted; however, Arthur was uniquely calm and seemed a bit amused by the whole turn of events. He watched as those around him sweated, complained, and catastrophized. He patiently let the more frenetic travelers get seated before he slid into a window seat with his climbing pack at his side. Arthur had already faced an earlier cancellation with a five-hour delay. Despite it all, Arthur remained focused, energized, and unaffected. Is this the kind of person you want on your Climbing Team?

When I asked him why he climbs, his answer revealed some of the things we seek in the people we hire. He leaned over and explained passionately, but with a grin, "When you put yourself at risk, you realize how precious life is. Climbing is a celebration of life, which makes me grateful for every day. I love the fact that challenges like the Grand Teton dwarf my day-to-day difficulties. Each day, I solve problems as a programmer, and when you rock-climb, you solve problems and must go around difficulties constantly. There is no doubt that climbing mountains helps me climb through challenges at work."

I asked Arthur what he would do if his employer, Prodigy, were bought out tomorrow, and his ideas could not be implemented because of new levels of bureaucracy. "If I was really convinced I couldn't penetrate the layers, I'd be looking for a job. Life's too short." I asked about his significant stock options and impending retirement. His gaze intensified.

"It's not about money," he replied. "It's about impact. I need to work for a place that makes a difference." This is how Climbers think!

You need not be the Lead Climber, CEO, or an organizational development specialist to influence the resilience of the culture where you work. By applying the insights and tools provided in this book, and the Cultural AQ Cycle included in this chapter in particular, you can have a *significant* impact. Of course, it is easier to influence the culture of a small enterprise, but this can be accomplished in larger organizations as well.

Within larger organizations, the cultural topography can vary dramatically, from high ledges bustling with Climbers to chasms that are void of morale and productivity where good people and resources fall, never to be seen again. Creating a topographical map of your culture will help you uncover the high-AQ pockets and low-AQ ravines.

To take on Cultural AQ and complete the Cultural AQ Cycle you must combine and apply the skills and concepts you've gathered throughout this book. This chapter and cycle will, therefore, pull together all the elements of AQ to create your own cultural climbing gear.

You probably have noticed that every time you add a person to a group, the complexity of the relationships and decision making doubles. The same is true of the patterns of behavior within an organization as you evolve from individuals, to pairs, to teams, and eventually to cultures. Despite the apparent complexity, anyone can influence Cultural AQ—the most powerful level at which you can affect your organization. According to the Cultural AQ Cycle (see Exhibit 10.1), you must first consider your *organization's aspirations*. Next, to strengthen Cultural AQ you must *assess its current state, or Cultural AQ*. Assessing your Cultural AQ involves a much richer and more multifaceted approach than those used in Chapter 9 to assess Team AQ.

When you assess Cultural AQ, you are reading the cultural topography of your organization, with all its variations, factors, and unique characteristics. For this reason, much of this chapter is dedicated to providing you with the tools required to complete this portion of the Cultural AQ Cycle.

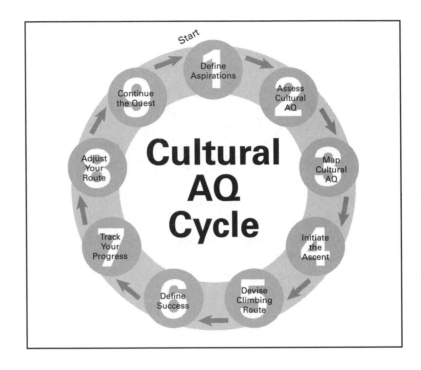

Exhibit 10.1 Cultural AQ Cycle

There is a tremendous personal, practical value to assessing your Cultural AQ. It provides you with new information about your workplace. Cultural AQ also gives you priceless information on how to succeed within your organization's norms, values, and so on. It also helps you assess the degree of alignment you feel between yourself and your organization's Cultural AQ. As in any relationship, AQ plays a deep and pivotal role in the health and sustainability of your fit with your workplace.

The following pages will show you several ways to assess your Cultural AQ or topography with the AQ Cultural Glance, along with a variety of commonsense approaches to understanding your organizational operating system. You can use this information to assess those areas in which your culture can be most easily and powerfully strengthened, and those in which it is currently most effective when faced with adversity.

You must then *map your Cultural AQ* by graphing your Cultural CORE and constructing your own Cultural AQ Profile. This will give you insights into specific cultural strengths, weaknesses, and tendencies in light of which you can decide future strategies.

You will then *initiate your cultural ascent* by drawing from a list of Twenty-two Ways to Upgrade Your Cultural AQ. From the list you will *devise a climbing route* based on your initial strategies for improvement. You must *define success*, so you can know when you have made meaningful progress in strengthening your Cultural AQ. Like any Climber, you must *track your progress* along the way, so you can *adjust your route* accordingly to stay on track and *continue your quest.*

DEFINE YOUR ASPIRATIONS

The first step in the Cultural AQ Cycle is to define your organizational aspirations. Pinpoint where you are striving to go and what you are striving to become. Be precise and bold in your vision. Ideally, your answers should reflect the sentiments of the organization's leadership and workforce. Before you can move to the next step of the Cultural AQ Cycle, we need to define culture and Cultural AQ.

CULTURE AND CULTURAL AQ DEFINED

Edgar Schein, a longtime expert on corporate culture, described culture as the interlocking system of attitudes, beliefs, norms, rules, values, and assumptions we use to guide our language, behavior, and decisions. Simply put, your culture is your organizational operating system, because it is the spoken and unspoken code of conduct that determines how things really get done. It defines the work you do. Exhibit 10.2 displays some of the facets of your culture that shape its propensity to Camp or Climb.

Based on this definition, how do you rate *your* culture? Does it resemble a campground? Does it possess the resilience, fortitude, and persistence of the Climber poised to thrive in difficult, chaotic, and uncertain times?

Your answers may initially tell you a lot about your Cultural AQ. This ultimately forms your organizational operating system and determines your agility, optimism, innovation, problem-solving ability, and cultural identity.

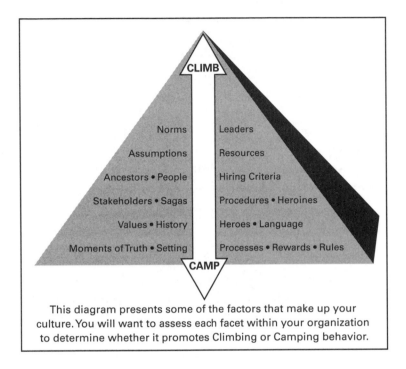

This diagram presents some of the factors that make up your culture. You will want to assess each facet within your organization to determine whether it promotes Climbing or Camping behavior.

Exhibit 10.2 Cultural Scan

ASSESSING YOUR CULTURAL AQ

No matter what kind of in-house analysis you may have conducted in the past, this will be your *first* Cultural AQ. There are a variety of ways to get at your organization's operating system, some more in-depth than others. Let us begin with some simple and powerful insights into *your* cultural operating system.

The Communication of AQ

Messages are made of symbols or words. Communication is the flow of cultural symbols. Embedded within your organization's formal and informal communications are some powerful and useful indicators of your Cultural AQ. Pay keen attention to the following facets of communication.

Leaders' Rhetoric: Leaders create and disseminate the vocabulary of an organization's culture. You can probably think of some terms that you associate with a specific leader, terms that are now pervasive within your culture. An effective leader uses language that persuades people to ascend to levels they might otherwise never reach.

What do *your* leaders say, and *how* do they say it? Specifically, you will want to listen to their CORE whenever they describe any challenge, setback, or difficulty. What does their language say about what is or isn't acceptable behavior? When Paul Mayes, European vice president of sales for Cypress Semiconductor, was faced with repeated refusals from Nokia (the largest company in Europe) for larger deals, his response was, "It's not a matter of if, but when. Even if it takes years, we will find a way to win their business." Listen to your leaders' CORE.

As you assess your leaders, ask yourself how much their language instills a sense of Control (see Exhibit 10.3). Do their words foster Ownership in those around them? How well do their words contain the Reach and Endurance of the adversity? In moments of truth, when they are facing real adversity, how do they respond? Do they ever lose control, rant and rave, or resort to tantrums? When stressed, does the leader have outbursts? Or, does the leader remain calm, with a strong resolve to deal with the adversity?

It is important to note that in addition to influencing Cultural AQ, a leader's rhetoric can also be influenced by Cultural AQ. It works both ways.

Assessing Cultural AQ Through the Rhetoric of the Leader

When adversity strikes:

- How effectively does the leader communicate what you can *Control* or influence in a situation to make it better?
- To what extent does the leader take *Ownership* for bettering the situation, regardless of its cause?
- How well does the leader limit the *Reach* of the adversity in how it is described and in terms of its predicted fallout?
- How effectively does the leader limit how long the adversity *endures* by seeing past it and helping others to do the same?
- What metaphors or analogies does this leader use in describing the organization or a specific adversity?

Exhibit 10.3 **Assessing the Leader's CORE**

Listen to the metaphors people use to describe their endeavors and the challenges they face. Do they indicate a high- or low-AQ culture?

Joe Kaempfer, chief executive of BAA McArthurGlen UK Ltd., now the largest outlet shopping center developer in Europe, introduced a new way of shopping to the United Kingdom and the European continent. He envisioned architecturally splendid and tastefully designed factory-outlet villages. Joe described his team's success at introducing the new shopping concept as being "salmon-like swimming upstream. We swim relentlessly. Then, when we hit a calm pool, we position, strategize, and rejuvenate for the next leap. It can be grueling, but we have reached and will continue to reach our destiny. Frankly, I have little patience for complaining. Deal with it, and get it done, do you know what I mean?"

This is a high-AQ metaphor for his organization's collective endeavor. It demonstrates Control and Ownership, while limiting the Reach and Endurance of the adversity.

In contrast, a vice president of a prominent pharmaceutical company that had recently experienced an onslaught of lawsuits described her division as follows: "We are like a multiple-stab-wound victim. No matter which wound you try to cauterize, another will keep gushing." This low-Control response indicates a far-reaching, long-enduring adversity.

The metaphors and responses a leader exhibits profoundly influence the Cultural AQ. High-AQ leaders articulate the ascent, passionately attack the challenge, and shape the Climbing Team to move forward and up. They may scare or inspire Campers. Some may be afraid of losing the stability and comfort they have fought so hard to maintain. They may leave to find another place to stake their tent. Others will feel compelled to join in the ascent. In either case, the Campground is likely to become history.

Leaders' language can be found in a variety of media, including Web sites, annual reports, meetings, conversations, corporate memos, E-mails, presentations, videos, and interviews in newspapers, magazines, television, and radio. Even though you may not always be able to influence your leader's rhetoric, you can study it to get a read on the Cultural AQ and influence your own language.

You can shape your culture every day regardless of your title. Apply the questions provided in Exhibit 10.3 to your own language, and you will help shrink the Campground and upgrade your culture.

Putting the Cultural Scan into Practice: The language used throughout your workforce can also be a bountiful source of information about Cultural AQ. Just as adversity shapes an individual's character, it also shapes the operating system of your culture. The exchange of symbols or language throughout the workforce regarding adversity is particularly important to understanding the operating system. There are some specific ways to explore this language (see Exhibit 10.4).

Wear your AQ lenses. Go through your day with an AQ lens; look for and listen to the CORE response to challenges, even annoyances, as they inevitably arise through the natural course of events. You should be able to discern whether these responses indicate higher versus lower Cultural AQ. Listen for the cultural topography. What areas of your organization seem to have the highest AQ? In what areas do people speak most confidently and with the grittiest determination? Which are the cultural chasms or pits of whining filled with hopeless or jaded Campers? How do people in different areas of your organization respond to an unanticipated change? How well are they dealing with their current changes and uncertainties?

AQylize meetings. Analyze the resilience demonstrated by different groups as you attend meetings where some difficult news is announced. How do people respond? What sort of questions are asked? Are these questions focused on fears or on possibilities?

Do you recall the following dialogue from Chapter 9?

TOM (TEAM LEADER): Okay, everybody, as you know, today is a big day. We need to get a lot accomplished and come up with some concrete actions for moving toward our goal *(high Control, strong Ownership Endurance)*. No more sitting on our hands *(high Ownership)*. Now, here's—

BOB: I have to object to this false sense of urgency. We have been gathering data, and we need more data in order to make the decisions we're being asked to make. Now, I think—*(strong Ownership, but weaker on Reach and Endurance)*.

JANICE: Can't you guys see this is impossible *(low Control)*? I mean, we're being asked to cut tens of millions from our budgets while preserving the quality of care and the integrity of our academic programs. I think it's time we just admit to ourselves our days of being world-class are over *(terribly low Endurance and*

Reach)! (Tom shakes his head slowly side to side.) And we're going to lose our prized faculty, because this is just the beginning—*(low Reach)*.

JOE: I don't mean to interrupt, but, I'm sorry, I have to disagree with Janice. *(Janice rolls her eyes and slumps back.)* The sky is not falling *(higher Reach)*. We're not the first group of people to face this kind of challenge; we may be the most dysfunctional, but—

MARIO: We can't get this done under this kind of pressure. I think this is the wrong way to go about this whole—*(low Control, moderate Ownership)*.

DAVE: In orthopedics we tried this and it failed there, so we need to—*(low Control and Reach)*.

JANICE (SLAMMING THE TABLE WITH THE PALM OF HER HAND): That's my point exactly!

As you AQylize this interaction, what do you notice? What words would you circle that indicate a lower-than-ideal AQ for Janice or Mario? Notice the italicized notes coding the different statements and the Ripple Effect those statements have upon the team and its productivity.

In your meetings, how do people describe authority figures or those with power? Are they seen as insurmountable obstacles to getting a task completed? Are they "the ones doing this to us"? Or, are they seen as vital resources for the ascent? Is energy wasted whining over the injustice of it all? Or do people refuse to accept injustice and make sure their contribution is meaningful and recognized as such? Listen to the words people choose when discussing something that went wrong. Do people take Ownership, pause, learn, and move on, or is there instant deflection and blame? Blame can happen with the most trivial issues.

I remember when the topic of a new copy machine came up in a meeting of administrative staff that I was observing. One of the more senior assistants announced, "The reason we will never get funding for this purchase—or any purchase, for that matter—is that the upper management has it in for us and has had it in for us ever since we tried to implement some changes around here." Others joined the frenzy, and the next half hour was spent discussing the various ways the company's management was determined to see them fail. Needless to say, this low-Control, low-Ownership, far-reaching, long-lasting response to the adversity killed any effort to request a new machine.

AQylize customer service or anyone on the front line with clients. More than ever, how these frontline people treat the customer has a more profound impact on the business than much of what happens in the executive suites. For this reason, you must know how the customer service folks respond when someone is absolutely rude or unfair. What is said when their computer system goes down or a request simply cannot be fulfilled at that moment? What happens when there is an unexpected flood of upset customers? How easily flustered are they when they face adversities? To what extent do they demonstrate the agility to reroute by improvising whatever it takes to delight the customer? Or do they justify themselves by giving logical reasons why the customer's request cannot be met in a timely manner, thereby unleashing a self-fulfilling prophecy? How much control do you give them to solve problems, or can they hide behind some substantial reasons why things cannot be done?

When I called the main customer service number for one of the better-known home-accessories stores to trace a long-overdue delivery, the customer service person spent several minutes asking for information. I figured she must be pinning down the precise location of my order. However, once she had gathered every imaginable piece of data, she firmly declared, "I'm sorry, I have no information on your shipment, sir." When I asked her why she couldn't find any information, she replied, "That's in furniture. They're a whole different department. You will have to call them yourself." I asked if her computer screen told her anything about where my shipment might be. She paused and let out a long sigh. "Well, even if it did, I'm really not supposed to answer questions about furniture. I'm in accessories. Besides, if what it says here turns out to be wrong, you will just take it out on me, right?" Obviously, she did not work in a high-Control, high-Ownership culture.

Seek the elders. How do the influential, seasoned veterans respond to events? Chances are they represent and have shaped the culture over time. If you want to know how Norwegian food affects health, study Norwegians. If you want to know about your Cultural AQ, go to those who have been consuming and propagating the culture for the longest time.

How do the veterans describe the organization to others? Does their style and tone emit pride, determination, and accomplishment? Or does it communicate resignation, compromise, and disillusionment? When I worked with a now-defunct division of Honeywell in the early 1980s, I remember a thirty-five-year veteran describing the company in this way: "Look out that window, Paul. See that Chevy pickup truck? We're like that truck—no awards for style, speed, performance, or value—we're just basic, solid, and we eventually get the job done." The other elders in the room nodded in agreement. His analogy with the truck said it all. Back then, Honeywell was a third-quartile performer, and its leaders struggled for years to shake up the campground and get back to the mountain.

AQylize what is written. Written documents often capture language that can provide useful insights into your Cultural AQ. You can find these cultural clues in annual reports, memos, marketing materials, announcements, updates, E-mails, correspondence, informational documents, policy manuals, and so on.

Try this exercise: Using the following excerpts from an internal memo from Microsoft founder Bill Gates, circle and label every AQ-related word or phrase. I circled a couple of phrases as examples. Would you characterize this as a higher- or lower-AQ message? Specifically, what CORE dimensions do you find to support your conclusion?

> Redmond, Wash., July 21, 1998—Microsoft just completed another amazing fiscal year, with revenue of $14.5 billion, a 28% increase over 1997. Our leadership in developing software that improves people's lives is more evident today than ever before. The computer industry is changing the world, and great software is at the center of this transformation. Yet in a business where technological change is constant, we cannot stand still. So today I want to talk about some of our exciting goals, and let you know how I am broadening Microsoft's management team to achieve them. . . .
>
> We are now entering a new phase—one that finds us with greater opportunities and challenges than ever before. Companies and employees everywhere are realizing the power of an information infrastructure that manages the flow of knowledge and data within a corporation—what we call a Digital Nervous System—and which allows it to leverage that knowledge more effectively than ever before. At the same time, people are starting to adopt a Web Lifestyle. No longer are they using Web only as a source of occasional information; they are routinely using it to pay bills, buy cars, check movie schedules, book restaurants and plan vacations. The Web is becoming a central part of lives. And

at the heart of all this—at the center of communication and commerce—is software. Microsoft will work in partnership with other industry leaders to provide people with great software that will make a difference to how they work, learn and play. . . .

The opportunities for all of us to contribute to this new phase are immense. We are just at the start of the digital age. The original vision of "a computer on every desk and in every home" will only be fulfilled by your work. We will look back on today's computers and software as unnatural and incredibly rudimentary. . . .

We need to use advanced technology to make our Internet sites the best. Every one of these goals requires work across several of our product teams. I will measure myself by how much I can facilitate ambitious goals that will help customers and put us further ahead if we move quickly. . . .

Microsoft is almost a quarter-century old, but we are just at the beginning. The future makes me very excited about my job and working with all of the Microsoft team to continue to surprise the world with our achievements. We can all be incredibly proud of what we've built so far. But the future opportunities will far surpass everything we've achieved to date. I'm more enthusiastic about and committed to Microsoft than I've ever been.

Now take one of your organization's memos and repeat the process. To what extent do these documents and the words you circled communicate higher- or lower-AQ intentions, behavior, language, and direction? How do these statements (formal communication) compare with what *really* goes on (informal rules)?

Assessing Cultural AQ

Wear your AQ lenses. Look and listen for how people describe and respond to everything from small annoyances to major disasters.

AQylize meetings. Listen to the words people choose in how they describe people with power, upset customers, obstacles, challenges, problems, and frustrations. Take away the words: what is the tone or feel of the room when adversity strikes?

AQylize the front line. Go to those who are on the front line with customers. How do they respond when overwhelmed? What effect is adversity having upon them—their demeanor and their health?

Ask the elders. How do the seasoned veterans respond to adversity? Is there resignation or is there pride?

AQylize written documents. Circle all CORE- and AQ-related words. What does this communicate about your culture? How well does your culture live up to how leaders, marketing, and recruiting folks describe it to others?

Exhibit 10.4 AQylize the Language

In addition to these methods for examining your culture qualitatively, there are also some useful ways to examine and measure your culture quantitatively.

ASSESSING YOUR CULTURAL AQ: THE AQ CULTURAL GLANCE

As a starting point in getting a *quantitative assessment* of your cultural topography, consider the AQ Cultural Glance in Exhibits 10.5 to 10.8. Even this abbreviated version of the full AQ Cultural Profile will provide a useful platform for assessing your culture more closely and seeing how the results compare with the previous communication exercises. It starts what should be a meaningful conversation.

Answer each of the following questions by circling your best and first response.

1) How effectively do people in your organization deal with unexpected challenges or setbacks?

1   2   3   4   5   6   7   8   9   10
Terribly   Extremely well

2) How likely is it that people will be demoralized by an unexpected turn of events or an impending change?

1   2   3   4   5   6   7   8   9   10
Extremely   Extremely
likely   unlikely

3) When adversity strikes (no matter how bad it is), to what extent do people tend to focus and act upon those facets that they can positively influence?

1   2   3   4   5   6   7   8   9   10
Not at all   Completely

4) When adversity strikes, how likely are people to give up?

1   2   3   4   5   6   7   8   9   10
Extremely   Extremely
likely   unlikely

5) When adversity strikes, how likely are people to step up to improve the situation, regardless of its cause?

1   2   3   4   5   6   7   8   9   10
Extremely   Extremely
unlikely   likely

6) How likely are people to resort to blaming others or deflecting accountability?

1   2   3   4   5   6   7   8   9   10
Extremely   Extremely
likely   unlikely

7) When adversity strikes, how likely are people to let the adversity reach over into or poison other areas of the job, team, or organization?

1   2   3   4   5   6   7   8   9   10
Extremely   Extremely
likely   unlikely

8) When adversity strikes, how likely are people to keep it in its place?

1   2   3   4   5   6   7   8   9   10
Extremely   Extremely
unlikely   likely

9) When adversity strikes, how likely are people to let it drag on?

1   2   3   4   5   6   7   8   9   10
Extremely   Extremely
likely   unlikely

10) How likely are people to see and get past complex challenges?

1   2   3   4   5   6   7   8   9   10
Extremely   Extremely
unlikely   likely

Exhibit 10.5 **The AQ Cultural Glance (Part One)**

Total all of your answers and multiply by 2 to get this snapshot measure of your Cultural AQ. Compare your results with the ranges shown below.

Question

#1____ + #3____ + #5____ + #7____ + #9 =____

#2____ + #4____ + #6____ + #8____ + #10 =____

TOTAL 1–10 =____ × 2.0 = **AQ**

155–200 **The High-AQ, Response-Able Culture.** You may have a relatively high-AQ Culture. Before you celebrate, ask yourself what numbers you would get if you asked these questions of people from all walks of your organization? To what extent do you suffer from high-altitude blindness? The higher you go, the harder it is to distinguish your own perceptions from what is real. If everyone's answers match yours, you are probably a high-AQ Culture capable of attracting and nurturing Climbers.

138–154 **Moderately High-AQ Culture.** Five years ago you might have been elated with these scores and how people deal with adversity. Today, you know you need a more resilient culture to withstand and learn from the mounting challenges. You do well with most challenges but remain vulnerable to the complexity, uncertainty, and difficulties that now define life.

113–137 **Moderate-AQ Culture.** You probably have your fair share of Campers, and their tent stakes are firmly implanted. Although you may be considered "successful," that status is in danger. Change is difficult, as is hanging on to your Climbers. People get beaten up unnecessarily by daily challenges.

96–112 **Moderately Low-AQ Culture.** You probably have a Campground on your hands. People are happy to maintain the status quo, if not adamant about it. Change is brutally slow. People are tapping a low percentage of their available potential and do not do well with adversity. The uncertainty and complexity that now define your reality are taking a toll on your people.

20–95 **Low-AQ Culture.** Climbers reroute for more promising conditions and prospects. Challenges become problems, and problems may become tragedies. People get mired down, if not depressed. Sick days and turnover are high, and loyalty is low. Blaming, whining, and helplessness may be rampant. The majority of potential goes untapped. Attempts at empowerment fail. Leaders are frustrated and possibly confounded.

See where your Cultural AQ score falls within the organization-wide range of scores. See how your Cultural AQ compares with your Team AQ (Chapter 9), and your individual AQ (Chapter 3).

Cultural AQ Score____ Org. Range of Scores____ Team AQ____
My AQ____

Score your CORE: To derive the CORE Profile for your organization, consider the simple scoring key provided below.

C = Questions 3–4, × 2.5   Org. Score____ Team Score____ My Score____

O = Questions 5–6, × 2.5   Org. Score____ Team Score____ My Score____

R = Questions 7–8, × 2.5   Org. Score____ Team Score____ My Score____

E = Questions 9–10, × 2.5   Org. Score____ Team Score____ My Score____

***Exhibit 10.6* The AQ Cultural Glance (Part Two)**

The following questions will help you interpret your Cultural AQ. Take a few minutes to follow this process and address these questions.

Your Score

1) What range did your score fall within?
2) What does this say about your organization and its prospects for an adversity-rich future?
3) Does your Cultural AQ help influence people to Climb, Camp, or Quit?
4) How do you see the Cultural AQ affecting your organization's agility, problem solving, morale, innovation, customer service, communication, leadership, hiring, retention, performance, and health?
5) How does your Cultural AQ influence your ability to compete (if applicable)?
6) What would you guess your chief competitors' AQs to be?

7) How does your Cultural AQ affect your enthusiasm and energy for contributing to this organization?

8) How do you see the Cultural AQ affecting people? What toll does adversity tend to take on people within your organization?

9) What role does AQ play in the overall success of your organization?

Their Scores

1) What range did others' scores fall within?

2) How does their Cultural AQ score compare with yours?

3) How would you explain any discrepancies?

4) How would they explain any discrepancies?

5) What do their scores say about your organization and its ability to navigate an adversity-rich future?

6) How is AQ affecting the way others approach and respond to adversity and opportunities?

Exhibit 10.7 Interpreting Your AQ Cultural Glance

I strongly advise you to have as many people as possible, from different areas of your organization, complete the AQ Cultural Glance. It's likely that individuals from different parts of your organization will score Cultural AQ from a different and vital perspective. Remember, a leader, no matter how adored, will likely be kept in the dark, to some degree, concerning the true perceptions of others. Whether out of fear, compassion, or concern, people want to protect the leader from bad news, so they naturally filter information. Therefore, a leader may not have the same view on your Cultural AQ that others share. It is worth finding out.

My experience in measuring Cultural AQ is that leaders often rate their organizations the highest, but those executing the frontline responsibilities may share a different perspective. They see daily challenges arise and know how people do and do not respond. Therefore, it is a very useful exercise to see how people in different areas of the organization perceive and score the organization culture.

You may be in for a surprise! Sometimes substantial discrepancies emerge between the score and perceptions from different areas of an organization. They may exist for any number of reasons. Primary among them is the leader.

Leaders are the single greatest cultural influence. They guide the subcultures, often forming Climbing Teams within camping organizations or campgrounds among Climbers. You may already know or suspect which facets of your organization are led by high- or low-AQ leaders. You can check your instincts with the AQ Cultural Glance.

It is common for some pockets or subcultures to score the culture higher or lower than others. Given the strength of some discrepancies, it is sometimes hard to believe that people are describing the same organization.

On the other hand, a high degree of consistency reflects a highly influential umbrella culture that pervades and even dominates the subcultures. The advantage is less dissonance among different facets of the organization. If the dominant culture is not as high-AQ as you might prefer, that is a definite disadvantage.

Interestingly, a high degree of inconsistency in how people score Cultural AQ reflects a place where subcultures are more influential than the umbrella culture. Just as different people in a national park often experience natural wonders in entirely different ways, people in your organization are experiencing their workplace differently. There can even be contrary findings within and among subcultures.

Most organizations of any size have subcultures. These can vary by geography ("Have you ever been out to our Sydney office? It's *very* different!), function ("The global logistics part of the business is entirely different"), or tenure ("This is the newest and most dynamic part of our business"). They can also vary by cultural background, gender, age, marketplace, history, title, and, of course, *leadership*. As subcultures vary, so can their subcultural AQs and their views on the grander Cultural AQ.

Mapping Your Cultural AQ: Interpreting Your Results

Although the AQ Cultural Glance is an abbreviated version of the full AQ Cultural Assessment, it can still be of substantial value. Just as a doctor can sometimes assess your condition simply by depressing your tongue, asking how you're doing, and carefully looking you over, this AQ Cultural Glance can give a meaningful first reading.

High Cultural AQ (155–200): If your organization's Cultural AQ falls in this range, it has an exceptional capacity for dealing with challenges and setbacks. It is likely a vibrant, energizing, innovative, and fulfilling workplace. Leaders are likely to demonstrate high-AQ relentlessness and may be highly demanding. Customers are drawn to the optimism and resilience the workforce demonstrates when faced with an obstacle. You likely draw and keep Climbers.

Moderately High Cultural AQ (138–154): Cultural AQs in this range indicate a workplace fairly well poised to handle uncertainty, change, and challenges. You are likely to be one of the stronger enterprises in your industry, and Climbers are drawn to be a part of what you do. There may be times when you feel that one more challenge will be too much to handle. Somehow people generally get it all done.

Moderate Cultural AQ (113–137): If your organization's Cultural AQ falls in this range, it is like the majority of enterprises in that it can deal with only so much adversity before suffering some negative consequences. When things go smoothly, your organization may effectively optimize its workforce and their talents. However, as adversity mounts, people may become stressed and performance may suffer. There is likely to be some substantial untapped potential.

Moderately Low Cultural AQ (96–112): If your organization's Cultural AQ falls in this range, you probably have a hard time attracting and/or keeping Climbers. People get demoralized easily and may hide from challenges that could help them improve. Performance, morale, and innovation fluctuate significantly, depending on the level of adversity people are facing during a given week or month. This can be improved as Cultural AQ is raised.

Low Cultural AQ (95 and below): Organizations with Cultural AQs in this range are sitting on a huge pool of untapped potential that they can bring forth as they raise their Cultural AQs. People may be frustrated, bitter, resentful, and/or negative. Challenges can bring productivity to a grinding halt, and people may blame one another for each new problem or failure. Organizations in this range experience the most dramatic improvements as they raise their Cultural AQs.

Insert your four Cultural CORE totals in the boxes and graph your Cultural CORE.

	C	O	R	E
	☐	☐	☐	☐

AQ		C	O	R	E
High	200	50	50	50	50
	190	48	48	48	48
	180	46	46	46	46
	170	44	44	44	44
	165	42	42	42	42
	160	40	40	40	40
	155	38	38	38	38
	150				
Moderately	145	36	36	36	36
High	140	34	34	34	34
	135	32	32	32	32
Moderate	130	30	30	30	30
	125	28	28	28	28
MEAN	120	26	26	26	26
	115	24	24	24	24
Moderately	110	22	22	22	22
Low	105	20	20	20	20
	95	18	18	18	18
	85	16	16	16	16
	75	14	14	14	14
Low	70	12	12	12	12
	60	10	10	10	10
	50				
	40				

Exhibit 10.8 Graphing Your Cultural CORE

Mapping Your Cultural CORE

It is one thing to get an abbreviated snapshot of your cultural AQ. It is quite another to explore the CORE differences. The former is like a road map, the latter a topographical map that provides the detail necessary to successfully navigate the terrain.

Take a moment and graph your organization's CORE Profile in Exhibit 10.8. Then apply the questions in Exhibit 10.9 to understand your results more fully and deepen the value you get from this activity. Exhibit 10.10 provides a more graphic description of how your CORE may be affecting people's likelihood to Climb, Camp, or Quit. It is useful to compare the Cultural CORE Profile with that of your team as well as yourself. At the bottom of Exhibit 10.6 you can compare these different CORE scores. Ranges are provided within each CORE dimension to better assess where your culture scores in comparison with others.

Use the following questions to get a deeper understanding of your Cultural CORE Profile from Exhibit 10.8:

Strengths

- On what CORE dimension(s) did you score your organization highest?
- What did others score highest?
- How do you explain any discrepancies (if applicable)?
- What does this say about your culture and what you do particularly well when facing adversity?
- What does this imply about your organization's Response Ability?

Weak Spots

- On what CORE dimension(s) did you score your organization lowest?
- What did others score lowest?
- How do you explain any discrepancies (if applicable)?
- What does this say about your culture and your potential weak spots when facing adversity?
- What does this imply about your organization's Response Ability?

Overall CORE Assessment

- How is your Cultural CORE influencing your ability to deal with current challenges?

- What does your Cultural CORE Profile say about your ability to successfully face and overcome adversity?
- How might it influence your success in the future?

Exhibit 10.9 Interpreting Your Cultural CORE

Cultural Climbing Tendencies

There is an immediate focus on what we *can* control.	People step up and take Ownership for making things better.	Adversity stays in its place.	Adversity is fleeting.
People believe they can positively influence the situation.	People focus on solutions over blame.	People keep perspective.	Few things endure.
People tend to persevere.	We enjoy high trust and interdependence.	People compartmentalize challenges.	People see past challenges and remain optimistic.

Cultural Camping Tendencies

People have a reasonable sense of Control.	People have a reasonable sense of Ownership.	Some things bleed into other areas.	Some things drag on.
People may get overwhelmed when adversity piles up.	People may resort to blame when tired, tense.	As adversities mount, it gets harder to separate each one.	Hope and faith are good, except when adversity is high.
Adversity can wear people down.	Ownership could be stronger.	People get burdened.	Realism is valued.

Cultural Quitting Tendencies

People respond as though we have little, if any, Control.	People deflect Ownership.	People get overwhelmed.	Things drag on and on.
People may develop learned helplessness.	People resort to blame, pointing fingers.	We are besieged with catastrophes.	Aversity endures more than necessary.
People give up.	People are guarded.	Little difficulties blow up.	Hope gives way to cynicism and sarcasm.

Exhibit 10.10 Cultural Tendencies

As Exhibit 10.10 indicates, the lower your Cultural "C," the more it implies that people not only do not feel a strong sense of Control in their work but also lack the optimism to better the situation. The lower the C score, the more likely people are to Camp or even Quit.

But if C is the high point, people are more likely to feel a strong sense of control and share the belief that they can positively influence even daunting situations. This suggests genuine and pervasive empowerment, innovation, and a potentially inspiring place to work.

Control is deep and fundamental to what people seek in their work today. In fact, there is a large-scale global shift afoot as people seek more Control over their work, decisions, and life. It is the driving criterion for many neophyte entrepreneurs, who are tired of having insufficient Control over their opportunities and adversities. They are willing to take on more headaches in order to have more Control. A low-Control culture is highly vulnerable to being buffeted by outside forces, such as changes in the marketplace, economy, customers, competition, technology, and so on. As a result, its people get beaten up, and, quite sensibly, *Camp.*

If your culture scores low on O, then there is a norm or pattern of deflecting accountability, focusing on blame, or both. This can ravage trust, agility, and interdependence. It also induces people to be inherently protective of information and their individual turf. Customers are likely to be dissatisfied, if not irate. Employee and customer turnover may be adversely affected.

If your culture scores high on O, then the opposite is true. People step up and take Ownership for improving the situation and dealing with the challenge du jour, regardless of its cause. This high-accountability culture is likely to inspire trust and interdependence and foster good relationships. The result is increased productivity and a renewed resolve to finish the job. This can greatly influence people's will to stay with their current employer and organization.

If your culture scores low on R, people may get bogged down in problems, which are perceived as substantial and far-reaching. When adversity strikes, people may respond as though it is a dramatically large difficulty: a given event becomes a "situation," and a setback becomes a "crisis." This can unnecessarily dampen the spirits of higher-AQ people, who are driven to limit the Reach of the adversity, which they likely view as a small obstacle rather than a major catastrophe. Low-R scores indicate many sizable boulders that can halt and even terminate the ascent.

If your culture scores high on R, then people's ability to keep adversity in its place is likely to result in quicker solutions and action. Staff can handle more adversity when each event is contained and, if your culture also has high Ownership and Control scores, the event is dealt with swiftly. People take the same challenges in stride, like trail runners weaving through and jumping over rocks and roots.

If your culture scores low on E, then people are likely to respond to events as if they are long-lasting and potentially formidable. Hope and faith can be diminished or destroyed in a low-E culture. This low-AQ behavior quickly wears thin for the high-AQ Climbers who want to get past the adversity and continue the ascent and have difficulty understanding why others insist on drawing things out so mercilessly.

If your culture scores high on E, people have the optimistic tendency to see past even the most complex and daunting adversities. This helps them remain more buoyant in difficult times. If your culture also has high R and C scores, people are unlikely to see any adversity as insurmountable. They may be energized by the challenges and if they also score high on O, take it upon themselves to grow the opportunity embedded within adversity. Such tendencies draw, affirm, and fuel Climbers, who refuse to let difficulties drag on any longer than necessary.

You will be glad that you invested the time and effort to map your Cultural AQ. It provides everyone with the same vantage point and information from which you can strengthen your Cultural AQ.

DEVISING A CLIMBING ROUTE: TWENTY-TWO WAYS TO UPGRADE YOUR CULTURAL AQ

Over the past dozen years the PEAK team, with the help of some inspirational high-AQ leaders, has implemented various strategies to upgrade Cultural AQs. For the purpose of this book, I have boiled down this extended list to the twenty-two most practical ways to upgrade your Cultural AQ. Take note: many of these strategies are deceptively easy to implement, at least *at first*. *Sustaining* these commitments, while holding true to them especially when people are tested, ultimately defines whether they are superficial initiatives or enduring improvements. As with most things that matter, it is in times of adversity that you will be most tempted to break your commitment to these principles, but it is precisely at those moments that they matter most.

1. Redefine Your Organization Around the New Economy: The New Economy offers an unprecedented opportunity to flourish. It combines technology and humanity in a new marriage that offers fresh freedoms and challenges. It also represents a whole new game that no one completely understands, with rules that are being rewritten every day. In short, *no one is bored.* Climbers relish New Economy opportunities in much the same way they would clamor to an unexplored summit.

Whether your organization is for profit, not-for-profit, private, public, huge, or tiny, you can apply New Economy principles to your culture. Innovation, knowledge, technology, Human Capital, connectivity, virtual work, and interdependence are the new powers you must embrace. These also represent some of the principles under which Climbers thrive. Shifting to the New Economy means investing in, integrating, and leveraging New Economy powers earnestly and doggedly. You will unearth hidden dynamism, excitement, and creativity in the process. Campers will begin to Climb.

2. Clear Your Gear: On May 10, 1996, eleven people died on the face of Mount Everest. Many mistakes were later revealed that had led to their demise. One tragic error in judgment was made when the expedition leader requested that a Sherpa carry several luxury items up to the highest base camp in the Dead Zone, where every ounce matters. According to Jon Krakauer, author of *Into Thin Air,* the Sherpa's fatigue from carrying extra weight and short-roping another climber drained his energy and ability to make necessary and repeated rescue ascents. Yet he was ethically obligated to try. Carrying such items to the upper reaches of the planet and short-roping is considered by Sherpas to be not only dangerous but also a slight against the gods. This tragic event reminds us that to sustain our ascent we must have the *right* gear. Anything extra or outdated will simply add weight and endanger our progress.

If you could toss out of your cultural backpack those artifacts that really add nothing, what would remain? Which meetings, rituals, rewards, and ways of communicating would you keep? Would you change the rules on parking, reimbursements for expenses, decision making, or getting approval for a change? Exhibit 10.11 helps you consider what belongs and what goes.

Consider those aspects of your culture that are most important to your ascent and those that weigh down your progress.

- If you could wipe the cultural slate clean and start over, what would you want to build?
- Specifically, what facets would you keep?
- What facets (rituals, norms, rules, assumptions, practices, procedures, etc.) would you eliminate?
- Given your answers to these questions, what facets of your current culture are worth changing?
- Which facets of your current culture are not worth changing?
- What are the consequences of keeping those you will not change the same?

Exhibit 10.11 Clear Your Gear

A director of operations at an Asian electronics manufacturer told me about his dilemma: "We have many rituals in the workplace designed to strengthen the team. They provide comfort, security, and a sense of belonging. The implied rule is, 'You must attend.' Yet many of our people must spend more and more time in the field in order to meet our customers' demands. They have to respond immediately to every request. If they are gone, they are not seen as team players. If they stay, they cannot excel at what they were hired to do." This is a good example of how certain cultural gear (implied rules, assumptions, rituals) can hinder the ascent and frustrate your Climbers.

> You become your playmates.
>
> —Ram Dass

3. Surround Yourself with Climbers: One of the most powerful ways to dump a lot of weight off your climbing rope is to rid your organization of the lower-AQ vendors, customers, directors, and alliances. These individuals and entities demand an undue amount of energy and time. This purging takes time, courage, and effort. Conversely, surrounding yourself with Climbers means forming relationships with people who have the strongest spirit of relentless resilience and a history of getting fired up when difficulties mount. You will find that your culture will be not only liberated but elevated when those supporting and interacting with it are true Climbers.

One way to do this is to select a challenge and see who steps up most quickly, completely, and relentlessly. You can even measure their AQs. Why not share with them part of what you are striving to become? People are generally intrigued to learn more about themselves and why you selected them to run a project or handle a specific task.

Earlier in the book I referred to the story of how the PEAK team built our new facility on top of a mountain at the end of an impossibly steep road. Ten contractors refused to consider our "impossible situation." The eleventh had a twinkle in his eyes; he could see the vision. Fully cognizant of the adversity, he *relished* the challenge and creativity it would take to succeed. Each day he faced several setbacks—from quicksand to trucks rolling off the road—and he always addressed them the same way: "There's nothing we can't handle, Paul." When the lumberyard told him the project was impossible, he said, "So, it can't be done? Hah! How about I drive them up here in a few months and show them how we did it?" Frankly, I believe he found the project *invigorating!* Needless to say, this high-AQ vendor helped us shape our future.

Surrounding your organization with Climbers can do the same for you. It requires looking through the lens of AQ at the people you choose to be involved with. In most cases you cannot choose to surround yourself with only Climbers. Given the relatively low percentage of Climbers, such an ideal would be tough to achieve. Instead, you want to focus on upping the proportion of Climbers who influence your work, projects, and success.

What about your formal or informal board of directors? High-AQ directors are the ones who step into a tense do-or-die meeting with the resilient determination to succeed, based on their clear sense of the original purpose of the enterprise. Such Climbers can literally shift the direction of conversations, refocusing the team on the future ascent rather than the chasm over which they are carefully stepping. Climbers of this sort can save an organization from a dangerous chasm. The decision to surround yourself with Climbers can make each day a lot more sane, and the ascent that much freer.

Conversely, at some point you may have experienced a scene like the one I witnessed when I passed through the employee break room at a large retail department store. "There's no *way* we're getting out of here at ten tonight," one clerk announced to her coworkers.

"No kidding. We're supposed to be ready for tomorrow's sale, and my manager has not even given me the new price sheet," added another.

Across the table, a weary-looking gentleman exhaled slowly and added his two cents; "I'm just going to throw a bunch of stuff on the shelf and let that idiot who comes in the morning deal with it. Our whole department is a mess anyway. It's not like I'm getting paid to figure it all out! This whole sale is a disaster anyway." Quitters and Campers everywhere. No Climbers in sight!

To the extent that you can influence the roles people fill and the projects they're engaged in, consider the fit through the lens of AQ. Put your highest-AQ people in the roles that require the greatest relentlessness and your lower-AQ people in roles where they will be less likely to feel helpless and influence others to feel the same.

While you may not choose your formal reporting and work structure, you can greatly influence the informal structure, or the people you spend time with to get things done who may not fit in the formal chain of command. These people form your informal network of Climbers—those who draw upon one another to find ways to get things done while others are still arguing over whether anything can be done. I find it useful to have some Climbers in each area of my work. If your job comprises three main areas of responsibility, begin by pinpointing one or two Climbers in each area. Meet with them, discuss your shared passion for getting things done, and offer them your help. They will spot you as an ally and probably seek you as an informal member of their Climbing Team. In this way you can expand your network and reduce your frustrations at work.

If you want a culture that drives change and prides itself on its work, surround yourself with Climbers.

4. Develop Lead Climbers: Leaders have the greatest influence on shaping the culture. If anyone can get Campers to Climb, it is your Lead Climbers. They determine the route and pound in the first anchor to secure the team to the rock. In essence Response-Able leaders shape Response-Able cultures, which inspire others to ascend. Through their formal or informal power, they have the greatest leverage for creating a high-AQ culture and serve as the logical starting point for your quest. Leaders need to understand AQ and the human operating system, beginning with their own and eventually those of their people. To quickly create substantive change, you must teach leaders the principles of AQ; you must infuse these precepts into their bloodstream, vocabulary, and practices, so that others can be inspired to do the same.

Chances are you have already spotted several Climbers within your organization. Develop them into Lead Climbers by giving them accountability for leading smaller expeditions. This can be done at any level within the organization. Start with challenges that stretch them but are not overwhelming. Accept and guide them to learn from their failures. Make it clear that it is *how* they fail, not *if* they fail, that matters. Give them ever more challenging terrain to ascend, along with responsibility for leading others. Their sense of mastery and their passion for helping Campers to Climb will grow and be contagious; it will also help you attract and retain Climbers.

Convene your Lead Climbers to discuss the organization's culture. Consider those elements that are hindering the ascent and those that can nurture Climbing behavior. Frank dialogue can reveal some weak spots that can be crippling your ability to grow and prosper to the fullest possible extent.

Poll your organization on the same questions of Climbing obstacles versus Climbing helpers. If they are allowed to respond confidentially, you might be surprised by what you learn. Leaders usually have blind spots and may not realize that certain norms, values, assumptions, and implicit rules can be crippling their Climbers. You need to fully engage your Lead Climbers to optimize your Cultural AQ.

A passionate, high-AQ leader can shake up the campground and help many Campers to get "on rope." One need not be the formal leader or have the highest title to achieve such inspiring results.

5. Offer Climbing School: It may be cheaper to hire Climbers than to grow them, but you must consider the cost of *not* growing them. To deny people the opportunity to measure and permanently rewire their AQs robs them of the skills they need to ascend a steep incline. It is equivalent to yelling "Climb!" without providing the training or a rope. Leaders have an ethical obligation to provide their current workforce with the opportunity to get on rope. You do this by providing the fundamentals of AQ, the opportunity to measure their AQs, and the skills to implement this technology directly into their daily challenges, and through Climbing School. Upgrade the operating system of your people, and your culture will evolve. This can strengthen people holistically, affecting all facets of their lives and, inevitably, their behavior and belief system at work.

Climbing School is a way to strengthen your Cultural AQ in units of one. You create individual pockets of resolve, Response Ability, and climbing behavior. Each serves as an ambassador of the Climb, and a seed that grows in different pockets of your organization.

People need to (1) measure their AQs, (2) strengthen their CORE awareness, and (3) use the LEAD Sequence to dispute and rewire their patterns of response to adverse events.

More specifically, you can integrate Climbing School into employees' development plans, so they have a path to upgrade their operating systems and make Response Ability the epicenter of their effectiveness and accountability for their own development.

Climbing School should be built around *your* culture, challenges, and burning issues. That is why AQ training must be customized to each organization's culture. You can use your culture's current assumptions, norms, history, and rules as a meaningful starting point for seeing in what areas you can best improve and strengthen your Cultural AQ. Then apply the tools from this book and beyond to permanently rewire how people deal with adversities, big and small.

6. Institutionalize the LEAD Sequence: Many years ago, the PEAK team devised and tested the LEAD Sequence as a way to dispute and rewire one's responses to adverse events. Since then, we have discovered that the LEAD Sequence is much more than that. It is one of the most elegant, compassionate, efficient, and significant methods for working through any challenge within yourself, among individuals, or within a team. The steps are universal and apply across cultures, industries, and situations. Make it standard practice to LEAD each other through any challenge and watch agility, clarity, and individuals become strengthened in the process.

Climbing School is the first step toward institutionalizing the LEAD Sequence, but it takes more. If you use the LEAD Sequence during meetings, when faced with challenges, and when adversities arise, you will give it the visibility and importance required to infuse it into your cultural veins. Make a concerted effort to include facets of the LEAD Sequence in presentations, documents, and conversation. Communicating it formally and informally will help it take root within your culture.

Within Cypress Semiconductor, use of the LEAD Sequence began as a part of a mentoring program for a select group of salespeople. As it spread into Cypress's team training, coaching process, and general approach to problem solving, the LEAD Sequence became more and more institutionalized. As a result, it now goes beyond a training program and has become a standard part of the cultural vocabulary.

7. Build Response-Able Climbing Teams: While many teams are formed unnecessarily, Climbing Teams have a defined and compelling reason to exist. Those that understand and apply the principles of AQ, CORE, Response Ability, Response-Based thinking, and the Significance Scale have the mental gear they need to climb into the rarefied air well above the tree line. Use your Lead Climbers to form, guide, teach, and inspire high-AQ Climbing Teams. Make the LEAD Sequence standard problem solving within teams to embrace each member's dignity and contribution (see Chapter 9). Begin with intact high-AQ teams, and let them serve as a meaningful example to the rest of the organization of what *can* be done and how adversities can be consistently overcome.

It is particularly useful to hold your highest-AQ team up as an example of what succeeds within your culture and why. Explain to others what's unique about this team and why it was able to persevere when others gave up—all in the language of AQ. Let it serve as a lesson of how teams shape the culture, even on limited resources and under tremendous pressure. This can go far to mitigate whining and victimhood while inspiring others to Climb.

8. Build a Base Camp, Kill the Campground: Obviously, it may be impractical, undesirable, not to mention unethical, to fire your Campers. Instead, you want to help people shift their energies and resources from the Campground to Base Camp. It is important for everyone to recognize his or her role as "climb-critical," or vital to the ascent.

People often wonder if they can be Climbers if they are staff-level employees, or if they decide not to compete for the next promotion. I'm often asked, "If I have stayed in the same staff job for the past twelve years, does that mean I am a Camper?" This apparent confusion stems from two misunderstandings. First, people have to examine *why* they stay in a particular job. If it's to avoid change or challenges, they are clearly camping and risk suffering atrophy; if it's because that job best leverages their gifts toward a meaningful purpose, then they can climb there for many years to come.

The second misunderstanding arises when people mistake camp-grounds for *Base Camp*. There is a fundamental difference between the two. One is about comfort, the other is critical to the ascent. Base Camp is made up of that climb-critical set of individuals who coordinate, support, and provide resources for those on the actual rope. They face tremendous challenges in the pace and demands of their jobs. Any Climber will tell you that the people in Base Camp are as much a part of the Climbing Team as those on the summit.

When Edwin Siew, a member of the first Singaporean team to summit Everest, reached the top, the first thing he did was call Base Camp. "We all screamed, cried, and hugged," he explained. "Because we knew we had done something so incredible together." Edwin, a staff member of the globally acclaimed Singapore Outward Bound, and his partners knew that those in Base Camp were as vital to their success as were those who stood on the summit.

Though Climbers embrace those in Base Camp, they do not feel the same way about the Campers. There is a fundamental difference between a Campground and a Base Camp. One takes up space, the other helps the ascent. Who in your organization can staff a true Base-Camp, climb-critical role? Who is just deadweight on the rope? Every organization should have its Base Camp.

FedEx accepted one of the most unusual shipments it ever carried: several thousand copies of the Koran on CD-ROM, destined for an important event on Spain's Mediterranean coast. In Paris the cargo weighed in at four tons, twenty times heavier than the shipper had reported. Yet these CDs were a gift from the Saudi Arabian king and his ambassador to Spain. They had to arrive on time. The plane was clearly not large enough. The operations team in Spain sprang into action and, working with the team in France, located a 727, then spent three hours negotiating with Spanish authorities for special permission to land the plane. Their agility paid off, and their shipment arrived ahead of the guests. This is the behavior of a well-trained Base Camp team. They help everyone to ascend.

One practical way to create a Base Camp out of a Campground is to find one specific area of your organization that is most obviously camping. Work with this area to develop a compelling, visible, significant quest in which everyone can play a role. Ideally, it will be riddled with challenges, not impossibilities. Make sure people in support functions recognize and can communicate the role they play in their department's success. Show keen interest in their progress and support them along the way. Celebrate each time they overcome an obstacle and give credit to the Base Camp personnel. It can change the way people approach their work.

9. Define Climbing Roles: Jack Welch, chairman of General Electric, is famous for asking people what they have done each day to contribute to the bottom line. You might consider a slight rewording of this challenge and ask yourself and others, "What have you done to contribute to the ascent today?"

Define organizational functions and individual accountabilities in terms of the ascent. How, and to what extent, does each person and position contribute to the ascent? Those who do not contribute should not be a part of the team or your organization. Sound harsh?

Running a campground helps no one. Employing people who do not add value also denigrates the person, the mission, and your integrity. You must have the courage to let those who cannot, or will not, contribute to the ascent, either in Base Camp or by being on rope, leave to find a place where they can be significant. Simply put, deadweight on the rope demoralizes everyone and *endangers* the ascent.

Ultimately, the high and compassionate road is to help your entrenched Campers find another mountain, not to accept their decision to Camp. Once you turn your workforce into a shelter for the motivationally impaired, you grant implicit permission to be merely sufficient and mediocre, and thus weaken the entire culture.

10. Allot Resources to the Ascent: Climbers don't bargain-shop when buying gear. They know their success and survival depend on having the best and only the most essential resources for the climb. Extra stuff just slows them down. The same is true in creating a Climbing Culture. Walk the hallways, tour the cubicles, peruse the workplace. What resources assist in the fulfillment of your mission, and which ones are really just adding weight to the rope? Where do you spend your resources? Are you padding the campground or equipping people for the ascent? For each piece of equipment and investment, ask yourself, "What does this do to contribute to the ascent?"

The rule on resources is simple: if it is not "climb-critical," lose it. If it is, buy the best.

11. Be the Guardian of the Mountain: People often forget that the mountain is *not* about performance, profitability, title, market share, or shareholder value. It is about something higher, deeper, more meaningful, and more compelling, *your defining purpose.* The rest of the words listed above are outcomes of assembling Climbers for a clearly articulated and shared ascent. Purpose is not soft, New Age consulting babble. It is as concrete and real as the granite of the mountain where you skin your knees and where you pull your team.

Send or support a message to everyone in your organization about what matters. Let people know, "We are *dedicated* to the ascent. Our mission/purpose is real, not a papier-mâché mountain. To fulfill our purpose and accomplish our vision, we hire and nurture Climbers."

Be the guardian of what is sacred. "Remember the mountain" can be your mantra, so Climbers can stay on path, focused, and worthwhile. Climbers are drawn to places and people who take purpose seriously and live it every day.

Whether or not we realize it, each of us has within us the ability to set some kind of example for people. Knowing this, would you rather be the one known for being the one who encouraged others, or the one who inadvertently discouraged those around you?

—Josh Hinds

12. Assess on Performance: Performance is the primary measurable criterion upon which one can be assessed and compensated, and it is the only one Climbers care about, right alongside purpose and significance. Performance as a criterion transcends gender, ethnic background, seniority, and other potentially cancerous criteria. Instead of dreading the exception to the cultural norm (for example, a young, eyebrow-pierced woman excelling in a situation where a traditional male-based succession plan still exists), embrace and highlight it, so every individual knows that he or she, too, has a chance to ascend without artificial limitations resulting from anachronistic rules, norms, and assumptions. Stay true to your word, and this will set your coworkers free. People will extol the fairness and the opportunity to contribute to the ascent from Day One.

It is easy to spot cultures where performance is given lip service but not rewarded. Academia is famous for blacklisting successful professors for gaining too much popularity and acclaim for their teaching. Rather than increasing the compensation for these educators, administrators and colleagues may increase their course load instead, or threaten their quest for tenure because they obviously "lack rigor" or make their peers look bad by raising the bar. It has taken most outstanding professors I know decades to be appreciated for their classroom accomplishments.

13. Leverage Technology for the Ascent: Technology can play a vital role in creating and sustaining a high-AQ Culture by facilitating the agility, creativity, and interpersonal communication that Climbers demand. This is why even the most hard-core climbing purists embrace technology. Use it to improve vital communication between Climbers and Base Camp. Use technology to create seamless communication and information sharing among all members of the extended Climbing Team. Give anyone dealing with the customer the real-time information he or she requires to solve a customer's needs on the spot. Banana Republic now programs its customers' Palm Pilot organizers to keep them posted on upcoming sales. In this way the customer and the salesclerk become partners in making sure the customer knows when a given item might be discounted.

In the airport, I sat next to a Frito Lay regional sales manager who was using his personal digital assistant to download E-mail from his home office and field sales force. "I can schedule, communicate, coordinate, and execute everything I need from this little device," he explained. "So the old dilemma of being away from the home office is now resolved." Technology can help anyone to transcend, even shatter, old boundaries and power structures that have become barriers to true interdependence and the sharing of time-sensitive wisdom to further the ascent.

14. Expect the Best: . . . And you just might get it! Contrary to the advice of some motivational theorists, set the highest possible expectations for yourself and your coworkers, then work arduously to live up to it. High expectations coupled with a worthy cause (mountain) are Climber magnets. Climbers will come from near and far to be a part of a culture that offers both. The expectations must apply to all members of the workforce—starting with you—with *no* exceptions. And they must be adhered to, *especially* in moments of truth. This gives both the expectations and the people setting them integrity and elevates the people and the culture in the process.

ADP is the leader in providing information and transaction processing to the financial services industry. Its relentless quest to be the "preeminent provider" has resulted in its current state of zero client turnover and 150-plus quarters of double-digit growth. Its management team enjoys unusually high retention and tenure, as people are consistently challenged, stretched, and rewarded for their ascent. ADP expects to be the best at what it does, without compromise, and every day that expectation pays off.

15. Control What You Can: . . . And let go of what you cannot. There are many facets of Control, which may require fine-tuning, even overhauling, in order to create an authentically high-AQ Culture. Establish the norm of focusing on the facets of the situation you and others *can* influence for the better, and clearly set aside those elements you cannot. Holly Threat, managing director of quality and process improvement at FedEx, makes a clear delineation every day. "You cannot control Mother Nature," she explained, "but you can influence how you respond to her challenges." This is why FedEx employees practice deicing drills throughout the summer and why their technology is specifically designed to help the planes with the biggest loads land when rain or snow backs up traffic. They master what they can control so that they can optimize their Response Ability.

Emotional Control is of paramount importance in shaping the hopes and aspirations of a workforce. Unfortunately, as authority grows, so does the right to "lose it" with employees or teammates. Sadly, many leaders still rant and rave, throw tantrums, and blow gaskets—all in the name of conviction, passion, and motivation. Typically, such tactics backfire terribly. They deplete respect and crush inspiration, modeling the opposite of what is needed. A charismatic CEO of a European business venture has long struggled with his temper. His tirades are legendary among his leadership team. Many have quit or had to seek therapy. Most live in constant fear that they will be the next to fall within his crosshairs. It is unfortunate when such an otherwise effective leader compromises his or her ascent by using power to render others helpless.

The human antitantrum mechanism is Response Control. In Chapter 4, we explored the Hierarchy of Control, including the consummate level of control, *Instantaneous* Response Control. Cultural response control begins with leaders and is subconsciously mimicked by others. No matter what your position, you can influence the norms of Response Control by controlling your *own* response when adversity strikes.

16. Infuse Ownership: Ownership is about *consistency,* holding true to your values regarding accountability *precisely when it is most difficult to do so.* This means holding people accountable for dealing with situations as they arise, regardless of their role. Ownership means creating a blame-free culture where covering one's backside at the expense of meaningful action is not only frowned upon but never tolerated. "Forget about blame, I am interested in *learning,*" explained Jim Campbell, a senior manager with Andersen Consulting. "I mentor people every day, and I believe it is up to me to make sure they learn the freedom and opportunity that comes with a sense of Ownership."

Look for situations where *you* can take it upon yourself to improve a situation that someone else may have caused. It will inspire others to do the same. When people take accountability for bettering difficult situations they had no responsibility for causing—that's *Ownership.*

17. Contain the Reach of Adversity: Establish a norm of containing adversity the moment it strikes, and you will already lift a terrible burden off your would-be Climbers. Every time a challenge arises, work through the LEAD Sequence to develop specific actions for containing the fallout of the adversity. Develop standard containment strategies for those adversities that regularly occur. Containment strategies are essential so that adversity cannot ripple into other areas. Such strategies provide people with the means to remain agile when adversity strikes, which can be exhilarating—a stark contrast to the overwhelming burden they can feel when annoyances explode into disasters.

Specifically, this means being on the lookout for the first sign of an adversity that could reach over into other areas of the business and people's lives and immediately addressing how it can best be contained. Such strategies add considerably to organizational resilience.

The president of a manufacturing company sensed that his accounting firm was not really doing the job. So, he fired it and hired a new firm. Soon thereafter, he walked into his office to find his new firm waiting. Their grim expressions could not begin to tell what would follow. The accountants looked him in the eye and declared, "You are worse than broke." He discovered that due to his previous accounting firm's mistakes, his company was facing a complete financial meltdown. He was informed that his company was in default of every single bank loan. The banks said they would not cover the debt, nor would they cover the next day's payroll.

Immediately, his sales manager created a panic, which induced the top five salespeople to jump ship, decimating the company. But the horror was far from over. Within a couple of hours, he was told that his closest friend's son had been killed in a car accident, and another friend's home had burned down.

To make matters worse, his now-elderly parents' names were on one bank note, and he had to sit next to his seventy-one-year-old father as the banker described precisely how he would be completely wiped out financially within thirty-six hours. He had also been experiencing some marital troubles. When he went home to tell his wife that he had hours to figure out a solution before everything they had built would be destroyed, she responded, "Well, that's your problem. *I'm* going skiing." And she left, ending their marriage. He had every reason to throw in the towel. The adversity appeared far-reaching, beyond his Control, and sure to affect all facets of his life.

Instead, this Climber bit the bullet and called personal friends for loans—which he could not promise to repay—to cover his expenses and buy some time. Next, he pulled his team members together and figured out a survival strategy that would allow them to meet their bills while they rebuilt the company. Thanks to their containment strategies, the company now enjoys unprecedented profitability. "We never would have reached this level of success had we not faced that adversity," he explained. "It was essential to getting us to where we are today." When asked how he views the adversity, he said, "I would not trade it for the world. I look back on it as enriching, strengthening, and fulfilling. Now we know what we are really made of."

18. Look Past Each Adversity: I recently walked through the cafeteria of a government agency and overheard a manager saying to her friend over lunch, "It takes *forever* for someone to get fired around here!" She was referring to a specific individual who was highly disruptive and, at times, verbally abusive to others. In her mind, the adversity was going to endure for a long time. This seemingly harmless venting of frustration communicates a deeper problem—the perception that this and probably many other adversities can drag on for a torturously long time, if not forever. I could hear the resignation and frustration in her voice.

The longer an adversity is allowed to endure, the greater the toll it takes on everyone and everything. Therefore, it is imperative to see past a given setback or challenge and go through the often difficult mental exercise of envisioning precisely what life will be like when this formidable difficulty is over. This process can begin to uproot and eradicate the weedlike assumptions that adversity must last forever, allowing healthy optimism to flourish.

19. Factor Failure into the Equation: Erik Weihenmayer is a Climber. He has climbed El Capitan in Yosemite National Park, which is the largest rock face on earth, as well as Mount McKinley and Mount Aconcagua, the tallest peaks in North and South America, respectively. These are admirable accomplishments made all the more remarkable by the fact that Erik is blind. You may be wondering how a blind person can climb a rock face without someone to call out the next handhold or foothold. "I factor failure into the equation," Erik explained. "I know I will fail a bunch of times in order to succeed, so I just factor that in."

Like so many Climbers in life, Erik climbs by *feel*. He literally has to run his hands and feet over the rock to make his way along the face. Based on what information he can gather, he then makes his move. He falls and gets stuck, but he ultimately succeeds—ascending rocks few sighted people would dare to attempt.

Unfortunately, most organizations do not allow their people to fall, scrape, and continue. They have destructive norms regarding failure that induce people to camp. They play it safe because the implicit rules say to do so, no matter what the leader said in his or her recent speech to the troops. Instead, seek failures that you can celebrate both for the spirit in which and the cause for which they occurred. Fail, and then fail better.

> If you want to increase your success rate, double your failure rate.
> —Thomas J. Watson Sr., founder of IBM

20. Live in the Learning Zone: The Learning Zone is the place where lessons are optimized so that you can avoid repeating past mistakes and grow wiser in your decisions. It is that degree of introspection from which you will improve; anything beyond it is unnecessary or destructively morphed into blame. Learning requires a pause. You must stop to harvest the lesson from each adversity. It demands that you establish a norm of asking, "What did we (or I) learn? What could we (or I) do better? What would we (or I) do differently if we (or I) were to encounter this situation again in the future?" It means getting past blame and celebrating the lessons from which everyone can grow. It means focusing on your own learning, both formal and informal, both inside and outside your workplace. Inspire others with your lifelong pursuit of learning so that they, too, can be nourished by its fruits.

How pervasive is learning in your culture? What percentage of your budget is spent on training, educational benefits, and learning resources? When people leave your organization, their Human Capital (knowledge) is lost, unless you have a software system for storing and accessing the lessons people learn while engaged in their work. In this way, the Human Capital stays after the person leaves. Case examples of dealing with client problems, new product launches, design projects, and new initiatives are but a handful of experiences that should be captured and stored for future teams and individuals to learn from as they take on challenges with similar characteristics. There are now a variety of knowledge-management software packages specifically suited to this purpose. You may also need to dedicate people to oversee organizational learning.

Learning systems and resources draw and retain Climbers, who are deeply compelled by the chance to make mistakes, learn, and improve (see number 19, page 292). A lack of learning in an organization is a serious impediment to the ascent.

21. Reward Climbing Behavior: Surprisingly few organizations reward Climbing behavior over Camping. The way to show that you really value intelligent risk taking, resilience, and fortitude is to reward it when things don't turn out so well. This clearly states that you believe that the right behavior is more important than getting the right result every time. Celebrate the great failures! Issue a Pickax Award or Best Fall Award for the ugliest mistake of the week. But Climbing behavior is about more than taking risks and falling down. Climbers innovate, learn, explore, persist, and inspire.

Invest your time and attention first and foremost in your Climbers. This means a lot to them and will be a welcome deviation from what usually happens in most organizations. Most leaders and managers spend the most time on those contributing the least. Reverse the equation. If you nurture your Climbers, more will grow.

Cypress Semiconductor holds a special AQ session for its high performers, fondly referred to as "Hypos," as a way to focus resources on and reward the group of individuals who are driving the success of their business.

You will also want to reward selflessness, renewal, tenacity, agility, and a person's commitment to the mission or mountain. Make renewal a priority by making it sacred. Do not let others invade renewal time, like vacation, with the daily brushfires or urgencies that pack your day and are so easily spread via pagers, cell phones, E-mail, and fax. Unless you run a cadre of neurosurgeons or a chemical-spill response team, I suggest that you pull people "off grid" when they are in training, on vacation, or merely taking a mental health break. Do it yourself first, so your coworkers know you mean it.

Mentally revamp your reward system and reassemble it with only those pieces that reward genuine Climbing behavior. Are you surprised by what little remains? What are people paid for—accomplishing outstanding feats or keeping the status quo? How are their lives different if they stick their heads out of their warm tents and resume the climb? Are they rewarded for this behavior, or are they in fact punished by the sneers and resentments of their Camping coworkers?

22. Grow Significance: The Freeplay Group is a young, fast-growing maker of self-powered devices based in Cape Town, South Africa. It prides itself on "doing good [for the world] while making money." Its innovative hand-cranked radios and lanterns are equally welcome in executive suites and remote African schools, where they are used to enhance learning, communication, and safety. The Freeplay Group attracts and keeps top people through the sense of significance each person feels as he or she contributes to the larger mission. "We have a real sense of commitment," said John Hutchinson, Freeplay's director of engineering. "It comes from doing honest work for an honest wage to make a product that's meaningful." This has helped Freeplay grow from zero to $35 million in five years and improve the lives of hundreds of thousands of people. Freeplay's momentum was palpable as people crowded its booth at the International Consumer Electronics Show in Las Vegas.

Significance is the experience or sense of mattering, of feeling vital to the overall ascent. Purpose is *why* your organization exists. It defines the mountain you have chosen to ascend together. As mentioned earlier, it should align strongly with your personal mountain. In other words, you should feel that your work is a meaningful way in which to live and hopefully fund your own ascent. There is clear alignment. You must feel that your role is climb-critical, or you will not give your all.

Several years ago Motorola set forth on a new path called Individual Dignity Entitlement to make sure every employee feels significant within the Motorola culture. One of the questions that must be answered yes by every employee is, "Do you have a substantive, meaningful job that contributes to the success of Motorola?" All workers must have the opportunity to contribute to the ascent. If they do not, Motorola guarantees corrective action to make sure every employee has a significant role.

How does *your* company grow, demonstrate, and deliver significance to your people? Significance is not about an obligatory pat on the back. It is about consistent, authentic caring, listening, and letting people matter, *especially* when it is inconvenient to do so.

I'll never forget a student of mine from my professorial days. He had done a stint as a marine and had the privilege of serving as a personal guard for President Reagan on Air Force One. He was also a 100 percent dedicated Republican. I asked him why he felt so strongly, and he replied, "There was this one day when Air Force One landed and I was in position by the president as he was to greet Soviet President Mikhail Gorbachev. Reagan paused, looked me in the eye, and asked, 'How are your college plans coming along, John?' Then he patiently waited for an answer. I was stunned. There's the Russian president, and Reagan is asking about *my* little life. Wow! I would have taken a bullet for that man." *That's* significance.

DEFINE SUCCESS

Once you have selected which strategies you will employ to strengthen your Cultural AQ, the next step is to define success. In other words, you and your partners-in-climb must ask yourselves, "Specifically, how will we know when we have succeeded?" There may be specific changes in behavior, retention rates, performance, employee surveys, innovation, problem solving, customer service, or other variables that will determine the success of your Cultural AQ–strengthening strategy. Pinpoint the improvements you seek, and describe them as specifically as possible.

INITIATE YOUR ASCENT

Take your first steps for implementing your new strategies. Begin the process knowing it may take a long time before you see any definable results. Engage co-Climbers to assist in the new direction so that it stands an even greater chance of gaining momentum. Communicate the rationale behind the new effort and the role it will play in helping you achieve the aspirations you defined in the first step of the Cultural AQ Cycle.

TRACK YOUR PROGRESS

Tracking your progress involves measuring improvements in AQ and other variables that you decided upon as the trail markers for your success. Constantly assess your progress by seeing how far you have come and how much further you have to go to have succeeded in your initial AQ-strengthening strategies. The more relevant data you gather, the better off you will be in accurately assessing your progress and communicating it to those involved.

ADJUST THE ROUTE

Climbers continually adjust to changes in the weather, knowing full well that the route they planned can change at a moment's notice. Since all organizations survive as open systems, you must adapt to changes in your environmental conditions and to the feedback you receive through the data you have gathered in the preceding step. Revisit your strategies, progress, and aspirations regularly as a way of keeping the Cultural AQ Cycle alive and at the forefront of your organizational consciousness.

CONTINUE THE QUEST

Most organizations turn meaningful efforts into conceptual Frisbees that fly over the heads of the workforce. They draw momentary attention and quickly disappear out of awareness and grasp. Even after you have successfully completed your first AQ-strengthening strategies, your challenge has just begun. To thrive in the New Economy, you must continue with your quest, continuing through the Cultural AQ Cycle. You will want to decide upon new aspirations for the future, and reassess and map your Cultural AQ, which leads to new strategies, new definitions of success, ongoing measurement, and continual adjustments in your route. The journey of creating and doing meaningful work never ends. That's the inspiration, the joy, and the challenge.

THE COLLECTIVE ASCENT

There are some ideas on our list of twenty-two that are going to be more easily implemented and readily embraced within your culture. Start with those. And recognize that this list is far from comprehensive and that the quest to create and sustain a high-AQ Climbing Culture is a never-ending ascent.

Jaded managers and hardened pragmatists sometimes question the likelihood of creating a true Climbing Culture. They wonder if they really want *all* Climbers and are threatened at the prospect of unleashing so much energy and potential chaos. They fear a loss of power, order, and predictability—the things they were promised back when they got their MBAs. I am often asked, "Don't you want to have at least *some* Campers? You know, to maintain the status quo?"

It all comes back to why you do what you do in the first place. If your significance comes from helping people get frozen into their comfort zones and slowly atrophy in the name of shareholder value, then pound in the stakes! But if your purpose has anything to do with unleashing people's true potential toward a worthy cause and doing something meaningful together, then the high-AQ Culture is your path, and you are the Lead Climber.

Topographical Map of Chapter 10
Building a Climbing Culture

Cultural AQ includes Norms, Leaders, Assumptions, Resources, Ancestors, People, Hiring Criteria, Stakeholders, Sagas, Procedures, Heroines, Values, History, Heroes, Resources, Language, Moments of Truth, Setting, Processes, Rewards, and Rules.

Assessing Cultural AQ

Wear your AQ lenses. Look and listen for how people describe and respond to everything from small annoyances to major disasters.

AQylize meetings. Listen to the words people choose when adversity strikes.

AQylize the front line. How do people on the front line respond when overwhelmed? What effect is adversity having on them, their demeanor, and their health?

Seek the Elders. How do the seasoned veterans respond to adversity?
AQylize written documents. Circle all CORE and AQ-related words.
Review the Communication of AQ within your culture
—Leaders' Rhetoric
—Workforce Language

AQ Cultural Glance is the instrument you use to measure your Cultural AQ.

Our Cultural AQ is:

What range does your Cultural AQ fall within?_____
What does this imply about your culture?_____
_____

Our Cultural CORE is:
C = _____
O = _____
R = _____
E = _____

Chapter 11

FORWARD AND UP!

The future is about more than superfast computers, designer genes, and neural networks. Answering life-altering questions posed by technology requires knowledge that goes beyond simplistic ideas about "progress." We need a more holistic intelligence—not just knowledge, but wisdom.

—Rajat Gupta, worldwide managing director, McKinsey & Co.

ADVERSITY. CHANCES ARE you have experienced it almost as many times as you have read the word "adversity" in this book. Now that you have reached the final chapter, do you view adversity differently? Has there has been at least one instance in your life or business in which you have altered or strengthened your response to adversity in some way? How has this journey affected *your* pattern of response so far? Perhaps you are more aware of how your AQ affects your Response Ability, energy, focus, and performance. You may now be keenly aware of the impact your CORE has on others. What lessons do you take forward?

What role has adversity played in *your* organization? How has it shaped your organizational character, integrity, values, prevailing culture, and the inspiration of the ascent? What moments of truth has your organization faced and how were they handled? Did adversity unleash the Nocebo Effect, weakening the hopes, expectations, and resolve of the workforce? Or did it somehow make the culture stronger and better?

At a recent presentation in Singapore on applying AQ to the family, I was saddened to discover that even its family-oriented societal fabric is being dangerously frayed by the demands placed on each person to remain viable and competitive in a globalized world. As the United States imports goods and services, we seem to export our frenetic pace, long hours, and adversities. It seems as if the whole world is impacted by the Age of Adversity and its mounting toll.

Every day people all over the world feel their Required Capacity being stretched as they struggle to keep their Existing Capacity out in front of the curve. This is the fastest-growing source of chronic stress. Their operating systems and those of their coworkers strain under the mounting demands that threaten their Accessed Capacity.

However, instead of being a source of constant strain, *adversity can be profoundly invigorating to the world's and the day's growing demands.* Work represents an opportunity uniquely well suited to experiencing this potential exhilaration.

> It's all about seizing opportunities to find meaning.
>
> —George Gendron, editor-in-chief, *Inc.* magazine

WORKING THROUGH YOUR ASCENT

This book has focused on one arena of the human experience: collective endeavor, or *work*. Work is the expression of our gifts and quest for significance. Ideally, it is a way that we leverage what we have and who we are toward something that ultimately matters and has meaning for all involved. That is the quest. However, *the quest cannot be fulfilled without adversity.* In fact, the more inspiring the vision, the more compelling the mission, the more elevating the goal, the more adversity you will face along the way, regardless of your job, your industry, or the size of your organization.

I hope you have learned that, regardless of your title or length of employment, you influence your enterprise's ascent. You can use AQ to find and hire Climbers, as well as to coach, mentor, and lead yourself and others. You can use these methods to build Climbing Teams and a high-AQ Climbing Culture. In so doing, you unleash the higher elements of those around you and deepen your legacy.

AQ is, therefore, not simply about being more productive or boosting your business's bottom line. While now proven to assist in these areas, AQ goes much deeper, to the wellspring of human energy, motivation, fortitude, and aspiration.

Which mountain you choose to ascend during the finite moments of your life is perhaps the most important decision you will make. Ideally, it will challenge you, better those around you, elevate your spirit, inspire greatness, provide meaning, and leave a legacy for others to follow. Regardless of your title, your work provides a structured, interdependent way to fund, express, and further your ascent. But AQ is also about a different sort of ascent.

THE ASCENT TOWARD WISDOM

How can you remain a Climber when your pack is overloaded, the view is obscured, and the weather is threatening? This is why Camping appears to be a rational choice, at least until we assess its costs. Rather than sacrificing your growth, inspiration, hope, potential, and fulfillment by Camping, there is another way to lighten your load, improve your navigational prowess, and sustain your ascent. Ascend with *wisdom*.

If your hard drive is overloaded with competing software programs, it cannot function. Nor can you. It would be ludicrous to load yet more software onto your system. Yet this is what people do every day in their quest to remain viable, let alone lead, in their respective industries and endeavors. Some of the software we seek comes in the form of training, knowledge, and information, which we use to guide our actions and decisions. Much of it bogs us down, however, infecting and infesting our hard drives. There are times when less *is* more.

What does it take to successfully navigate adversity and uncertainty? Those who assume they must accumulate and carry more ideas, models, skills, and tools to survive might be missing the point. Cody Lundin is one of the leading experts on wilderness survival and runs the Aboriginal Living Skills School in Prescott, Arizona. Lundin is alarmed that most people load their backpacks with gadgets and lots of stuff. By loading themselves down, they risk their lives. It's not about having more stuff, it is about having the *right* stuff. Lundin teaches people how to dump their tents, sleeping bags, and backpacks and to survive on the essentials instead. He reverts back to ancient aboriginal wisdom to equip people with only what they need to handle any situation. He says most people realize an incredible sense of freedom when they can dump their overloaded packs and travel lighter and better into the wilderness.

Consider the Ascent Toward Wisdom model presented in Exhibit 11.1. At the base of the mountain is a thickening fog bank, which most people never escape. At the trailhead is *noise.* This is the deafening hum of the random stimuli that pound our senses throughout the day. Noise saps energy, strength, and resources while providing no inherent value. If we persist, we rise above the noise to *data,* which is merely organized noise. Today, the amount of data one must slog through to get to a decision or meaningful insight is formidable and growing exponentially.

Higher on the mountain is *information,* or organized data. The Internet is the gateway to boundless information. Ascending through information is like hiking through 10 feet of fine, powdered snow. You can slip 3 feet backward for each step forward. Getting a handle on these first three levels is akin to mapping the universe. It expands too quickly to ever be grasped. Efforts to master information are, therefore, futile.

If you are fortunate enough to get some semblance of a foothold on information, you can gain *knowledge,* which is a higher order of information. Knowledge represents and grows expertise. It is selected, ideally relevant and useful, stored information. But greater knowledge does not guarantee that you will achieve greater clarity, accuracy, or effectiveness. The fact that you have effectively stored certain information does not mean it will prove vital to the ascent. For example, training is one way to enhance knowledge. It is information selected for its supposed relevance to the collective ascent. Such training is endless and might include information about new products, developments, trends, competitors, one's job, and so on. Those lessons that become embedded into your hard drive become knowledge, whereas that portion of the training materials and lessons that simply ends up on the shelf or in a file remains information, or may even degrade to data and noise. So when gurus report that we are now in a knowledge-based economy, driven by knowledge-based workers, they are essentially warning that your success is driven by your ability to sift through mountains of information, data, and noise to extract and deliver higher value.

But, as everyone wrestles with accumulating more knowledge, some advantage is gained by rising to the next level, *intelligence.* You improve your intelligence as you get better and better at discerning which knowledge to access in making decisions and solving problems. Intelligence, in this sense of the word, is a higher order of knowledge. It is skilled selection of knowledge used to make effective decisions. It enables you to act more quickly and effectively. In the past, intelligence would often suffice when it came to navigating the challenges of a given day or enterprise. Today, we pay top dollar for proven intelligence. We seek it in our leaders and best people. Ideally, it would exist at all levels within an organization.

Consider, however, the *amount* of noise and data and information you must sort through to form knowledge and grow the level of intelligence your job now demands. It is like *climbing into an oncoming avalanche*. No matter how tenaciously you scramble, you simply cannot keep your head above the onslaught. Relying on intelligence is fraught with adversity. This battle to stay on top endangers leaders' ability to remain strong and make clearheaded, focused decisions.

Being a successful Climber or leading a successful Climbing Team cannot just be about *more* data, information, knowledge, or simply intelligence. It is impossible to gather all you need, and you can be literally stymied in the process. As Cody Lundin teaches, you can endanger your ascent with too much stuff. More is not the answer.

To achieve clarity, you must ascend toward *wisdom*. Wisdom is the intersection of experience, intuition, and knowledge. It comprises simple timeless truths that you can use to navigate all facets of your life and your venture.

In this model, AQ ideally serves as both a source of wisdom and a way to ascend toward wisdom in all that you do. AQ is the scientific explanation and measure of what we have always known to be true: people who respond more effectively to adversity get more out of and go further in life. No matter what ancient teaching you consult, the great lessons are built on humankind's relationship with adversity. These are timeless truths.

AQ is also what is required to slog through the noise and data and struggle past the Infofog to the higher levels of clarity and understanding. As these lower levels expand, it gets harder and harder to escape their grasp, and your AQ becomes more important in elevating to the next level. AQ defines the discipline of Response Ability. It provides you with the Climber's mind, or the ability to respond effectively to whatever comes your way. It enables you to maintain clarity, focus, and direction in the face of mounting challenge, uncertainty, and chaos. In this way AQ grows your wisdom. As you improve your Response Ability, you gain some deeper insight into what enables you to preserve and expand meaning, significance, and potential throughout life and your endeavors. AQ defines what you need to successfully struggle and ascend toward wisdom.

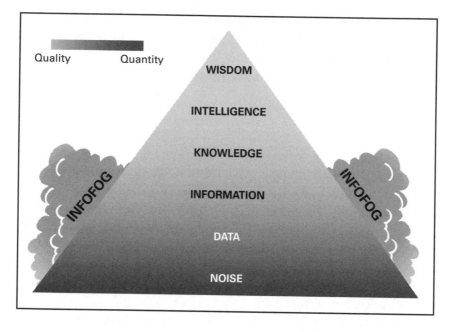

Exhibit 11.1 The Ascent Toward Wisdom

The mountain represents your purpose, and so much more. By ascending along your purpose with the resources you have, you commit to lifelong learning, improvement, growth, and some humbling falls. So why is the ascent so universally compelling? Perhaps, as renowned climber Ed Bernbaum points out, it is because "a mountain is actually a pyramid, and as you reach the top, you also reach the center."

Collectively, as you move toward the center, you start to work and live in harmony with your CORE values and your central beliefs. Life becomes simpler as you and your Climbing Team become more centered on timeless truths about appreciating and navigating the challenges inherent in the ascent. Together, your growing Response Ability strengthens your operating system, which is not about being a better computer, but being better people, better able to rise to any challenge. As it strengthens, your Response Ability enables you to navigate ever more challenging terrain with ever greater alacrity and grace. You flourish while others flounder.

When you look back on your life and career, you will see how, as you moved toward the center and top of your mountain, life gained more meaning, and your role became more significant. Ultimately, it will be your AQ, not your IQ, that enabled you to stay true to your mountain and inspire so many others to Climb. So listen to the mountain, let it humble you, and never relent.

"Forward and up!"

THE ADVERSITY RESPONSE PROFILE 7.0

ARP Overview. The full-length Adversity Response Profile (ARP) version 7.0 is the only instrument in existence that measures a person's AQ, or Adversity Quotient, and is the exclusive property of PEAK Learning, Inc. The ARP is intentionally designed to be simple, precise, and economical. Its uses include hiring,* coaching,* training, managing change, improving performance, and individual and team development. Given the advantage of exceptionally high reliability (88 percent overall) the ARP requires fewer items and, therefore, less time to complete (eight to twelve minutes) than most assessments.

The ARP consists of fourteen situations with four questions per situation, for a total of fifty-six questions (see Chapter 3 for an abbreviated version). Abbreviated versions, which appear as snap quizzes on Web sites and in the world's print media, should not be used for hiring or training.

Current Database: At the time this book went into print, the Adversity Response Profile had been completed by more than 100,000 people worldwide, representing a broad array of careers, industries, cultures, and ethnic backgrounds.

Format: The ARP comes in printed and Web-based versions. It takes approximately eight to twelve minutes to complete. The printed version

---

* To use the ARP for hiring or coaching, a person must be certified by PEAK Learning, Inc. (see Appendix B) and must also use only the full-length ARP.

takes five minutes to score. The Web-based version includes embedded automatic scoring and graphing.

No Adverse Impact: Because it has no adverse impact (does not discriminate against any gender or background), AQ is safe and proper for use as part of the overall applicant screening process. Which version you employ will depend on your technology and your needs. Both versions will provide instant results. Both provide an individual's AQ and CORE Profile, as well as some interpretative guidelines so you may assess those areas in which the person is strongest and weakest and how those areas fit with your company culture and expectations.

For more information on the uses, pricing, and availability of the Adversity Response Profile, contact PEAK Learning, Inc., at (800) 255-5572, (805) 595-7775, (805) 595-7771 (fax) or via E-mail at info@peaklearning.com. Additional information is also available on the Web site www.peaklearning.com.

THE ADVERSITY RESPONSE PROFILE CERTIFICATION PROGRAM

This exclusive 1½-day program certifies and trains a highly select group of professionals to administer and utilize the Adversity Response Profile (ARP) technology within their companies, organizations, and institutions. Those certified join an elite group of professionals worldwide who are granted the exclusive right to integrate this one-of-a-kind tool into their personal coaching and selection.

What Is Included?

- The Adversity Response Profile certification supporting materials
- Certification to use the ARP for hiring and coaching
- On-call coaching from PEAK Learning on AQ-related issues
- Discount pricing on the Adversity Response Profiles
- Ongoing electronic updates of the technology and research discoveries

What Is Required?

Those selected for this certification program must meet the following qualifications:
- Experience in coaching, human resources, counseling, and/or training
- A basic understanding of the AQ concept and applications
- The opportunity to have a significant impact helping others
- The ability to grasp *basic* statistical concepts

• A commitment to purchase a minumum number of ARPs within twelve months of the certification program

For additional information about the certification program, dates, and costs, please check our Web site at www.peaklearning.com or call 1-800-255-5572 or (805) 595-7775.

TEAM AQ SCORE RANGES AND INTERPRETATION

GROUND LEVEL (*MEAN 147.5*)

High Ground Level Team AQ (178–200): If your team average AQ is in this range it possesses a rare, extremely strong, and expanding capacity for challenges and adversity. Any setback is likely to be quickly handled, and accountability is shared. The group probably thrives on difficult tasks and is made up of agile problem solvers. Leaders are likely to seek your team to take on the most daunting challenges. It is probably exhilarating to be a part of this team. You can fine-tune your skills and expand your capacity by further strengthening your Team AQ.

Moderately High Ground Level Team AQ (161–177): If your Ground Level Team AQ falls in this range, your team is probably considered a high-performance team. You tap and expand a significant portion of your Existing Capacity. Its members are skilled problem solvers and decision makers and demonstrate a can-do spirit. The group probably remains resilient and perseveres when faced with most challenges. There may be moments when adversity piles up and becomes more of a burden than necessary. By strengthening the Team AQ to the next level(s) you will expand your potential and capacity for even greater challenges.

Moderate Ground Level Team AQ (135–160): The majority of teams have Ground Level Team AQs within this range. If this describes your team, then it probably fares well with most challenges. However, when adversity piles up and the team's capacity is stretched, your team's decision making, innovation, problem solving, and agility may start to fray. The team may at times become demoralized or overwhelmed. You tap less than full capacity. As the team strengthens its Team AQ, it will replenish its fortitude in dealing with all sorts of challenges.

Moderately Low Ground Level Team AQ (118–134): If your team scores in this range, it may deal with some issues sufficiently well. However, when the team is faced with multiple challenges, difficult setbacks, or severe time pressures the team's performance and dynamics may suffer unnecessarily. Significant capacity goes untapped. It is difficult for the team to experience true synergy while working through challenges.

Low Ground Level Team AQ (117 and Below): For a team that scores in this range, conflicts are probably commonplace, capacity goes untapped, and problems are rarely resolved. This team is tapping a small portion of its Existing Capacity. This team can experience dramatic improvements by gaining awareness of and strengthening its Team AQ at all three elevations. Meetings are likely to become more energizing and productive.

MID-MOUNTAIN (*MEAN 130.5*)

High Mid-Mountain Team AQ (161–200): Your team has a healthy faith in its resilience and ability to deal with whatever comes its way. The team sees itself as Response-Able. It has a substantial capacity for problem solving and taking on daunting challenges. You access much of your Capacity, and it continues to expand. Your team may be offered tough situations that others can't resolve. The team is unfazed by most setbacks and obstacles.

Moderately High Mid-Mountain Team AQ (144–160): If your Mid-Mountain Team AQ falls in this range, your team is stronger and accesses more of its Capacity than most. It deals with setbacks and difficulties effectively except when buried under multiple challenges. The team solves problems, makes decisions, and may elevate other individuals to try things they otherwise would not attempt. Even so, the team will access and expand greater capacity as it strengthens its AQ.

Moderate Mid-Mountain Team AQ (119–143): Like most teams, this one has a moderate capacity for difficulties of all magnitudes. Some capacity goes untapped. Your team may move along efficiently until sideswiped by some unexpected change or difficulty. Or when adversity piles up and your capacity is stretched, this team's decision making, innovation, problem solving, and agility may start to diminish. The team may lose its spirit and resolve when faced with daunting challenges.

Moderately Low Mid-Mountain Team AQ (103–118): If your team scores in this range, it probably does best when dealing with more predictable, stable situations. Capacity is underaccessed and does not expand to meet what is demanded of the team. Highly volatile, sensitive, and challenging problems may bring out some negativity. People may whine or complain. The team is unlikely to be synergistic.

Low Mid-Mountain Team AQ (102 and Below): A Low Mid-Mountain Team AQ is a team that accesses only a small portion of its capacity, resulting in frustration, conflict, and apathy. Challenges threaten the interpersonal fabric of the team, and people may behave ineffectively when facing an obstacle. This team can experience dramatic improvements as you raise your Team AQ.

SKY LEVEL (*MEAN 133.5*)

High Panoramic Team AQ (163–200): Your team is widely perceived as superior in the face of adversity. Chances are you are at your best when faced with "unsolvable" problems or impossible tasks. You pride yourselves on taking on tasks others wouldn't touch. Trust and interdependence are likely to be strong and based on the trials and successes of past challenges. You waste no time on blame, you focus on what you *can* do to improve the situation, and ownership is shared among the team. Others are impressed by your expanding capacity. You solve problems adeptly, and others seek your help. You have a significant impact on the success of your organization, and your team members are likely to be highly loyal to the team.

Moderately High Panoramic AQ (146–162): Your stakeholders perceive that you are stronger than most at dealing with adversity. You access much of your Capacity to meet growing demands. You have relatively strong

Response Ability, and others are likely to respect your ability to use a large portion of your Existing Capacity. In times when challenges are particularly keen and/or the adversity stacks up, your team may still fall short of its full potential. Severe adversities may take an unnecessary toll on your team members. You will enlarge your Accessed and Existing Capacity as you strengthen your Team AQ.

Moderate Panoramic Team AQ (121–145): Your team, like most, is likely to be reasonably effective at handling some challenges. When adversity strikes, your team may lack the Response Ability to perform optimally. Others notice that your Accessed Capacity sometimes falls well short of your Existing Capacity, and your Existing Capacity does not always meet what is required. Trust may be compromised when people respond destructively to each new challenge. You probably solve some problems but struggle unnecessarily with others.

Moderately Low Panoramic Team AQ (105–120): Your innovation, problem solving, and decision making are compromised when you are working in adversity-rich conditions. These abilities are at their strongest when conditions are calm. As things intensify, people may refuse to fully invest in improving the situation or getting the job done. You access only a portion of your Capacity, causing frustration and disappointment. Your team may at times feel helpless when faced with what seem like unreasonable demands.

Low Panoramic Team AQ (104 and Below): Your team faces the chronic difficulty of expanding and tapping enough of its Capacity. Chances are the members are disengaged, if not completely apathetic. Outside stakeholders may have voiced frustrations with your team and/or given up on using your team to get the job done, especially when challenges arise. Your interactions are likely rife with blame, and they are low on problem solving, innovation, and aspirations. People on low-AQ teams usually dread meetings, since they can get more accomplished by themselves than they can as a team. This is called "team entropy."

APPENDIX D

PEAK LEARNING, INC.

PEAK Learning, Inc., was founded by Dr. Paul Stoltz in 1987 and has grown into an international firm of select professionals focusing on applying, researching, and expanding the AQ philosophy, science, and methods to address a broad range of issues. PEAK has licensed international affiliates in the Nordic Region and Singapore, and others soon to follow.

PEAK Learning works with client organizations from small to large, representing various industries in dozens of countries worldwide. Among PEAK's clients are ADC Telecommunications, ADP, Cypress Semiconductor, Deloitte & Touche, Federal Express, Hunt-Wesson, the Institute for Management Studies, Marriott International, SBC Telecommunications, and various U.S. government agencies.

PEAK is the exclusive and original creator of the AQ measure, programming, and change processes. The PEAK team of professionals provide the following services:

- Keynote presentations on AQ and related New Economy topics customized to each group
- AQ programs customized to each client's challenges and needs
- Web-based AQ programs
- AQ consulting to strengthen culture, teams, processes, and leadership
- AQ coaching to provide individual managers with in-depth and personalized guidance
- Conference-learning design for select clients seeking leading-edge content for their next conference event
- Customized experiential learning programs

PEAK Learning and AQ have been featured in the world's top print and broadcast media outlets, including CNN, Business News Asia, CNBC, the *Wall Street Journal, Investor's Business Daily,* Bloomberg TV, the *Washington Post, Asia 21, Business Week, Entrepreneur, Fast Company,* and *Success.*

If you would like to learn more about AQ, PEAK Learning, or how AQ can benefit your enterprise, please call (800) 255-5572 or (805) 595-7775 or E-mail us at info@peaklearning.com. The PEAK Learning, Inc. Web site is www.peaklearning.com.